C000302568

HARDPRESS.NET
HOME OF HARD-TO-FIND BOOKS

Narrative of the Voyage of H.M.S. Rattlesnake
by John Macgillivray

Copyright © 2019 by HardPress

Address:
HardPress
8345 NW 66TH ST #2561
MIAMI FL 33166-2626
USA
Email: info@hardpress.net

UC-NRLF

B 3 821 531

LIBRARY
UNIVERSITY OF
CALIFORNIA
SANTA CRUZ

LIBRARY
UNIVERSITY OF
CALIFORNIA
SANTA CRUZ

AUSTRALIANA FACSIMILE EDITIONS No. 118

Reproduced by the Libraries Board of South Australia from a copy held in the State Library of South Australia.

Adelaide
Libraries Board of South Australia
1967

The State Library of South Australia
has catalogued the original of this facsimile as under:

MACGILLIVRAY, John, 1822-1867

　　Narrative of the voyage of H.M.S.
Rattlesnake, commanded by the late Captain Owen Stanley..., during the years
1846-1850, including discoveries and
surveys in New Guinea, the Louisiade
archipelago, etc.　To which is added the
account of Mr. E.B. Kennedy's expedition
for the exploration of the Cape York
peninsula, [by William Carron.]
London, T. & W. Boone, 1852.

　　2v. ill. fold. map, 22cm.

　　Ferguson　11972

1. New Guinea -Description
2. Louisiade Archipelago -Description
3. Cape York Peninsula -Discovery and
　　　exploration
4. Kennedy, Edmund Besley Court, 1818-
　　　1848
5. Rattlesnake, ship
I. Carron, William, 1823-1876

　　　　　　　　　　　　　　　919.5

NARRATIVE OF THE VOYAGE

OF

H.M.S. RATTLESNAKE,

COMMANDED BY THE LATE

CAPTAIN OWEN STANLEY, R.N., F.R.S. &c.

DURING THE YEARS 1846–1850.

INCLUDING DISCOVERIES AND SURVEYS IN

NEW GUINEA, THE LOUISIADE ARCHIPELAGO,

ETC.

TO WHICH IS ADDED THE ACCOUNT OF

MR. E. B. KENNEDY'S EXPEDITION

FOR THE EXPLORATION OF THE CAPE YORK PENINSULA.

BY JOHN MA GILLIVRAY, F.R.G.S.

NATURALIST TO THE EXPEDITION.

PUBLISHED UNDER THE
Sanction of the Lords Commissioners of the Admiralty.

IN TWO VOLUMES.
VOL. I.

LONDON:
T. & W. BOONE, 29, NEW BOND STREET.
1852.

Facsimile edition 1967

DU
21
M19
1852a
v. 1

TO

MRS. STANLEY,

This Work is Dedicated

AS A TRIBUTE OF RESPECT TO THE

MEMORY OF HER SON,

UNDER WHOSE DIRECTION THE PRINCIPAL OBJECTS

OF THE

VOYAGE OF THE RATTLESNAKE

WERE SUCCESSFULLY ACCOMPLISHED.

PREFACE.

IT was originally intended that an account of the Surveying Voyage of H.M.S. Rattlesnake should have been undertaken conjointly by the late Captain Owen Stanley and myself, in which case the narrative would have been constructed from the materials afforded by the journals of both, and the necessary remarks upon hydrographical subjects would have been furnished by that officer, whose lamented death in March, 1850, prevented this arrangement from being carried out. Not having had access to Captain Stanley's private journals, I considered myself fortunate, when the Lords Commissioners of the Admiralty—in addition to sanctioning the publication of my account of the Voyage in question—directed that every facility should be afforded me in consulting the manuscript charts and other hydrographical results at their disposal, and to Rear-Admiral Sir F. Beaufort, C.B., Commander

C. B. Yule, R.N., and Lieut. J. Dayman, R.N., I beg to express my thanks for the liberal manner in which they carried out their Lordships' intentions.

To the other gentlemen who have contributed Appendices to this work—George Busk, Esq. F.R.S., Dr. R. G. Latham, Prof. Edward Forbes, F.R.S., and Adam White, Esq., F.L.S.—I have also to offer my best thanks. It also affords me great pleasure to record my obligations to T. Huxley, Esq. R.N., F.R.S., late Assistant-Surgeon of the Rattlesnake, for the handsome manner in which he allowed me to select from his collection of drawings those which now appear as illustrations; and I may express the hope, which in common with many others I entertain, that the whole of his researches in marine zoology may speedily be laid before the scientific world. My own collections in Natural History have been submitted to the examination of various eminent naturalists. Many of the novelties have already been described, and the remainder will appear from time to time.

CONTENTS OF VOL. I.

CHAPTER I.

CHAPTER IV.

CHAPTER V.

CHAPTER VI.

CHAPTER VII.

CHAPTER VIII.

APPENDIX.

ERRATA.—VOL. I.

p.	line.		
13	20	for *los* read *dos.*	
34	12	„ *breach* read *breech.*	
35	28	„ *pantherina* read *mauritiana.*	
50	6	„ *astrea* read *astræa.*	
58	28	„ *Louis* read *Curtis.*	
92	16	„ *second* read *first.*	
102	31	„ *occulata* read *oculata.*	
103	18	„ *meandrina* read *mæandrina.*	
104	29	„ *sordidus* read *sordida.*	
288	28	„ *Pritchard* read *Prichard.*	

p.	line.		
356	22	„ *cube* read *cup.*	
357	10	„ *oval* read *oral,* also p. 370, l. 7 ; p. 372, l. 20 ; p. 380, l. 9.	
358	10	„ *fine* read *five.*	
367	11	„ *dichotoma* read *furcata.*	
367	20	„ *marginata* read *Torresiana.*	
375	1	„ *flexilis, n. sp.* read *Johnstoniæ.*	
375	27	„ *Janiero* read *Janeiro.*	
395	14	„ *fluxure* read *flexure.*	

LIST OF PLATES.

VOL. I.

VOYAGE

OF

H. M. S. RATTLESNAKE.

CHAPTER I.

OBJECTS OF THE VOYAGE—ADMIRALTY INSTRUCTIONS—HYDRO-
GRAPHER'S INSTRUCTIONS—SAIL FROM PLYMOUTH—ARRIVE
AT MADEIRA—FUNCHAL—VISIT TO CURRAL—TRY FOR DEEP
SEA SOUNDINGS—CROSSING THE LINE—ARRIVE AT RIO DE
JANEIRO—CITY OF RIO AND NEIGHBOURHOOD—DREDGING IN
BOTAFOGO BAY—SLAVERY—RELIGIOUS PROCESSIONS—BRAZI-
LIAN CHARACTER—CROSS THE SOUTH ATLANTIC—TEMPERA-
TURE OF THE SEA—OCEANIC BIRDS—PELAGIC ANIMALS—
ARRIVE AT SIMON'S BAY—SURVEY THE BAY—CAFFRE WAR
—OBSERVATIONS ON THE WAVES—ARRIVE AT MAURITIUS—
PORT LOUIS—VISIT TO PAMPLEMOUSSES—LA POUCE MOUN-
TAIN—TRY FOR DEEP SEA SOUNDINGS—ARRIVE AT HOBART
TOWN.

H.M.S. RATTLESNAKE, one of the old class of
28-gun ships, was commissioned at Portsmouth on
September 24th, 1846, by the late Captain Owen
Stanley, with a complement of 180 officers and men.
The nature and objects of the intended voyage will
best be conveyed to the reader through the medium
of the following instructions from the Admiralty, for
the use of which I am indebted to Lieut. C. B. Yule,

VOL. I.   B

who succeeded to the command of the Rattlesnake, upon the death of our late lamented Captain, at Sydney, in March 1850, after the successful accomplishment of the principal objects of the expedition.

" By the Commissioners for executing the Office of Lord High Admiral of the United Kingdom of Great Britain and Ireland, &c.

" Whereas, it being the usual practice of vessels returning from the Australian Colonies, or from the South Sea, to proceed to India through Torres Strait; and most of those vessels preferring the chance of finding a convenient opening in the Barrier Reefs to the labour of frequent anchorage in the In-shore Passage, it was thought fit to send out an expedition under Captain Francis Blackwood, to determine which was the best opening that those reefs would afford, and to make such a survey thereof as would ensure the safety of all vessels which should continue to adopt that mode of reaching the Strait:

" And whereas, although that specific object was successfully achieved by the survey of Raine Island Passage, and by the erection of a durable beacon there to render it the more accessible, yet it appears that much is still to be done in those seas in order to make the approach to the Strait more secure and certain, as well as to afford the choice of another entrance farther to the northward in case of vessels overshooting the latitude of Raine Island by stress of wind, or current:

" We have, therefore, thought proper to appoint you to the command of the Rattlesnake, for the purpose of carrying out these objects; and you are hereby required and directed, when that ship is in every respect ready for sea, to proceed in her to Madeira for the verification of your chronometers—from thence to Simon's Bay at the Cape of Good Hope, for a supply of water, and to land the £50,000 you have been ordered to convey to that colony; then to make the best of your way to the Mauritius, to land the treasure (£15,000) entrusted to your charge for that island; and having so done, to proceed to King George's Sound for the purpose of carrying its exact meridian distance to Sydney, where you will lose no time in preparing for the execution of the important service entrusted to you.

" The several objects of that service have been drawn up under our direction by our Hydrographer; but notwithstanding the order in which they are placed, we leave to your own discretion the several periods of their performance, and likewise the times of your return to Sydney to re-victual and refit—being satisfied that your zeal in pushing forward the survey will never outstrip your attention to the health and comfort of your crew.

" You will take the Bramble and her tender, the Castlereagh, under your orders, and employ them in those places which require vessels of a lighter draft of water than the Rattlesnake. They are to be attached as tenders to the Rattlesnake, and to be manned from that ship; and such of the present crew of the Bramble as may have served five years continuously, and volunteer to remain on the surveying service in Australia, are to be entered in the Rattlesnake under the provisions of the Act of Parliament. The books of the Bramble are to be closed, and she is to be considered as no longer in commission; and you are hereby authorized, after being joined by her and by the Castlereagh, to enter ten supernumerary seamen for wages and victuals in the Rattlesnake, (making her total complement 190,) to enable you effectively to man the said two tenders.

" In stretching off from the Barrier Reefs to the eastward, in order to explore the safety of the sea intervening between them and Louisiade and New Guinea, you will have occasion to approach those shores, in which case you must be constantly on your guard against the treacherous disposition of their inhabitants, all barter for refreshments should be conducted under the eye of an officer, and every pains be taken to avoid giving any just cause of offence to their prejudices, especially with respect to their women.

" A naturalist having been permitted to accompany you, every reasonable facility is to be given him in making and preserving his collections.

" In the event of this country being involved in hostilities during your absence, you will take care never to be surprised; but you are to refrain from any act of aggression towards the vessels or settlements of any nation with which we may be at war, as expeditions employed in behalf of discovery and science have always been considered by all civilized communities as acting under a general safe-guard.

" You will consider yourself under the command of Rear-Admiral Inglefield, the Commander-in-Chief of Her Majesty's ships and vessels on the East India station, while you are within the limits of that station; and we have signified to him our desire that he should not divert you from the survey, nor interfere with your proceedings, except under the pressure of strong necessity; and that upon all fit occasions he should order you to be supplied with the stores and provisions of which you may stand in need; and all officers senior to yourself, with whom you may fall in, are hereby directed to give you any assistance which may be requisite.

" Notwithstanding the 16th article of the 4th section of the 6th chapter of the Admiralty Instructions, you are, besides your reports to your Commander-in-Chief, to send brief accounts to our Secretary of your proceedings, state,

and condition : and you will make known to him, in due
time, the nature and quantity of any supplies of which you
may be absolutely in want, and which may have to be
forwarded to you from England.

" With our Hydrographer you are by every opportunity
in your power to keep up a constant correspondence; you
are to report to him in full detail all your proceedings; and
you are to transmit to him, whenever possible, tracings of
all charts and plans that you may have completed, accompanied by sailing directions, and with notices of any facts
or discoveries which may be of interest to navigation.

" Having completed the service herein set forth, you are
to return in the Rattlesnake, along with the Bramble, to
Spithead, when you will receive directions for your further proceedings. If the Bramble should, however, by
that time be in an unfit state to undertake the voyage to
Europe, it may perhaps be prudent to dispose of her,
under the sanction of the Commander-in-chief.

" In the event of any unfortunate accident befalling
yourself, the officer on whom the command may in consequence devolve, is hereby required and directed to carry
out, as far as in him lies, the foregoing orders and instructions.

" Given under our hands, this 1st December, 1846.

    (Signed)   " CHAS. ADAM.

              " JNO. D. DUNDAS.

" To OWEN STANLEY, Esq.,

  " Captain of Her Majesty's

" Surveying Vessel Rattlesnake, at Plymouth,

    " By command of their Lordships,

      (Signed)   " H. G. WARD."

In connexion with the preceding general instructions to Capt. Stanley, it will be necessary to give

a portion of those more explicit directions furnished by the Hydrographer, Rear-Admiral Sir Francis Beaufort.

Extracts from Hydrographic Instructions for Capt. Stanley.

"On your arrival at Sydney you should take the earliest opportunity of communicating with Lieut. Yule, in order to learn how much has been executed, by the Bramble and her tender, of the orders which he received from Capt. Blackwood, and you will no doubt avail yourself of his long experience in those seas in digesting your plan of future operations.

"A letter from the Colonial Office having recently apprized their Lordships that it is the intention of her Majesty's Government to form a new settlement at Harvey Bay, and having requested that it may be duly examined with that view, your first undertaking, after leaving Sydney, should be to repair to that place, and to make an efficient survey of the whole bay, extending it down through the channel into Wide Bay, and marking the best anchorages, the most convenient landing-places, and the several parts where water may be found. And as it appears that Colonel Barney, R.E. is engaged in the same inquiry, it will be prudent to act in concert with him, and to give him a copy of such parts of it as may suit his purposes.

"In your way to this district, and indeed on every part of the shores of Australia, you should lose no fair opportunity of verifying the positions—of multiplying the soundings—and of improving the smaller details of the coast as laid down by Capt. P. P. King in his excellent Survey, but which he had not time or means to effect with the same accuracy that will be in your power. By carrying on this system of correction and improvement in our present charts from Harvey Bay along the narrow navigation which is generally known by the name of the In-shore Passage, between the coast and the Barrier Reefs, a very great benefit will be conferred on those masters of vessels who would be the more readily inclined to adopt that channel, if certain parts of it were so clearly delineated, and the soundings so spread on either side of the tracks, that they could sometimes continue under sail during the night. However necessary it was, and is, to contribute as much as possible to the safety of those vessels who choose the outer voyage by the Barrier Reefs, it is not the less our duty to facilitate the navigation of the In-shore Passage to all vessels who prefer its tranquillity and security to the risk of the former; and your labours for the accomplishment of this object will prove to be of peculiar importance when steam communication between Singapore and Sydney shall be established.

" In the general and searching examination of those parts of the Coral Sea which are likely to be traversed by ships steering for Torres Strait, you will be obliged to regulate your movements by the periodic changes of the weather and monsoons—probably beginning to windward, and dropping gently to leeward by close and well-arranged traverses, and by spreading out your three vessels to a convenient distance apart. This great expanse of sea, which may be said to stretch from Lord Howe's Island to New Caledonia and to the Louisiade, would no doubt require many years work in order to accomplish that object; but, by dividing it into definite zones or squares, and by fully sifting those which you may undertake, a certain quantity of distinct knowledge will be gained. Navigators in crossing those zones will then be sure of their safety, and future surveyors will know exactly on what parts to expend their labours.

" In carefully exploring the northernmost, and apparently the safest entrance from the Pacific, which may be called Bligh's Channel, you will connect the islands with a survey of the coast of New Guinea, as well as with the edge of the Warrior Reef, and as there are throughout moderate soundings, you will probably be able to draw up such clear directions as will enable the mariner to use it in moderate weather by night, and to beat through it at all times.   Characteristic views of the coast and hills of New Guinea, as well as of each island, both from the eastward and westward, will greatly assist him by the immediate certainty of his landfall, and will also materially add to your means of giving proper marks and bearings for avoiding the dangers.

" In Torres Strait you will find much to do ;—not only has a new rock been discovered in the middle of the Endeavour Channel, but the water in its western opening is only four and a-half fathoms, and there seems no reason for not believing that Prince of Wales Channel is safer, easier, and more direct.   But before we can decide upon that point, an accurate survey must be made of it, throughout its length and breadth, including the adjacent islands, and showing their anchorages and watering-places, as well as the nature of the soil, and the kind of timber they produce, along with a full investigation of the tides.

" The connexion of that Strait with Bligh's Farewell should also be examined, for many circumstances may render it highly necessary that the Admiralty should be made aware of what means there are to pass from one ocean to the other, without being observed from Cape York.

" On this latter Cape Government have for some time contemplated a station, and it will therefore be very desirable to fix upon a convenient but secure anchorage in its neighbourhood.   Our latest surveys do not show much promise of finding such a port; but, perhaps, inside the reefs beyond Peak Point, or more likely between Albany Island and the main, a snug place may be discovered for that purpose.

" In tracing out the approach to Bligh's Farewell, you will be led to examine the southern face of New Guinea as far as Cape Valsche; but after verifying the position of this point, it will be prudent to quit the shores of that island, and not to meddle with any part of it over which the Dutch claim jurisdiction.

"When you have arrived at this distant point, the S.E. monsoon will probably render it necessary to repair to Port Essington for such supplies as may by previous arrangement have been sent there for you from Sydney; or perhaps unforeseen events might render it more expedient to proceed for refreshments to some of the islands in the Arafura Sea, or it is possible to one of the Dutch settlements in Java. And in either of these two latter cases you should make a complete survey of the island to which you have proceeded, or you should select any one of the eastern passages from Bally to Floris most convenient to the object you have in view, and then lay it down with precision. Of the many well-known passages between the innumerable islands of that great Archipelago, there is not one which has ever been charted with plausible accuracy; and it cannot be too strongly impressed on your mind that hydrography is better served by one accurate chart than by ten approximate sketches.

" The several objects of this highly interesting expedition having thus been briefly enumerated, I have only to remind you that their Lordships do not prescribe to you the order in which they are to be executed, leaving it to your own prudence, and to your experience in those climates, so to arrange them that each part of your survey shall be complete in itself, and that each step in your progress shall be conducive to its successor.

(Signed)　　　　　　" F. BEAUFORT,
　　　　　　　　　　　　Hydrographer."

The Rattlesnake left Spithead on December 3rd, and on the 11th took her final departure from Plymouth, which place we had called at to complete her fittings, swing the ship a second time to ascertain the amount of local attraction, and receive some specie for the Cape of Good Hope and the Mauritius. Being favoured by strong northerly winds, we reached Madeira on December 18th, after a quick, but most uncomfortable passage; during the greater part of which the main and lower decks were partially flooded, owing to the inefficiency of the scuppers, and the leaky state of nearly every port and scuttle in the ship.

Dec. 20th.—The scenery of Madeira has been so often described by voyagers, who, from Cook downwards, have made it the first stage in their circumnavigation of the globe, as to render superfluous more than a few passing allusions. When near enough to distinguish the minor features of the island, the terraced slopes of the mountain sides converted into vineyards and gardens studded with the huts of the peasantry, presented a pleasing aspect to visitors, whom a week's sailing had brought from the snow-clad shores of England. Here and there a white-washed chapel or picturesque villa lent a charm to the scenery by contrasting strongly with the patches of green upon the slopes, the deep blue of the ocean, and the delicate white of the ever-changing clouds of mist which rolled incessantly along, while the rugged summit of the island, and the deep ravines radiating towards the coast-range of precipitous cliffs, gave an air of wildness to the scene.

The town of Funchal, said to contain about 25,000 inhabitants, is situated upon the slope of an amphitheatre of hills, behind the only anchorage of the island. The finest view is obtained from the balcony of a church dedicated to Nossa Senhora de Monte, situated at a considerable elevation above the town. Here one looks down upon the numerous quintas and cottages of the suburbs embosomed in gardens and vineyards, the orange groves and clumps of chestnut trees, the snow-white houses of Funchal with its churches and public buildings, the citadel frowning over the town, the calm waters of the bay with the vessels at anchor gently heaving to and fro on the long westerly swell, the Ilheo rock and batteries, the bold 1   dlands, and the dim outline of the distant Desertas. Some of the streets are pleasantly shaded by rows of plane trees (*Platanus occidentalis*). Several deep ravines passing through the town are carefully walled in, to prevent damage being done by the torrents which occasionally sweep down the mountain, carrying everything before them. From the steepness of the narrow roads and streets, wheeled vehicles can scarcely be used,

and sledges drawn by small bullocks supply their
place, while the wine, the chief article of export, is
conveyed into the town in goat-skins carried on
the shoulder.

Dec. 23rd.—Few strangers remain long in Madeira
without paying a visit to the Curral, and a large
party of us left the ship for· that purpose this
morning.   At first the road led through a series of
narrow lanes frequently separated from the fields
and vineyards on either side by hedges of roses,
honeysuckle, jasmine and fuchsias ; now and then
passing under successions of trellis work covered by
the vines when in full vigour, and then forming long
shady vistas.   For several miles we wound our way
along the hill sides, down deep ravines, and up
steep rocky slopes.   In spite of the ruggedness of
the path, our horses progressed with wonderful
alacrity, although occasionally impeded by the
additional weight of the attendant burroqueros
holding on by the tail, and laughing at our efforts
to dislodge them.   On reaching the shoulder of one
of the hills, we found the ravines and valleys below
us filled with dense mist.   Here, at an elevation of
2500 feet, a species of spruce-like pine appeared to
thrive well.   The path, which at times is not more
than three feet wide, now winds along the sides of
the mountain with many sharp turnings ; heading
numerous ravines, the frightful nature of which
was partially concealed by the obscurity of the
mist.

We halted at the Pass of the Curral, to which Captain Stanley's barometrical observations* assign an elevation of 2700 feet above the sea. Shortly afterwards the mist gradually dissolved, unveiling the magnificent scenery below and around. The Curral gives one the idea of a vast crater† of irregular form, surrounded by a rugged wall (upwards of a thousand feet in height) of grey weather-beaten rock cut down into wild precipices, intersected by ravines and slopes of debris mixed up with masses of crumbling rock, and towering upwards into fantastic peaks. A winding path leads to the bottom—a small fertile valley watered by a streamlet which leaves it by a deep gorge on the left, and forms a picturesque waterfall on its way to the sea. The scattered rustic huts and snow-white chapel of the Curral complete the picture of this peaceful and secluded spot, buried in the very heart of the mountains.

* The height of the Pico los Bodes, determined in the usual way by the mountain barometer, was found by Lieut. Dayman to be 3677 feet ; his observations on the magnetic dip and intensity (for which, see the Appendix) are interesting, as shewing a great amount of local attraction at the summit.

† There is reason to suppose the Curral to have been the principal, although not the only centre of that submarine volcanic action, during the continuance of which Madeira first emerged from the sea, an event, which the evidence afforded by the limestone fossils of St. Vincente (on the north side of the island) associates with the tertiary epoch. See Paper by Dr. J. Macaulay in Edinb. New Philos. Journ. for October, 1840.

Although it is now the middle of winter, to-day's excursion afforded many subjects of interest to a naturalist. Some beautiful ferns, of which even the commonest one (*Adiantum Capillus-Veneris*) would have been much prized by an English botanist as a very rare British species, occurred on the dripping rocks by the roadside, and many wild plants were in flower on the lower grounds. Even butterflies of three kinds, two of which (*Colias Edusa*, and *Cynthia Cardui*) are also found in Britain, occurred, although in small numbers, and at the Pass of the Curral coleoptera of the genera *Pimelea* and *Scarites*, were met with under stones along with minute landshells, *Bulimus lubricus*, *Clausilia deltostoma*, and a *Pupa*.

After a stay of eight days, we left Madeira for Rio de Janeiro, and on January 2nd picked up the S. E. trade wind, and passed through the Cape de Verde Islands to the southward between Mayo and St. Jago. Two days afterwards, in lat. 9° 30′ N., and long. 22° 40′ W., a slight momentary shock, supposed to be the effect of an earthquake, was felt throughout the ship. On the 11th an attempt was made to strike deep sea soundings, but failed from the drawing of a splice used to connect two portions of the spun-yarn employed. On the following day the attempt was repeated by Captain Stanley, unsuccessfully, however, no bottom having been obtained at a depth of 2400 fathoms. Still a record of the experiment may be considered interesting. At three P.M., when nearly becalmed in lat. 1° N., and long. 22° 30′ W. (a few hours previous to meeting the S. E. trade), the second cutter was lowered with 2600 fathoms of line (six yarn spun-yarn) in her, coiled in casks, and a weight consisting of twelve 32 lbs. shot,—in all, 384 lbs., secured in a net bag of spun yarn. The jolly-boat was in attendance to tow the cutter as fast to windward as she drifted, so as to keep the line during the time it was running out as nearly up and down as possible. The following table shews when each 100 fathoms passed over the stern, the whole 2400 fathoms of line having taken 38 minutes and 40 seconds to run out :—

Fathom Mark.	Time of Passing.		Fathom Mark.	Time of Passing.	
	Min.	Seconds.		Min.	Seconds.
100	1	0	1300	17	5
200	2	5	1400	19	0
300	2	30	1500	20	50
400	3	35	1600	22	30
500	5	0	1700	24	25
600	6	15	1800	26	30
700	7	35	1900	29	10
800	9	0	2000	31	0
900	10	35	2100	32	55
1000	12	40	2200	35	0
1100	13	30	2300	36	55
1200	15	10	2400	38	40

The forenoon of January 13th was employed in

the performance of the usual ceremonies on "crossing the line," a custom now happily falling into
desuetude—I allude to it merely for the purpose of
mentioning its unfortunate consequences in the present instance; for, although the whole proceeding
was conducted with the greatest good humour,
we had soon afterwards to lament the occurrence of
a fatal case of pleurisy, besides another scarcely less
severe, believed by the medical officers to have been
induced by forcible and continued submersion in
what is technically called " the pond," one part of
the performance which novices are obliged to sub-
mit to during these marine Saturnalia.

The most interesting occurrence in natural history
during the passage, in addition to the usual accom-
paniments of flying fish, dolphins, physaliæ and
velellæ, was our finding, in the neighbourhood of
the equator, considerable numbers of a rare British
bird, *Thalassidroma Leachii*, a species of storm-
petrel, not before known to extend its range to the
tropics; it was distributed between the tropic of
Cancer and lat. 5° S.

As we approached the South American coast, the
rates of several of our seventeen chronometers (fifteen Government and two private ones) were found
to have strangely altered, thus reducing the value
of our meridian distance between Madeira and
Rio; this effect was ascribed to the firing of shotted
guns when exercising at general quarters, a practice
which in consequence was not afterwards repeated.

January 23rd.—I shall not soon forget my first
view of the shores of the new world.   The morning
was beautifully fine, and with a light breeze scarcely
sufficient to cause a ripple on the water, we were
slipping past the high and remarkable promontory
of Cape Frio, which at first appeared like an island.
A long beach of glittering sand stretched away to
the westward, and was lost in the distance ; behind
this a strip of undulating country, clad here and
there in the richest green, was backed by a range of
distant wooded hills, on which many clumps of
palms could be distinguished.   Few harbours in the
world present a more imposing entrance than that
of Rio de Janeiro.   Several islands lie off the
opening, and on either side the coast range terminates in broken hills and ridges of granite, one
of which, Pao d'Açucar, the Sugar Loaf of the
English, rises at once from near the water's edge
to the height of 900 feet, as an apparently inac-
cessible peak, and forms the well known landmark
for the entrance.

Passing the narrows (where the width is a mile
and a quarter), strongly guarded by fortifications,
of which Fort Sa. Cruz, an extensive work, with
several tiers of guns occupying a rocky point, is
the principal, the harbour widens out with beautiful
sandy bays on either side, and rocky headlands
covered with luxuriant vegetation.   Here the view
of the city of Rio de Janeiro is magnificent.   The
glare of the red-tiled buildings, whitewashed or

painted yellow, is relieved by the varied beauty of the suburbs and gardens, and the numerous wooded eminences crowned by churches and other conspicuous public edifices. Beyond the city the harbour again widens out to form an immense basin, studded with green islands, extending backwards some seventeen or eighteen miles further towards the foot of the Organ mountains, remarkable for their pinnacled summits, the highest of which attains an elevation of 7800 feet above the sea.

The harbour presented a busy scene from our anchorage. The water was alive with small craft of every description, from the large felucca-rigged boat down to the fishing canoe simply constructed of a hollowed out log, and steamers crowded with passengers plied between the city and the opposite shore. The sea breeze died away, and was succeeded by a sultry calm; after a short interval, the grateful land wind, laden with sweet odours, advanced as a dark line slowly stealing along the surface of the water, and the deep boom of the evening gun echoing from hill to hill may be said appropriately to have closed the scene.

Landing at the Largo do Paço, or palace square, my first favourable impressions of the city of Rio de Janeiro were somewhat lessened by the stench arising from offal on the beach, and the vicinity of the market, under the conjoined influence of a perfect calm and a temperature of 90° in the shade. The palace, now used by the emperor only on court

days, has two sides of the large irregular square in
which it is situated, occupied by shops and other
private buildings. Close by is the market, which
the stranger, especially if a naturalist, will do well
to visit. The variety of fruits and vegetables is
great, that of fish scarcely less so. On the muddy
shore in the back ground, the fishing canoes are
drawn up on their arrival to discharge their cargoes,
chiefly at this time consisting of a kind of sprat and
an anchovy with a broad lateral silvery band.
Baskets of land crabs covered with black slimy mud,
of handsome *Lupeæ,* and the large well-flavoured
prawns, called *Cameroons,* are scattered about, and
even small sharks (*Z, gœnæ,* &c.) and cuttle-fish are
exposed for sale.

The streets, which, with few exceptions, are very
narrow, are paved with large rough stones,—they
have usually a gutter in the centre, and occasionally
a narrow pavement on each side. For building
purposes, unhewn granite is chiefly used, the walls
being afterwards smoothed over with a layer of
plaster, whitewashed nd margined with yellow or
blue. The two principal streets are the Rua Direita,
the widest in the ci , and the principal scene of
commercial transactions, and the narrow Rua do
Ouvidor, filled with shops, many of which equal in
the richness and variety of their goods the most
splendid establishments of European capitals. Of
these the most tempting, and the most dangerous
to enter with a well-filled purse, is the famous

feather-flower manufactory of Mme. Finot, where the
gorgeous plumage of humming birds and others of
the feathered tribe is fabricated into wreathes and
bouquets of all kinds. Although the absence of
sewerage is everywhere apparent, the town is well
supplied with water from numerous large fountains,
filled by pipes from an aqueduct five or six miles in
length, communicating with the Corcovado mountain. One is struck with the comparative absence
of wheeled vehicles in the streets of Rio. Now and
then a clumsy calêche is driven past by a negro
postillion, in blue livery and jack boots, riding a
second horse yoked outside the shafts, and omni-
buses drawn by four or six mules, are not unfrequently met with, and seem to be much patronised.

Many of the walks in the neighbourhood of the
city are exceedingly beautiful; one of the pleasantest
leads along the line of the aqueduct. Here the
botanist fresh from Europe, will find subjects of
interest at every step, and the entomologist may
revel to his heart's content among gaudily coloured
Heliconiæ, Hesperiæ, and *Erycinæ,* or watch the
larger butterflies of the restricted genus *Papilio,*
slowly winging their lazy flight among the trees
just beyond the reach of his insect net. A common
butterfly here *(Peridromia Amphinome)* has the
singular habit of frequenting the trunks and limbs
of the trees where it rests with expanded wings,
and generally manages adroitly to shift its position,
and escape when swept at with the net. Some

large dark *Cicadæ* are common among the branches, and the air often resounds with their harsh grating cries, especially towards evening. On the trunks of various trees along the path, especially a thorny-stemmed *Bombax*, the pretty *Bulimus papyraceus* is common, with an occasional *B. Auris-leporis*, but I never during my walks was so fortunate as to find any of the more magnificent of the Brazilian landshells,—for example, *B. ovalis*, a noble species, four or five inches in length, of which I have bought live specimens in the market.

Some of the lanes, in which, on one occasion I lost my way, about dusk, would have reminded me of those of the south of England on a fine autumnal eve, were it not for the scattered palms and papaw trees in the hedge-rows, and the hedges themselves occasionally consisting of the coffee plant, conceal-ing clumps of banana and sugar-cane. The Cicadæ were singing their evening hymn from the branches overhead, and in due time the fire-flies came out in all their glory.

I had looked forward with eager anticipation to the result of the first dredging of the Voyage. None of the ship's boats could be spared, so I hired one pulled by four negro slaves, who, although strong active fellows, had great objections to straining their backs at the oar, when the dredge was down. No sieve having been supplied, we were obliged to sift the contents of the dredge through our hands,—a tedious and superficial mode

of examination.   Still some fine specimens of a
curious flat sea-urchin (*Encope marginata*) and a
few shells, encouraged us to persevere.   Two days
after, Mr. Huxley and myself set to work in Botafogo Bay, provided with a wire-gauze meat cover,
and a curious machine for cleaning rice; these
answered capitally as substitutes for sieves, and
enabled us by a thorough examination of the contents of the dredge, to detect about forty-five species
of mollusca and radiata, some of which were new
to science.   Among these acquisitions I may
mention a new species of *Amphioxus*, a genus of
small fishes exhibiting more anomalies than any
other known to ichthyologists, and the lowest organ-
ization found in the class; it somewhat resembles
the sand-eels of Britain in habits, like them moving
with extraordinary rapidity through the sand.   By
dint of bribery and ridicule, we had at length managed
to get our boatmen to work tolerably well; and
when we were alike well roasted by the sun and
repeatedly drenched, besides being tired out and
hungry, they had become quite submissive, and
exchanged their grumbling for merriment.   A more
lovely spot can scarcely be found, than the secluded
bay of Botafogo with its pretty village, and the
noble Corcovado mountain immediately behind, and
we paid it other visits.

One of the principal characteristics of Rio is
slavery.   Slaves here perform the work of beasts of
burthen; and in the business parts of the city the

attention of a stranger is sure to be arrested by
gangs of them heavily laden, proceeding at a jog-
trot, timing their steps to a monotonous song and
the noise of a tin rattle filled with stones, carried by
their leader.   What their domestic condition and
treatment may be, I know not, but, among the
slaves one sees out of doors, the frequency of iron
collars round the neck, and even masks of tin, concealing the lower part of the face, and secured behind with a padlock, would seem to indicate extreme
brutality in those capable of resorting to such means
of punishment.   Yet these, I was told, were rare
exceptions, the Brazilians not being worse task-
masters than the people of other slave-holding countries,— and such may be the case.

Whatever he may think of the true state of religious feeling, it soon becomes obvious to a stranger
that great care is taken to celebrate the numerous
festivals of the Church with all possible pomp and
splendour.   One day I happened to encounter a
procession in honour of St. Januarius, the patron
saint of Rio.   The number of ecclesiastics taking a
part amounted to several hundreds, and a body of
military brought up the rear.   The streets and windows were crowded with people in their holiday
costume, bands of music were playing, bells were
ringing, flowers were scattered about and showered
down from the houses.   The profusion of tinsel and
embroidery was very great, and the balconies and

windows in the line of procession were hung with rich brocade in all the colours of the rainbow.

A short stay, such as ours, afforded very limited opportunities of judging of the national character; and my impressions on this point were, probably, often erroneous. The Brazilians and English did not then reciprocate very cordially, on account of the existing state of international relations. Of late years great advances appear to have been made upon the mother-country, judging from the increasing liberality of their institutions, the establishment of commercial relations abroad, the freedom of discussion and influence of the press, the attention paid to public education (especially of the middle classes), the support granted to literature and science, and the declining influence of the priesthood in secular matters. The national character, however, can scarcely be considered as fully formed : the Brazilians have been too recently emancipated from the thraldom of a modified despotism to have made, as yet, any very great progress in developing the elements of national prosperity and greatness which the vast empire of Brazil so abundantly possesses, and the foul blot of slavery, with its debasing influence, still remains untouched.

On February 2nd we sailed from Rio for the Cape of Good Hope. The morning being calm, we were towed out by the boats of the squadron until a light air, the precursor of the sea-breeze, set in. While hove-to outside the entrance, a haul of the dredge brought up the rare *Terebratula rosea*, and a small shell of a new genus, allied to *Rissoa*. The remainder of the day and part of the succeeding one were spent in a fruitless search for a shoal said to exist in the neighbourhood, to which Capt. Stanley's attention had been drawn by Capt. Broughton, of H.M.S. Curaçoa.

At one P.M. of each day, when the weather was favourable, the ship was hove-to for the purpose of obtaining observations on the temperature of the water at considerable depths, under the superintendence of Lieut. Dayman. As these were continued during our outward voyage as far as Van Diemen's Land, and the number of observations amounted to 69, the results will more clearly be understood if exhibited in a tabular form, for which the reader is referred to the Appendix. "Two of Sixe's thermometers were attached, one at the bottom of the line of 370 fathoms, the other 150 fathoms higher up. The depth recorded is that given by Massey's patent sounding machine. As the same quantity of line was always used, the difference of depth of each day should be trifling, varying only in proportion to the ship's drift; yet on several occasions the depth recorded by the machine gives as much as 100 fathoms short of the quantity of line let out."*

While engaged in sounding, a process which usually occupied three-quarters of an hour, a boat was always at my service when birds were about the

* Lieut. Dayman, R.N.

ship, and the state of the sea admitted of going after them,—by this means many species of petrels were obtained for the collection. On one of these occasions, owing to a mistake in lowering the stern boat before the ship had quite "lost her way" through the water, one of the falls could not be unhooked in time; consequently the boat was dragged over on her broadside, and finally capsized with eight people in her. Some reached one of the life-buoys, which was instantly let go, the others managed to roll the boat over and right her, full of water. All were eventually picked up by the leeward quarter-boat; the weather one, from the shortness of the davits, would not clear the ship's side, but turned over on her bilge, dipping in the water, and was rendered ineffective when most wanted. This defect in the davits was afterwards remedied by the substitution of other and longer ones, which had formerly belonged to H.M. steam vessel Thunderbolt, wrecked at Algoa Bay a short time previously.

Among many interesting birds* procured in the above mentioned manner, I may allude to *Puffinus cinereus*, an European species of shearwater, which was found to be generally distributed across the South Atlantic between the meridians of 28° W. and 1½° E.; on two successive days, while in the

---

* For the occurrence of *Procellariadæ* during our outward voyage, with a view to determine the geographical distribution of the species met with by me, see "Contributions to Ornithology, by Sir W. Jardine, Bart." p. 94.

neighbourhood of Tristan da Cunha, myriads of these birds passed the ship to the westward, apparently coming from that island. A few days afterwards, while 480 miles from the nearest land, we caught a beautiful tern (*Sterna melanorhyncha*) hitherto considered to be peculiar to Australia.

On several occasions the towing net* produced a rich harvest, especially one day when almost becalmed in lat. 34° 40′ S. and long. 4° W. The surface of the water was absolutely teeming with marine animals. Of these a small *Physalia* and a *Velella* (*V. emarginata?*) were the most plentiful. The latter curious animal, consists of a flat oval expansion, an inch and a half in length, furnished below with numerous cirrhi and a proboscidiform mouth, and above with an obliquely vertical crest, the whole of a rich blue colour with white lines and dots, the soft parts conceal a transparent cartilaginous framework. The crest acts as a tiny sail

---

* Not having seen a description of this useful instrument, 1 may mention that the kind used by Mr. Huxley and myself, consisted of a bag of "bunting" (used for flags,) two feet deep, the mouth of which is sewn round a wooden hoop fourteen inches in diameter; three pieces of cord, a foot and a half long, are secured to the hoop at equal intervals and have their ends tied together. When in use the net is towed astern, clear of the ship's wake, by a stout cord secured to one of the quarter-boats or held in the hand, The scope of line required is regulated by the speed of the vessel at the time. and the amount of strain caused by the partially submerged net.

(hence the name), and communicates to the animal a slow rotatory movement while drifting before the wind. Two kinds of *Janthinæ* (*J. globosa* and *J. exigua,*) molluscs with a fragile, snail-like shell, and a vesicular float, were drifting about, and, together with a very active, silvery-blue *Idotea*, half an inch long, preyed upon the *Velellæ*. At another time, among many other pelagic crustacea, we obtained three kinds of *Erichthus*, a genus remarkable for the glassy transparency of its species, also *Hyalæa inflexa* and *H. tridentata*, curious pteropodous molluscs which swim near the surface.

On March 8th, we anchored in Simon's Bay; our passage from Rio de Janeiro, contrary to expectation, had thus occupied upwards of five weeks, owing to the prevalence of light easterly winds (from N. E. to S. E.) instead of the westerly breezes to be looked for to the southward of lat. 35° S. We were fortunate, however, in having fine weather during the greater part of that time.

The period of our stay at the Cape of Good Hope was devoted to the construction of a chart of Simon's Bay and its neighbourhood, which has since been incorporated with the previous survey of Capt. Sir Edward Belcher in H. M. S. "Samarang," and published without acknowledgment. The requisite shore observations were made by Capt. Stanley and Mr. Obree, while Lieuts. Dayman and Simpson conducted the sounding. Our detention was lengthened by a succession of S.E. gales, and the state of the

weather throughout was such that during the period
of twenty-one days the sounding boats were able to
work on six only,—the other fine days were devoted
to swinging the ships for magnetical purposes. It
was also intended to survey the Whittle shoal in
False Bay, but when we sailed, the weather was so
thick and unsettled, that Capt. Stanley was reluc-
tantly obliged to give it up.

Simon's Town is a small straggling place of
scarcely any importance, except in connection with
the naval establishment kept up here—dockyard,
hospital, &c.—this being the head-quarters of the
Cape station. It is distant from Cape Town twenty-
three miles. The neighbourhood is singularly dreary
and barren, with comparatively little level ground,
and scarcely any susceptible of cultivation. I have
often been struck with the great general similarity
between the barren and sandy tracts of this district,
and many parts of New South Wales, where sandstone is the prevailing rock. In both countries
there are the same low scrubby bushes, at the Cape
consisting of Heaths and Proteæ, and in Australia
of Epacridæ and Banksiæ,—the last the honey-
suckles of the Colonists. Even the beautiful sun-
birds of the Cape, frequenting especially the flowers
of the Proteæ, are represented by such of the Australian honeysuckers as resort to the Banksiæ.

We found the Cape Colony suffering from the
long continuance of the Caffre war. As a natural
consequence, the price of everything had risen, and

there was little specie left in Cape Town. All the troops had been sent to the frontier; a party of blue jackets from the flag-ship at one time performed garrison duty at Cape Town; the emergency was so great that even some detachments of troops on their way back to England after long service in India, having put in at the Cape for refreshments, were detained and sent to Algoa Bay. We were all heartily tired of Simon's Bay long before leaving it; not the less so from having this all engrossing " Caffre war " dinned into our ears from morning to night as an excuse for high prices, and sometimes for various extortions, which I had before supposed to be peculiar to new colonies.

On April 10th we left Simon's Bay for Mauritius. Our passage of twenty-four days presented little remarkable. We experienced every gradation between a calm and a heavy N.E. gale; during the continuance of one of the latter, we passed near the " Slot Van Capel " bank of the old charts, the existence of which it was of importance to verify;* but the heavy confused sea, such as one would expect to find on a bank during a gale, rendered it dangerous to heave-to to try for soundings.

During this passage some important observations were made by Capt. Stanley and Lieut. Dayman to

* I have since learned that H.M.S. Mœander, Capt. the Hon. H. Keppel, struck soundings on this bank, but have not been able to procure the particulars.

determine the height, length, and velocity of the waves. The results will be apparent from the following tabular view.*

Date 1847.	No. of Observations.	Force of Wind.	Speed of Ship.	Height of Wave.	Length of Wave.	Speed of Wave.	Remarks.
		No.	Knots	Feet.	Faths.	Miles.	
April 21		5	7.2	22	55	27.0	Ship before the wind with a heavy following sea.
,, 23	8	5	6	20	43	24.5	,, ,,
,, 24	6	4	6	20	50	24	,, ,,
,, 25	9	4	5		37	22.1	,, ,,
,, 26		4	6		33	22.1	,, ,,
May 2	6	4 & 5	7	22	57	26.2	Sea irregular, observations not very good.
,, 3	7	5	7 & 8	17	35	22.0	Wind and sea on port quarter.

Oceanic birds were plentiful in our wake, and gradually dropped off as we approached the tropic.

* The *height* was determined by watching when the crest of the wave was on a level with the observer's eye (the height above the trough of the sea being known), either while standing on the poop or in the mizzen rigging; this must be *reduced to one half* to obtain the absolute height of the wave above the *mean level* of the sea. The *length* and *velocity* were found by noting the time taken by the wave to traverse the measured distance (100 yards) between the ship and the spar towing astern. In column 3rd, the number 4 denotes a "moderate breeze," and 5 a "fresh breeze."

On May 2 the vicinity of land was denoted by the
appearance of four tropic birds (*Phaëton æthereus*)
and a tern; and next evening, shortly before sunset,
we sighted the Island of Mauritius, the Bamboo
Mountain at Grand Port being the first part seen.
We rapidly closed in with the land, and during the
night were near enough to see the surf on the
coral reefs fringing the shore, it assuming the appearance, in the bright moonshine, of a sandy beach
of glittering whiteness.

Captain Stanley remarks, that " the reef on the
east side of the island projects further than is laid
down on the Admiralty chart, and as from the prevalence of the S. E. trade a current is constantly
setting to the westward, vessels approaching this
part of the island should be very cautious, even
with a leading wind, not to get too close in with the
land until the passage between Gunner's and Round
Island is well under the lee. At night, also, the
distance from the land, when off the N. E. end of
the island, is very deceiving, as the plains of Pamplemousses are very low. The Rattlesnake, in passing at night between the Gunner's Quoin and Flat
Island, experienced a strong set of nearly three
miles an hour to the westward, which at times is
said to be much stronger, and partakes in some
measure of the nature of a tide."

May 4th.—When I came upon deck I found that
we had rounded the north end of the island, and
were beating up for Port Louis. It was a delightful

morning, with bright sunshine, smooth water, a gentle trade wind, and an unclouded sky. The view was very beautiful, and quite equalled my expectations, based, though they were, upon the glowing descriptions of La Pierre. The extremes of the island are low, but the centre is occupied by the partially wooded crest-like ridge, rugged and pinnacled, connecting La Pouce with the famous Peter Botte. Viewed in a mass, the country looked burnt up, of a dull yellowish red hue,—the higher hills were dark green, and the lower grounds partially so. To the left was the fertile plain of Pamplemousses, even now, in the beginning of winter, one mass of green of various degrees of intensity. As we approached we began to make out more distinctly the sugar plantations, the groves of cocoa-nut trees and casuarinas, the features of the town, and the dense mass of shipping in the harbour. We hove to off the Bell Buoy (denoting the outer anchorage), for the steamer which towed us to our berth abreast of Cooper's Island.

The harbour of Port Louis is of singular formation. It is entered by a narrow passage or break in the coral reef surrounding the island, leading into a large basin, the central portion only of which has sufficient water for shipping. The bottom is mud, which, they say, is fast accumulating, especially in a small bight called the Trou Fanfaron, where a few years ago a line-of-battle ship could float, but which has now scarcely water enough for a large corvette. The reefs about the entrance are nearly dry at low water, at which time one may wade to their outer margin, as is daily practised by hundreds of fishermen.

Passing through the closely packed lines of shipping, and landing as a stranger at Port Louis, perhaps the first thing to engage attention is the strange mixture of nations,—representatives, he might at first be inclined to imagine, of half the countries of the earth. He stares at a Coolie from Madras with a breach cloth and soldier's jacket, or a stately, bearded Moor, striking a bargain with a Parsee merchant; a Chinaman, with two bundles slung on a bamboo, hurries past, jostling a group of young Creole exquisites smoking their cheroots at a corner, and talking of last night's Norma, or the programme of the evening's performance at the Hippodrome in the Champ de Mars; his eye next catches a couple of sailors reeling out of a grog-shop, to the amusement of a group of laughing negresses in white muslin dresses of the latest Parisian fashion, contrasting strongly with a mo-destly attired Cingalese woman, and an Indian ayah with her young charge. Amidst all this the French language prevails; everything more or less pertains of the French character, and an English-man can scarcely believe that he is in one of the colonies of his own country.

May 16*th.*—Few passing visitors, like ourselves,

leave the Isle of France without performing a
pilgrimage to Pamplemousses, a pretty village
seven miles distant, near which are the (so called)
tombs of Paul and Virginia, and the Botanic Gardens. For this purpose,—as we sail the day after
to-morrow, I started at daylight. The road, even
at this early hour, was crowded with people—
Coolies, Chinamen, Negroes, and others, bringing in
their produce to market, while every now and then
a carriage passed by filled with well-dressed Creoles
enjoying the coolness of the morning air, or bent
upon making a holiday of it, for the day was
Sunday. I breakfasted in one of the numerous
cabarets by the roadside, dignified with the name of
" Hotel de —, &c." Numerous small streams crossed
the road, and the country, so far as seen, exhibited
a refreshing greenness and richness of vegetation.

" Les Tombeaux " are situated in a garden
surrounded by trees, and a grove of coffee plants,
behind the residence of a gentleman who must
be heartily sick of being so constantly disturbed by
strangers. They exhibit nothing more remarkable
than two dilapidated monumental urns on opposite
sides of the garden, shaded by a clump of bamboos
and casuarinas, the latter usually mistaken for
cypresses. In the coffee plantation close by, I was
delighted to find great numbers of a large and
handsome land shell, *Achatina pantherina,*—it burrows in the earth during dry weather, but some rain

which had fallen during the night brought it out in abundance.

The Botanical Gardens are close to the church. Among the plants are some magnificent sago palms, almost rivalling those I had seen in New Guinea, during the voyage of the Fly,* and many clove and nutmeg trees, the cultivation of which in the island it had been the intention of Government to introduce. Here are some very fine shady walks with ponds of water and rivulets, but although these cool retreats are admirably adapted for solitary rambles and the holding of merry pic-nic parties, I found with regret that the title of *botanical* had misled me.

On my return I was not surprised to see in an island colonised by the French—so little *outward* respect paid to the Sabbath. Many people were at work in the fields, and washerwomen in the streams, —a party of Chinamen were employed roofing a house, and blacksmiths hammered away within gunshot of the church, while many of the shops and all the taverns were open in the villages.

On a former occasion I had made an excursion to the summit of La Pouce, a remarkable knob-like peak on the sharp crateriform ridge behind Port Louis. Following a path, leading from the town directly to Wilhelm's Plains, one crosses a small

* Narrative of the Surveying Voyage of H.M.S. Fly in Torres Strait, New Guinea, and other Islands of the Asiatic Archipelago. By J. Beete Jukes.

stream and skirts the steep face of the hill over rough ground covered with burnt up grass, and straggling bushes. To this succeeds a region of evergreens (among which the wild mango is the prevailing tree), where a species of monkey introduced many years ago into the island has taken up its abode. I saw none, however, but occasionally heard their chattering as they hurried along among the bushes. Where the path crosses the ridge, it widens out into a succession of rounded eminences, with the summit of La Pouce rising suddenly from its centre in a thumb-like form. Its base is watered by a small gushing rill, and the vegetation now is very luxuriant from the continual supply of moisture. The most striking plants are the tree-ferns (*Cyathea excelsa* and *C. Bourbonica*), some of which attain a height of from fifteen to twenty feet. From the eastern margin of the ridge the view is very fine; a sloping precipice, several hundred feet in height, covered with stunted bushes, overlooks Wilhelm's Plains, nearly all under cultivation and studded with sugar plantations. The soil, when newly turned up, appeared of a dull red colour. Numbers of tropic birds were flying along the face of the cliff where they probably breed. Eight species of land shells were picked up here, either creeping up the grass or under stones and logs; they were of the genera *Caracolla*, *Helix*, and *Pupa*.

A narrow path, difficult to find among the long grass, leads to the summit of the mountain, 2,600 feet above the level of the sea. The view from the top embraces the greater part of this fine island. The coral reef fringing the shores is well seen,—the pale green of the shoal water is separated from the deep blue of the ocean by a line of snow-white surf.

For entomological purposes I frequently visited the Cemetery, numbers of insects being attracted by its flowers and trees. The road leading to it, one of the principal evening drives, is shaded by rows of magnificent casuarinas, from Madagascar. Some five or six widely-separated religious creeds may each here be seen practising their peculiar modes of interment—Chinese, Mahometan, Hindoo, and Christian; and among the last it was a novelty to me to observe, for the first time, the pleasing custom of decking the graves with fresh flowers, often renewed weekly for years, disposed in jars of various kinds, from the richly ornamented vase down to the humblest piece of crockery. All the low land hereabouts has been borrowed from the sea; it is a mixture of sand and fragments of coral; and the land-crabs have established a colony in one part of the cemetery, and run riot among the graves.

Although well aware of the productiveness of this fine island in marine objects, I was yet unprepared for the sight of upwards of one hundred species of fish, which I frequently witnessed of a morning in the market at Port Louis; but this to me was diminished by the regret that the most skilful taxidermist would signally fail, either to retain upon the prepared skin, or to reproduce, the bright colours for which so many of them are remarkable. Dredging in the harbour was perfectly unsuccessful; outside the margin of the coral reefs which fringe the entrance to Port Louis one finds a zone of loose blocks of living *Mæandrinæ*, *Astreæ*, and other massive corals, where dredging is impracticable; to this succeeds a belt of dead shells and small fragments of coral; and the remainder of the channel is tenacious mud, in which I found nothing of interest.

After a pleasant stay of twelve days, we left Mauritius, on May 17th, as soon as the last set of "sights" for rating the chronometers had been obtained, and in due time rounded the north end of the island to a light wind off the land. In the first watch a distant light was conjectured, with some degree of probability, to proceed from the well known active volcano of the Island of Bourbon.

During our stay at Port Louis, Captain Stanley had complied with a requisition from the Commissariat to take some specie to Hobart Town, consequently his previous intention of proceeding to Sydney, by way of King George's Sound, was abandoned.

On May 24th (our noon position being in lat. 28° 1′ S., and long. 67° 30′ E.) we tacked to the S. W., having found the impracticability of making a straight course for Cape Leeuwin without first getting well to the southward, and in due time we reached the latitudes where westerly winds prevail, and were enabled to proceed onward on our course.

On June 14th, when in lat. 40° 45′ S., and long. 123° 23′ E., the occurrence of a calm during the forenoon, although accompanied by a considerable swell, induced Captain Stanley to make a third attempt to obtain deep sea soundings. He had been much interested in the success of experiments of this kind, in which the grand desideratum has always been to produce *positive proof of having reached bottom* by bringing up a portion of its substance, hitherto unattempted on account of the great length of time required for the experiment, and the disproportionate strength of the line to the enormous weight employed, should any sudden jerk ensue from the heave of the sea. Captain Stanley had at length succeeded in contriving a very ingenious apparatus by which, upon striking soundings, the eight 32 lbs. shot employed would be immediately detached, leaving no greater weight to be hauled up than the iron framework to which the shot was slung, and a small bell-lead with the usual " arming" of tallow, to which portions of the bottom would adhere. The line was similar to that employed on January 12th, as then carefully coiled away in casks, each of which held from 800 to 1000 fathoms, and ran out remarkably well, without any tendency to " kink" or get foul; but, unfortunately, after 3500 fathoms (or forty yards less than four statute miles) had gone out, the line parted, from some flaw, it is supposed, as a piece of the same bore a far heavier weight when tested subsequently on board. The whole weight employed was equal to 280 lbs.; and the time taken by the line to run out was 1 hour, 59 minutes, and 56 seconds.

Fathom Mark.	Time of Passing.			Fathom Mark.	Time of Passing.		
	Hrs.	Min.	Seconds		Hrs.	Min.	Seconds
100	0	0	42	1900	0	38	11
200	0	1	49	2000	0	41	5
300	0	3	3	2100	0	44	3
400	0	4	23	2200	0	47	38
500	0	5	57	2300	0	50	47
600	0	7	39	2400	0	53	57
700	0	9	30	2500	0	57	6
800	0	11	22	2600	1	0	51
900	0	13	20	2700	1	6	15
1000	0	15	19	2800	1	12	25
1100	0	17	35	2900	1	20	27
1200	0	19	41	3000	1	26	34
1300	0	21	38	3100	1	32	45
1400	0	24	15	3200	1	39	49
1500	0	26	47	3300	1	45	37
1600	0	29	32	3400	1	52	47
1700	0	32	17	3500	1	59	56
1800	0	35	2				

On June 24th we entered Storm Bay, and next day arrived at Hobart Town. None of our Australian colonies — I had previously seen them all — reminded me of the mother country so much as Tasmania. The clearings on the shores of the Derwent looked very pretty, and almos English, particularly the spire of a small church peeping out from among the trees.

CHAPTER II.

WE left Hobart Town for Sydney on July 8th.
On the night of the 15th, saw the fine revolving
light on the South Head of Port Jackson, and next
morning anchored at Farm Cove. Our stay in
Sydney was protracted to a period of nearly three
months. During this time, in consequence of previous arrangements, the schooners Bramble, Lieut.
C. B. Yule, and Castlereagh, Lieut. D. Aird, were
paid off. Both these vessels had been left in
December, 1845, by Capt. F. P. Blackwood, of
H.M.S Fly, to continue the survey of New Guinea,
(as will afterwards be more particularly alluded to),
and had long been awaiting our arrival. The
Castlereagh, originally purchased in Sydney, being

reported to be quite unfit for surveying purposes, was sold to her former owner; and the Bramble was re-commissioned as tender to the Rattlesnake, and continued under the command of Lieut. Yule. Ten additional men were entered on board, increasing our complement to 190 officers and men, of whom 36 were placed on board the schooner. After a thorough refit, both vessels were at length quite ready for sea.

Meanwhile a minute survey was made by Lieutenants Dayman and Simpson of the inner entrance to Port Jackson, where a reef, called the Sow and Pigs, (distinguished by a beacon and a light vessel,) in the middle of the passage, leaves only a narrow available channel on either side. The exact boundaries of them, with the depth of water, were to be determined, especially to ascertain whether a line-of-battle ship, with her full armament, could pass into the harbour. The shoalest part of the west channel was found to have 21 feet, and of the east 24 feet at low water (the rise and fall of tide being from 5 to 8 feet); consequently, at high water there would be room for a three-decker to enter.* This work was in connexion with a proposed dry dock† on Cockatoo Island, above Sydney,

* It was found by comparison with Lieut. Roe's survey, made 25 years before, that the inner edge of the shoal had extended considerably to the southward.

† This has for several years been under construction; its importance will appear more evident, when it is considered that a

towards the expenses of which the Imperial Government were willing to contribute, provided it were made of such a size as to be available for large steamers and line-of-battle ships.

In compliance with a requisition from Sir Charles Fitzroy, the Governor of New South Wales, Capt. Stanley, in the Bramble, paid a visit to Twofold Bay, 200 miles to the southward of Sydney, a place of rising importance as a harbour, also in connexion with whaling establishments, and the extensive adjoining pastoral district of Maneroo. The bay was resurveyed, with a view to test the comparative merits of the two townships there,—one founded by government, the other by private enterprise. After all, I believe, the advantages afforded by each of the rival establishments are so equally divided, that the question still remains an open one.

Oct. 11th.—After a protracted stay in Sydney of very nearly three months, we were at length enabled to start upon our first cruize to the northward, the object of which was to make a survey of Port Curtis and part of the Inshore Passage leading up to Torres Strait. The Rattlesnake and tender got under weigh soon after daybreak and ran out of Port Jackson to the northward with a fine S. E. wind. In the evening the Bramble parted company, her present destination being Port Stephens,

large vessel in the Australian colonies requiring repairs, which cannot be effected by the process of " heaving down," will find no suitable place nearer than Bombay.

for the purpose of running a meridian distance, and ours Moreton Bay.

One day, while off Cape Byron, an interesting addition to zoology was made in a small floating shell-fish, which has since proved to constitute a new genus,* throwing light, I am informed, upon many fossil univalves in the older formations ; and a rare bird of the noddy kind (*Anous leucocapillus*) perched on the rigging towards evening, and was added to the collection ; for even the beauty and innocence of a tired wanderer like it was insufficient to save it from the scalpel.

On Oct. 18th we anchored in Yule's Roads, Moreton Bay, in 12 fathoms, sand, about a mile off shore, and remained there for sixteen days. During our stay, some additions were made to render more complete the former survey of this important sheet of water. Buoys were laid down to mark the intricate channels of the north entrance, now preferred for its greater safety to the south entrance, although lengthening by about 50 miles the passage to or from Sydney. The wreck of a steamer, and loss of most of those on board, had not long before caused a great sensation, and forcibly attracted attention to the dangers of the southern entrance.

Moreton Bay is an expanse of water 45 miles in length, and 20 in greatest width, enclosed between

* This mollusc, allied to *Litiopa*, Professor E. Forbes has done me the honour to publish in the Appendix as *Macgillivrayia pelagica*.

the mainland and Stradbroke and Moreton Islands. It is open to the northward, but sheltered on the eastward by the two islands forming that side, which run nearly north and south. The Brisbane river enters the bay about the middle of its western side, and, having been the means of opening up an immense extent of the finest pastoral country, it has conferred a considerable degree of importance upon the place as a harbour, although beset with numerous shoals and narrow winding passages, through which the tides run with great force. The entrance to the river has a depth of only 10 or 11 feet at high water, consequently, is available for small vessels only ; the best anchorage for larger ones is five miles distant. The banks are constantly shifting, and the channel is intricate. When to this is added that the settlement,— consisting of the townships of North and South Brisbane, and Kangaroo Point, is situated 14 miles from the river mouth—it was not surprising that a proposal had been made to establish a trading port elsewhere in the bay, so that the wool and other produce of the district, might be shipped direct for England.

For this purpose, Cleveland Point (at the southeast side of the bay) had been suggested, and the Colonial Government requested Captain Stanley's opinion on the subject :— which is as follows. "This," says he, " is the worst possible place I ever saw for such a purpose ; from the proposed site of the town, a low rocky point only a few feet above the level of high water, projects for more than a mile in the sea; and from both sides of this, mud-flats, that become dry at low water, extend for a very considerable distance. The anchorage off this point must be of necessity in the stream of tide, which, when it sets against even a moderate breeze, causes a heavy sea. And as the point affords no shelter whatever for boats, it will be absolutely necessary to build a breakwater, at least as far out as three fathoms at low water."

Moreton Island, under the lee of which the Rattlesnake was at anchor, is 19 miles in length, and 4½ in greatest breadth. It consists for the most part of series of sand-hills, one of which, Mount Tempest, is said to be 910 feet in height; on the north-west portion a large tract of low ground, mostly swampy, with several lagoons and small streams. The soil is poor, and the grass usually coarse and sedge-like. All the timber is small, and consists of the usual *Eucalypti, Banksiæ,* &c. with abundance of the cypress-pine (*Callitris arenaria*) a wood much prized for ornamental work. The appearance along the shores of the Pandanus or screw-pine, which now attains its southern limits, introduces a kind of intertropical appearance to the vegetation. Among the other plants are three, which merit notice from their efficacy in binding down the drift sand with their long trailing stems, an office performed in Britain by the bent grass (*Arundo arenaria*), here represented by another grass, *Ischæmum Rottboellioide*: the others are a handsome pink flowered convolvulus (*Ipomœa maritima*), one stem of which measured 15 yards in length, and *Hibbertia volubilis*, a plant with large yellow blossoms.

Among the marine animals of Moreton Bay are two cetacea of great interest. The first of these is the Australian dugong (*Halicore Australis*), which is the object of a regular fishery (on a small scale however,) on account of its valuable oil. It frequents the Brisbane river and the mudflats of the harbour, and is harpooned by the natives, who know it under the name of *Yung-un*. The other is an undescribed porpoise, a specimen of which, however, I did not procure, as the natives believed the most direful consequences would ensue from the destruction of one; and I considered the advantages resulting to science from the addition of a new species of *Phocæna*, would not have justified me in outraging their strongly expressed superstitious feelings on the subject. We observed that whenever a drove of these porpoises came close inshore, a party of natives followed them along the beach, and when a shoal of fish, endeavouring to avoid their natural enemies, approached within reach, the blacks rushed out into the water with loud cries, and, keeping their bag nets close together, so as to form a semicircle, scooped out as many fish as came within reach.

Our seining parties from the ship were usually very successful, but only at one particular time of tide,

or during the " young flood." Sharks are numerous
close to the beach, but are generally small and
harmless; one of the natives however had lost his
foot at the ankle joint, from the bite of one.

There were then no white residents upon Moreton
Island, but we found a party of about twenty
natives encamped near the watering place. Some
of the men were rather good specimens of the race,
but the reverse was the case with the females;
although the latter on the first day of our meeting
them evinced a desire to cover their persons, they
afterwards went about as naked as the men, — but the
female children wore a small fringe in front. The
married women had lost the last joint of the little
finger of the right hand,—one had three half-caste
children. The huts of these natives are of simple
construction, yet comfortable enough, and perfectly
waterproof,—a framework of sticks in a dome-like
form is covered with bark of the tea-tree (*Melaleuca*) and branches of trees.

While procuring materials for a vocabulary, I
found that even this small party contained individuals of two tribes, speaking different dialects.
It was curious to observe that although these
natives had had much intercourse with Europeans,
a party of them who came on board, could not be
persuaded to go below; and one strong fellow
(" one-eye," as he called himself) actually trembled
with fear when I laid hold of him by the arm, to
lead him down to the main-deck.

Nov. 4th.—Sailed from Moreton Bay for Port Curtis in company with the Bramble. The wind being at north, we had to beat out through the narrow channel leading between the banks of the north entrance, probably never before attempted by a square-rigged vessel.

On *Nov. 7th,* we rounded Breaksea Spit, and passed Lady Elliott's Island,—low, of coral formation, and one of the great breeding places of the sea-birds of this portion of the coast. Next day we anchored five miles off the south entrance of Port Curtis, and sent in two boats to sound. On their return with a favourable report, the ship was got under weigh, and ran in under the head sails to round Gatcombe Head, by the channel laid down in Flinders' chart; but, while following a boat ahead in charge of the master, the signal to "anchor immediately" was made, and we brought up as required, being then about the middle of the north channel.

We remained here until the boats had sounded the remainder of the approach to the port sufficiently to enable Capt. Stanley to move the vessel without risk to a safe anchorage inside, at a spot convenient for landing at all times to obtain the requisite observations for determining an astronomical position, and sufficiently central as a starting point for boat operations. This was effected on the 10th of November, when we anchored in 5 fathoms, mud, at three cables lengths distance from the shore.

In January, 1847, the recently proposed colony of " North Australia " was established by a party from Sydney, under Lieut.-Col. Barney, R.E., with a suitable staff of public functionaries. The colonists encountered more than usual difficulties and hardships even at the commencement. The transport conveying the first portion of the party, consisting of eighty-eight persons, struck on the shoal off Gatcombe Head, and required to be hove down, a fit spot for which purpose was fortunately found in a narrow but deep mangrove creek further up the harbour, at a place indicated upon the Rattlesnake's chart. The party were at first encamped upon the south end of Facing Island, but afterwards removed to the main land, upon a site for the new township of Gladstone having been chosen there. The settlement, however, was abandoned, after a short-lived existence of five months, in obedience to orders received from home, consequent upon a change in the plans of Government regarding the disposal of convicts, for " North Australia " had been originally intended to be a penal settlement, or one for the reception of " exiles." The expenses incurred by this experiment amounted to upwards of £15,000.

The survey of the harbour and its approaches occupied a period of three weeks. Although this work had ceased to be one of immediate importance, yet it will eventually be of considerable benefit to the colony of New South Wales, as the gradual extension of the squatting stations to the northward from the Wide Bay district must, ere long, call Port Curtis into requisition as a harbour, and thus enable the settlers to obviate the necessity of a long and expensive land carriage to Wide Bay, the nearest place resorted to by the small coasting vessels, communicating with Brisbane and Sydney.

In illustration of this important subject, I cannot do better than quote portions of a despatch from Colonel Barney to Sir Charles Fitzroy, dated Sydney, 20th July, 1847, published in a return ordered by the House of Commons.

" The extent of land fit for agriculture, within a few miles of the coast, far exceeds the expectations I had formed on my first visit. Timber for dwelling-houses and for shipbuilding is abundant, and of the best description, and within five miles of South Shore Head (the best site for a settlement) there is to be found pipeclay, brick-earth, ironstone, freestone, granite, trap, slate, indications of coal; and independent of a great supply of shells for lime on the immediate site, there is at the head of one of the navigable salt creeks a fine fresh-water stream running over a bed of limestone; a second creek, in which the ' Lord Auckland ' of 600 tons, is hove down, also navigable for ten or twelve miles, terminates in extensive water-holes; indeed within the port there are four inlets or creeks, navigable from ten to fifteen miles for vessels drawing eight or nine feet of water, each terminating in fresh water.

" The position and extent of Port Curtis, which I take to be the third harbour in importance in these seas, inferior only to Port Jackson and Hobart Town, must shortly lead to an establishment on its shore, offering security to numerous whaling vessels, which are now compelled to proceed to Sydney for repairs and supplies ; it must also become an important depôt for supplying steamers on passage to India with coal, which I have reason to believe will be found in abundance within a few miles of the coast. I have no doubt also that this port will become celebrated for shipbuilding, possessing, as it does, timber of the highest quality for such purposes, and favourable positions for building, as well as for the construction of docks.

"The country is capable of affording all the tropical, as well as a considerable portion of European produce, and will be found highly favourable for the breeding of stock; indeed, I believe I am correct in stating that numerous parties, with stock to a very large amount, are now within a short distance of Port Curtis, taking up stations, not only with a view to the supply of the projected settlement, but also to the shipment of wool, tallow, &c. direct to England."

A few days after our arrival at Port Curtis, the Asp, as our decked boat had been named, joined us, having made an important addition to the surveys of this portion of the coast. On his passage up from Brisbane, Lieut. Dayman, under the unexpected circumstances of finding that the Rattlesnake had sailed, instead of coasting along the eastern side of Great Sandy Island, thus involving the necessity of rounding Breaksea Spit, determined upon trying the passage between that island and the mainland leading into Hervey's Bay; this he fortunately succeeded in accomplishing, although under difficulties which his sketch (since published by the Admiralty), will lessen to those who may require to use the same previously little known channel.

Port Curtis, comprising a space of about ten miles in length, is enclosed between Facing Island on the east, or to seaward, Curtis Island on the north, and the shores of the main land on the western side,

leaving to the southward a wide entrance partially
blocked up by shoals.   Besides the narrow channel
described by Flinders as leading between the south
end of Facing Island and the large bank of shoal
water extending about six miles to the south-east,
a second, and much safer one, the least width of
which is upwards of a mile, was discovered between
the large bank and others of less extent towards the
main land.

We landed almost daily upon Facing Island,
which was traversed in every direction, but nowhere
could we find a practicable watering place for the
ship; in fact, during our excursions, it was found
necessary to carry a supply of water with us, not
being able to depend upon obtaining any on shore.
The island is 8½ miles long and 2¾ in greatest
width; it is generally low, the most elevated part,
Signal Hill, situated at its south end, measuring
only 275 feet in height.   Its aspect is various; the
shores, as well as those of the adjacent main land,
are often muddy, and covered with mangroves,
fringing creeks, and occupying swamps more or less
extensive, while the remainder of the country is
either covered with the usual monotonous gum-trees,
or, as over a large portion of the sea face, covered
with coarse sedgy grass and small bushes, on sandy
ground, which rises into a series of low sand hills extending along the coast.   During winter there must
be much water, judging from several nearly dried up
lagoons and swamps, and some empty water-courses.

In company with Mr. Huxley, I made an excursion of two days' duration, with the double view of seeing the country and adding to my collection. We started heavily laden with provisions, water, arms and ammunition, besides boxes, botanical paper and boards, and other collecting gear; and although taking it very easily, the fatigue of walking in a sultry day, with the thermometer at 90° in the shade, afforded a sample of what we had afterwards so often to experience during our rambles in tropical Australia. Towards the northern end of the island we found several creeks and lagoons of salt and brackish water, occasionally communicating with the sea, probably under the conjoined influences of spring tides and a strong easterly wind. Towards evening, finding among the contents of our game-bags several ducks, of two species—*Anas superciliosa*, the " black duck " of the colonists, the richest and best flavoured of all the Australian water-fowl, and *A. punctata*, or " teal," we had them cooked " bush fashion," for supper. The night being fine, we enjoyed our bivouac upon the top of a sand-hill, near the sea, by the side of a dead Pandanus, which served as firewood,—although it was judged expedient to keep watch by turns, and go the rounds occasionally, especially after the setting of the moon and before daybreak. We saw no recent signs of natives, however, during our absence from the ship; but former experience upon this coast had taught me how necessary it is to be ever on one's guard, even in apparently uninhabited places; and such watchfulness soon becomes habitual, and at length ceases to be irksome. Next day we returned to the ship, more than ever convinced of the comparative uselessness of the country which we had gone over for agricultural or even pastoral purposes, except on a very small scale. On our way back we met with two horses, both in good condition, which had been left by Colonel Barney's party.

On another occasion Mr. Huxley and myself landed at the site of the settlement of Gladstone, and were picked up in the evening by Capt. Stanley in one of the surveying boats, on his return to the ship. It is difficult to conceive a more dreary spot, and yet I saw no more eligible place for a settlement on the shores of the harbour. A few piles of bricks, the sites of the tents, some posts, indicating the remains of a provisional "Government-house," wheel-ruts in the hardened clay, the stumps of felled trees, together with a goodly store of empty bottles strewed about everywhere, remained as characteristics of the first stage of Australian colonization. Within 200 yards of the township we came upon a great expanse of several hundred acres of bare mud, glistening with crystals of salt, bordered on one side by a deep muddy creek, and separated from the shore by thickets of mangroves. The country for several miles around is barren in the extreme, consisting for the most part of undulating, stony, forest land. I have heard, however, that there is much good pastoral country at the back. We found no fresh water during our walk; of two wells which had been dug by the settlers, through stiff clay, one was dry, and the other contained a puddle of brackish water, not fit to drink. We met with few birds, but saw many tracks of emus and kangaroos.

During our stay at Port Curtis, we had no intercourse whatever with the natives, although anxious to establish friendly communication. With the aid of the spyglass, we could occasionally make out a few, chiefly women, collecting shell-fish on the mud flats of the main land, and their fires were daily seen in every direction. The employment of fire-arms against them on several occasions by the crew of the Lord Auckland (under, apparently, justifiable circumstances however), which left the harbour, after repairing her damages, only a few months before our arrival, had probably taught the natives to look with distrust upon white men; and they cautiously avoided our parties.

On Facing Island, our sportsmen found little inland to recompense them for their trouble, except blue mountain parrots and quail; but along the shore, curlews, oystercatchers, and godwits, were plentiful. One day I killed a bustard (*Otis Australasiana*), weighing 22½ pounds; the goodness of its flesh was duly appreciated by my messmates. Several small flocks of this noblest of the Australian game-birds were seen; but, from their frequenting the

open country, and being very wary, it is only by
stratagem or accident that they can be approached
within gunshot.   No land snakes were seen, but
sea snakes seem to be frequent in the harbour.
Sharks of enormous size appeared to be common ;
one day we caught two, and while the first taken
was hanging under the ship's stern, others made
repeated attacks upon it, raising their heads partially out of the water, and tearing off long strips
of the flesh before the creature was dead.   Another
swam off apparently as active as ever, although a
musket ball had been fired through its head.   On
several occasions a party was sent to haul the seine
upon a neighbouring mud flat covered at high
water, and generally made good captures, especially
of mullet and bream *(Chrysophrys)* ; in addition,
many other more curious fishes were caught, and
several rare and new crustacea— *Squilla, Lupea
Thalamita,* and a new genus allied to *Gonoplax,*
which will be found described in the Appendix.
Of landshells, only two kinds, a *Helix* and a
Succinea, were found upon Facing Island.   Of
marine species, 41 were added to the collection ;
the most important in a non-zoological point of
view is a kind of rock oyster of delicious flavour
and large size.

Nov. 29th.—Sailed from Port Louis for the
northward, in company with the Asp, the Bramble
being sent to Moreton Bay in order to communicate
the results of the survey to the Colonial Govern-

ment, and rejoin us at Cape Upstart. For the next two days light northerly winds prevailed, after which we had the wind from about E.S.E.

Dec. 3rd.—Percy Isles. The Asp having made a signal for assistance, and it being ascertained that she had lost her dingey and bumpkin by a sea which struck her while crossing a tide-race, it was judged necessary to run for the nearest place where the damage could be repaired. We consequently anchored under No. 2 of the Percy Isles, to leeward of its south-west point, in 10 fathoms, mud, between it and the Pine Islets of the chart.

Here it blew so hard from E.S.E. that a second anchor was let go; the yards were pointed to the wind, and the top-gallant masts sent on deck. A party which attempted to land were forced to return, nor was it thought expedient to repeat the attempt on the following day. We remained at this anchorage until the 7th, and found the gale to subside into the south-east trade.

This is the largest of the Percy Isles, being about twelve or fourteen miles in circumference. In structure, it may be said to consist of a series of hills running in ridges, many of them covered with gum-tree scrub; and all with long grass growing in tufts, concealing the loose stones, and rendering walking very laborious. On the western side of the island, about a mile from the anchorage, the sea communicates, by a narrow entrance, with a large basin partially blocked up with mangroves, among which a creek filled at high water, runs up for a mile. At the head of this hollow a deeply worn dried-up watercourse indicated the periodical abundance of fresh water ; and by tracing it up about a mile further, I found many large pools among the rocks containing a sufficient supply for the ship, but unavailable to us in consequence of the difficulty in getting at it. Signs of natives were frequently met with, but none were recent. From the quantities of turtle-bones about the fire-places, it is evident that these animals occasionally resort to a small sandy beach near the entrance of the basin above alluded to.

The botany of the island afforded at this unfavourable season not more than five or six species of plants in flower, some of which I had met with elsewhere. A species of pine, *Araucaria Cunninghami*, is found here in small quantities, but more plentifully on the adjacent Pine Islets, where it appears to constitute the only arboreal vegetation. A few cabbage palms, *Corypha Australis*, are the only other trees worth mentioning. Among the birds observed, black and white cockatoos, swamp pheasants, and crows were the most numerous. A fine banded snail, *Helix Incei*, was the only land-shell met with. A *Littorina* and a *Nerita* occur abundantly on the trunks and stems of the mangroves, and the creek swarmed with sting-rays (*Trygon*), and numbers of a dull green swimming crab.

During our stay, the bush was thoughtlessly set

on fire by some of our people, and continued burning for several days, until nearly the whole island had been passed over; the long dry grass and dead trees blazing very fiercely under the influence of a high wind. At night the sight of the burning scrub was very fine when viewed from a distance, but I did not forget that I had one day been much closer to it than was pleasant—in fact, it was only by first soaking my clothes in a pool among the rocks, emptying the contents of my powder flask to prevent the risk of being blown up, and then making a desperate rush through a belt of burning scrub, that I succeeded in reaching a place of safety.

Singularly enough, the Asp's dingey was picked up uninjured on one of the sandy beaches of this island, and on December 7th we left the anchorage with a strong south-easterly wind, and anchored for the night under one of Sir James Smith's group. On the following day we ran through part of Whitsunday Passage, so named by Cook, and anchored in Port Molle, in seven and a half fathoms, a quarter of a mile off shore. The best anchorage here appears to be in the second bay as you round the end of the island, forming the S.E. side of the harbour; it may be known by a sandy beach at the head.

During our stay of two days, search was made for water in every likely spot, but none could be found. In the dried up beds of three shallow lagoons (one of which I had seen half filled four years before), we found native wells, one dug to the

depth of six feet, but the water had disappeared.
Port Molle, besides being a well sheltered harbour
from all prevailing winds, has a much more pleasing
aspect than almost any place I have seen on the
north-east coast of Australia. To ourselves the
change was agreeable; instead of the monotonous
gum-trees and mangroves of Port Curtis and the
scantily wooded stony hills of the Percy Isles, we
had here many varieties of woodland vegetation,
including some large patches of dense brush or
jungle, in which one might observe every shade of
green from the sombre hue of the pine, to the pale
green of the cabbage-palm.

Some rare birds were procured in the brushes,—
two of them appear here to attain their southern
limits of distribution upon the north-east coast of
Australia; they are the Australian sun-bird
(*Cinnyris Australis*), reminding one of the humming birds from its rich metallic colouring, and the
Megapodius Tumulus, a rasorial bird, the size of a
fowl, which constructs great mounds of earth, leaves,
sticks, stones, and coral, in which the eggs are
deposited at a depth of several feet from the surface,
and left there to be hatched by the heat of the
fermenting mass of vegetable matter. In addition
to these, our sportsmen were successful in procuring
numbers of the pheasant-tailed pigeon, and the
brush-turkey (*Talegalla Lathami*), the latter much
esteemed, from the goodness of its flesh. Many
plants and insects as well as several land-shells, new

to science, which will elsewhere be alluded to, were added to the collection. Doubtless fish are also plentiful here, but we were prevented from hauling the seine by the remains of a wreck in the centre of a flat of muddy sand at the head of the bay where we were anchored; the vessel, I have since heard, had come in contact with a coral reef, and been run on shore here, in order to save a portion of her stores.

Dec. 10*th.*—In company with the Asp we ran up to the northward to Cape Upstart, a distance of about ninety miles, and anchored in five fathoms off the sandy beach inside the point. Two boats were immediately sent to search for water, but we found the pools where the Fly had watered, in 1844, completely empty; and it was not until the deep rocky bed of the torrent had been traced upwards of a mile higher up on the following morning, that fresh water was met with; but at too great a distance from the shore, to be available for our purposes. Judging from the almost total want of water at all the places hitherto visited on this coast since entering the tropics that there was little probability of our finding it at Goold Island, Captain Stanley determined to proceed no further, but return at once to Sydney, by way of Moreton Bay, and letters were left for Lieutenant Yule signifying this intention.

Dec. 15*th.*—Three days ago we sailed for Cape

Upstart on our return to the southward, working down the coast against a strong trade-wind, the Asp keeping in shore to survey the neighbourhood of the coast line, imperfectly and erroneously laid down upon the Admiralty chart. We had calms and light winds with thick rainy weather in the morning. While in Whitsunday Passage, a small bark canoe with two natives came off to within a quarter of a mile of the ship, shouting loudly and making gestures to attract attention, but we did not stop; in fact, every moment now was precious, as we were upon reduced allowance of water. Soon after noon we anchored in Port Molle, and next day the Asp was stripped and hoisted inboard.

Dec. 21st.—Since we left Port Molle, the winds have been variable from the northward and eastward, with calms, and the weather quite unsettled with occasional rain. While nearly becalmed, several opportunities were afforded for dredging from the ship, and many new and curious marine animals were procured. To-day we had the wind from E.S.E., gradually freshening to a moderate gale with the sea getting up, and in the evening it was judged expedient to bear up and run for an anchorage under the largest Keppel's Isle, where we brought up in five and a half fathoms, sand. A line of breaking water a quarter of a mile to leeward, was afterwards found to be caused by a dangerous reef not indicated upon the chart, where, instead, an anchorage was marked, a circumstance which might have led to serious results, had we run in during the night.

Keppel's Isle is from ten to twelve miles in circumference—it is distant from the mainland six miles. That portion of it seen from our anchorage presented rather a pleasant appearance; some fine verdant grassy looking places were, however, found on closer inspection to be poor stony or sandy ground, thinly covered with tufts of coarse grass. Behind a long sandy beach abreast of the ship, an extensive hollow apparently running back for two or three miles, flanked by low wooded hills, was found to be a mangrove swamp traversed by several branches of a salt-water creek, by which the flood-tide gains admittance. Here I found numbers of a singular fish of the genus *Chironectes* leaping with great activity over the mud among the arched roots of the mangroves, among which small crabs (*Ocypoda* and *Macrophthalmus*) were making for their burrows in all directions. Fresh water appeared scarce—I came upon one small well, and beside it a large shell for the purpose of drinking from. I followed the recent tracks of two natives, but they concealed themselves among the mangroves, with their usual caution, although armed with spears, as I could see by the marks left during their hurried flight, and they knew that I was alone. A small group of women and children were afterwards met with by a shooting party from the ship, but they ran off affrighted, leaving behind their baskets, which were filled with a small blue gregarious crab, common upon the sandy beaches.

After leaving our anchorage under Keppel's Island, we continued working to the southward against a strong S.E. wind. On the 24th while standing in for the land, about 11 P.M., the ship was suddenly found to be within a cable's length of the rocks off the N.E. end of Facing Island, on which we were fortunate in not having to spend our Christmas. Next day a water-snake (*Hypotrophis Jukesii*) four feet two inches long was caught when we were several miles off the land; it had accidentally been hooked by the tail by some one fishing for albacore, several of which fine fish were taken hereabouts. We rounded Breaksea Spit on December 29th, and two days afterwards arrived at Moreton Bay, where we found the Bramble.

During our stay at Yule's Roads, we had much gloomy blowing weather, with drizzly rain, and a heavy gale from N.E. to N.N.E. After replenishing our nearly exhausted stock of water, we sailed for Sydney, which we reached on January 14th, 1848. During this passage we were much aided by the strong current, and had usually the wind between S.E. and E.S.E., with occasional calms.

Feb. 2nd, 1848.—During our absence from Sydney, and since our arrival, some events of great importance to the colony had occurred. Public attention had been strongly directed towards the question of

Steam Communication with India and England, the facilitating of which was one of the principal objects of the Voyage of the Rattlesnake.*　Meetings to discuss the practicability of forming railroads† had also been held.　Dr. Leichhardt, the well-known, indefatigable traveller, had started with a party to attempt to traverse the Continent of Australia, and reach Swan River,—and Mr. Kennedy had returned from tracing the Victoria River of Sir Thomas Mitchell, which he found to become lost in the stony desert of Sturt, instead of disemboguing into the head of the Gulf of Carpentaria, as some had conjectured.

During our stay the 60th anniversary of the foundation of the colony was celebrated, and a large proportion of the 50,000 inhabitants of Sydney and the neighbourhood joined in the festivities and amusements commemorating so glorious a day in the annals of their adopted country.　When witnessing the gaieties of the regatta, I could not help reflecting on the simple narrative of the first founder of what may hereafter become a great empire, a mighty monument of the genius of the Anglo-Saxon race.　"The spot chosen for our encampment," says Colonel Collins, "was at the head of the cove

---

* This project, I regret to add, has not yet been carried into effect, nor does there appear to be any reasonable prospect of its speedy accomplishment.

† I have lately heard that the first Australian railroad has actually been commenced at Sydney.

near the run of fresh water which stole silently along through a very thick wood, the stillness of which had then, for the first time since the creation, been interrupted by the rude sound of the labourer's axe, and the downfall of its ancient inhabitants; a stillness and tranquillity which from that day were to give place to the voice of labour, the confusion of camps, and the busy hum of its new possessors."*

Finding that there was yet some time to spare before the arrival of the usual period for leaving Sydney to pass through Torres Strait, Captain Stanley resolved upon acting in accordance with the expressed wishes of the Colonial Government, that he should make an inspection of the various lighthouses in Bass' Strait, and for that purpose sailed from Sydney on February 2nd, with the Rattlesnake and Bramble. The Asp and one of the galleys accompanied us as far as Botany Bay, which they were to be employed in surveying during our absence, under the orders of Lieut. Simpson.

On February 8th, we passed between Kent's and Hogan's groups (in Bass' Strait); the lighthouse on the former of these, perched upon a hill 829 feet high, is admirably situated, and although the night was rather hazy, the light (revolving) shone out with great brilliance, and was afterwards seen from the Bramble's deck, when thirty-seven miles distant. We caught, in the narrows of the Strait,

* Collins's New South Wales, 2nd edit. p. 10.

numbers of baracoudas, a very bold and ravenous
fish, and withal a good eating one, measuring from
two to three feet in length ; they bite eagerly at a
hook towing astern, baited with a piece of red or
white rag, and are taken in greatest numbers when
several miles distant from the land, and the vessel
is going from four to eight knots through the water.

Two days afterwards, the weather being extremely
favourable for the purpose, I got several hauls with
the dredge in forty-five fathoms, sandy bottom,
and, in addition to many curious crustacea and
shell-fish, a number of very fine zoophytes, almost
all of them new to science, were in such abundance
as quickly to fill the net.

Feb. 11*th.*—While standing off and on the land
during a fog, a partial clearing up shewed the
entrance to Port Phillip, with its lighthouse,* and
after passing through between the heads, with the
usual strong tide ripple, we reached the anchorage
at Hobson's Bay after dark.

I found no alteration in William's Town, since a
former visit made two years ago. The place

* Of this Captain Stanley remarks—" In consequence of being
placed so far within the heads, the light is visible to seaward
only between the bearings of S$\frac{1}{2}$W. and S.W.$\frac{1}{4}$W. A better
position would be on Lonsdale Point, when the light would be
seen by vessels coming from the eastward as soon as they rounded
Cape Schank. It would also serve as a leading mark for navi-
gating the southern channel, but the tower would require to be
of considerable height to shew the light over Shortland's Bluff to
vessels inside the harbour."

appeared to be completely at a stand-still, as a small straggling village of 200 inhabitants, chiefly dependent upon the shipping for support.   Far different was it with Melbourne, the capital of the district.   On our way in a steamer up the Yarra-Yarra, several large and recently constructed boiling-down establishments in full work indicated the extensive operation of the tallow-manufacturing process.   The town (or city as it may, I believe, be termed) appeared to have wonderfully increased of late, and a quiet business-like air prevailed.   Everywhere we met bullock-teams and drays recently arrived with wool, or on their return to the sheep stations with supplies, but there were few loungers like ourselves in the streets, nearly every one seeming to have his time fully occupied.

It appeared to be the general and loudly expressed opinion, so far as we could judge, that the separation of the Port Phillip district from New South Wales, and its formation into an independent colony, would materially advance the interests and conduce to the prosperity of the former; and that the large surplus revenue which is annually transmitted to Sydney ought to be spent among the people who have raised it.*

One day some of us made up a party to visit

---

* These and other claims of the colonists have, I need scarcely add, been fully admitted by the recent separation from New South Wales of the Port Phillip district, now the colony of Victoria.

Geelong, the town in this district of next importance to Melbourne, from which it is distant, by water, fifty-five miles. The western shores of Port Phillip, along which we passed, are low, thinly wooded, and bear a very monotonous aspect. Vast numbers of a large " sea-jelly" (*Rhizostoma Mosaica*), gave the water quite a milky appearance. I was surprised to find the town, only a few years old, to be one already containing about 3000 inhabitants. It is built on a range of low gravelly banks facing the harbour, from which it extends backwards in a straggling manner towards the river Barwon, which, at the distance of a mile and a half, was then 100 yards wide, deep, and without current. The town of Geelong derives its consequence from being a convenient outlet for the wool and other produce of the southern districts of Port Phillip— perhaps the best sheep country in Australia. Four or five vessels were then loading for England. Unfortunately, Corio Harbour, on the shores of which the town is built, is blocked up by a bar, and vessels of moderate size are obliged to remain in Geelong Bay, about five miles off, while discharging or receiving cargo.

Five days after clearing the Heads of Port Phillip, we had crossed Bass' Strait,* and anchored

* For every information required by navigators passing through Bass' Strait, I would refer to Discoveries in Australia, with an account of the Coasts and Rivers explored and surveyed during the Voyage of H.M.S. Beagle, in the years 1837-43, by J. Lort

in Port Dalrymple, on the northern coast of Van
Diemen's Land, and remained there sufficiently
long to obtain rates for the chronometers, and connect it by meridian distance with William's Town,
and Sydney.*   The two lighthouses of Banks'
Strait only now remained unvisited, that on the
Kent Group, and another on Cape Otway, having
been left to Lieut. Yule.

March 3rd.—With the help of a strong westerly
wind we reached Goose Island at 5 P.M., and a
party from the ship landed immediately after anchoring.   The island is one and a half miles in
length, by one in greatest breadth.   The rock is a
coarse sienite, forming detached bare masses and
ridges, but none of considerable height.   In the
hollows the soil appears rich, dark, and pulverulent,
with much admixture of unformed bird-guano.   The

Stokes, Commander, R.N., and to the Admiralty chart by Capt.
Stokes.   On this subject I find a MS. note by Capt. Stanley:
"Stokes has mentioned in his chart that 'there is little or no
tide in Bass' Strait.'   Such may be the case, but I have invariably found a very strong current, depending both as to force
and direction upon the prevailing winds.   On one occasion, during
a westerly gale, it set to the eastward with a velocity of at least
three knots per hour.   I mention this circumstance, as, from
Capt. Stokes' remarks, strangers might be led to suppose there
were no currents in the Strait, and neglect to take the usual precautions."

* It is unnecessary to give separately the various meridian distances obtained by the Rattlesnake and Bramble, as these will be
found, with the various circumstances affecting their value, in the
Appendix.

scanty vegetation is apparently limited to a grass growing in tussocks, and a few maritime plants. The ground resembles a rabbit warren, being everywhere undermined by the burrows of the mutton-bird, a dark shearwater (*Puffinus brevicaudus*), the size of a pigeon. A person in walking across the island can scarcely avoid frequently stumbling among these burrows, from the earth giving way under his feet, and I was told by one of the residents that snakes are very numerous in these holes, living upon the mutton-birds; I myself trod upon one which, fortunately, was too sluggish to escape before I had time to shoot it, and ascertain it to be the well known " black snake" of the Australian colonists (*Acanthophis Tortor*), a very poisonous species. Among the sea fowl, a large gull (*Larus Pacificus*), was exceedingly plentiful, together with a smaller one (*Xema Jamesonii*), and a few penguins (*Spheniscus minor*). A fine flock of wild geese (*Cereopsis Novæ Hollandiæ*), was seen, but they were too wary to allow of close approach. About dusk clouds of mutton-birds came in from the sea, and we amused ourselves with chasing them over the ground among their burrows, and as many specimens as I required were speedily provided by knocking them down with a stick. As usual with the Petrel family they bite severely if incautiously handled, and disgorge a quantity of offensive oily matter, the smell of which pervades the whole island, and which the clothes I then wore retained for a long time afterwards.

The party in charge of the lighthouse have numbers of goats, pigs, and sheep, and also raise a few potatoes and other vegetables; still their life is a hard one—more so comparatively, than that of the keepers of the Eddystone or Bell Rock lights at home, as they communicate with Van Diemen's Land only twice a year, and are often in want of fuel, which they have to send for to a neighbouring island.

March 4th.—Aided by the remains of a strong westerly wind, with which we at one time logged ten and a half knots—a great feat for the old Rattlesnake, jury-rigged as she was for " surveying service," we passed through part of Banks' Strait, and anchored off Swan Island at 9 A.M. The rock is a fine grained basalt, exposed only on the shore, the remainder of the island being a series of sand-hills covered with low shrubs and luxuriant grass growing in tufts. Having left Captain Stanley's party on their way to the lighthouse, I found on the western side of the island a long sandy beach strewed with marine rejectamenta, among which were many new species of zoophytes; the number and variety of sponges was very great, but nearly all had suffered so much from exposure to the sun and weather, as to be useless as specimens. Returning to the ship before noon, we immediately got under weigh for Sydney.

March 9th.—Yesterday morning we picked up a strong S.S.E. wind, which brought us off Botany

Bay by 8 A.M., but the weather being thick with
rain, and the land doubtful, being seen only in
occasional glimpses, it was judged prudent to haul
off, standing in again during a clearing. At length
the lighthouse was distinguished, when we bore up,
and in little more than an hour reached our former
anchorage in Farm Cove.

CHAPTER III.

April 29th.—THE season for passing through Torres Strait from the southward having arrived, we left Port Jackson on a ten-months cruize, in order to complete the survey of the Inner Passage, or the clear channel between the north-east coast of Australia and the inner edge of the outer reefs, which again are bounded to seaward by the Great Barrier Reef, stretching from north to south, for a distance of upwards of 1000 miles.

In the evening we were joined by the Tam O'Shanter, a barque having on board a colonial overland expedition under Mr. Kennedy, which we are to accompany to Rockingham Bay, 1200 miles

north from Sydney, where we are to assist in the
disembarkation and starting of the party.

For the first nine days we averaged only thirty
miles a day, owing to a long continuance of calms
and light winds with a strong adverse current,
which on one occasion set us to E.S.E. fifty-three
miles in twenty-four hours. At length, on May 8th
we picked up a strong southerly breeze, accompanied
by a northerly set. On May 12th we rounded
Breaksea Spit, and Captain Stanley finding his
original intention of passing inside of Lady Elliot's
Island impracticable, or at least involving unnecessary delay, determined to bear up NW. by W.
keeping outside of the Bunker and Capricorn
Groups, and try the channel previously passed
through by Captain F. P. Blackwood in H. M. S.
Fly. Captain Stanley's remarks on this subject
are so important, that I give them verbatim :—

" After reaching Lady Elliot's Island, we steered
a course direct for the High Peak of the Northumberland Islands, so as to pass between Bunker's
Group and Swain's Reefs, which affords a far better
entrance into the Inner Passage, than the old route
round Breaksea Spit inside the Bunker Group ;
when the course requires to be changed, and the
channel is much narrower. We sounded every
half-hour without finding bottom, with from 80 to
120 fathoms, till we came to the soundings laid
down by the Fly, which we found to agree almost
exactly with ours.

" Our soundings were obtained by using Massey's patent lead, with which we found we could reach the bottom at twenty-six fathoms, when the ship was going 9.2 knots an hour; and with such a guide any error in the reckoning would be detected, even by night, as the Bunker Group gives warning by the soundings. For a steamer going to Sydney by the Inner Route, this channel would be invaluable as far as the Pine Peak of the Percy Isles. One direct course will lead out to sea clear of all the reefs, a distance of more than 200 miles, during which period there would be ample time to ascertain by observations of the sun, whether any current had been experienced sufficient to place the ship in danger, and, as the channel between Swain's Reef and the Bunker Group appears to be clear, there is a drift of thirty miles on each side the course from the High Peak."

May 15th. — After having at daylight sighted the land about Port Bowen and Cape Townshend, we passed the Northumberland and Percy Isles to the westward, the water being very smooth with light airs from S. to E.N.E. A very offensive smell which has been experienced in the after part of the ship for a week back, was to-day traced to some preserved meats prepared in Sydney; 1036 pounds of these being found quite putrid were condemned.*

* It is but justice to state here that the English invention of preserving meat in air-tight canisters had only recently been attempted in Sydney; and it was then to be regarded merely as

May 19*th.*—At length, after several days of light and contrary winds, the wind came round to S.E. and assumed the appearance of the trade, which we had at last picked up. We ran round the north-east end of the Cumberland Islands, passed Cape Gloucester, and in the evening anchored under Cape Upstart in our former berth.

During a solitary ramble next day, chiefly in order to search for a kind of rock wallaby, or small kangaroo, peculiar to this place, and which I failed on this occasion (as during two previous visits) to procure, I walked as far as the place where the Fly had watered some years previously. The large rocky basin which we had found dry in December last, when the whole plan of our first northern cruize had to be altered, in consequence of this unexpected result, was now nearly full. The aspect of the country had been considerably changed by the late abundant fall of rain, and the vegetation everywhere looked quite green. No signs of natives were seen — their visits to the immediate vicinity of the Cape appear to be made only at rare intervals; and the just

an experiment to try whether a new and important article of colonial export could not be produced. Since then, further experience in the process has enabled the introducers of the plan to succeed so perfectly, that afterwards, the colonial preserved meats supplied to the Rattlesnake, including some which had been kept for eighteen months, were always preferred by us to those prepared in England. The meat itself, I allude to beef and mutton, was of better quality, and the cost much less.

chastisement bestowed upon them some years ago, in consequence of a wanton attack made upon a seining party will, probably, for some time to come, render them cautious of coming in contact with white men. While wading about among the tall grass, the long sharp awns of the prevailing kind, an *Anthistiria*, were more annoying than can be described, having forced their way in hundreds through my thin clothing, causing an annoying and painful irritation; to which, the bites of clouds of musquitoes in a mangrove swamp which I had entered in chase of some bower birds, added a finishing touch, as if to test the powers of human endurance. Having expended my stock of dust shot, I tried fine sand—which I had somewhere read of as a substitute, but, although used under the most favourable conditions, the experiment proved a complete failure. "Sights" for rating the chronometers, to get which was the only object in coming here, having been obtained, we left for Goold Island in the afternoon.

May 21*st*. — Passing outside of the Palm Islands, and rounding Cape Sandwich, we entered Rockingham Bay, and anchored on the N.W. side of Goold Island, where we found the Tam O'Shanter. This island is about seven miles in circumference, gradually rising towards the centre, to form a peak 1376 feet in height. The shores are rocky, with occasional sandy beaches, and the island is well wooded up to its summit; Eucalypti (gum-trees), frequently of great size, being the predominant trees. The grass was very luxuriant and even difficult to wade through, indicating an abundance of water, of which several small streams were seen. One of these streamlets close to the anchorage is well adapted for watering a ship at, as boats can approach within a few yards; and the supply can never, I have good reason to believe, entirely cease.

The natives, a small party of whom were here, have had frequent intercourse with Europeans, and indeed the sight alongside the ship of eight canoes, four of which carried two unarmed men, and the others one each, would of itself, to most people, have been a convincing proof of a friendly disposition. That such apparent desire to be on friendly terms might often mislead strangers, is not to be wondered at. Yet these same people, a few years ago, made a sudden and most wanton attack upon a seining party belonging to H.M.S. Fly, and shortly after we left them, they attempted to cut off a small vessel which had called there for water.

Their canoes are very simply constructed of a single sheet of bark of the gum-tree brought together at the ends, and secured by stitching. The sitter squats down with his legs doubled under him, and uses a small square piece of bark in each hand, as paddles, with one of which he also bales the water out by dexterously scooping it up from behind him.

On May 23rd, a convenient spot for landing the overland expedition having been found on the shores of Rockingham Bay, we shifted our berth in the afternoon a few miles further to leeward, and anchored under the westernmost of the Family Islands, in order to be near the place of disembarkation. On the two following days everything belonging to Mr. Kennedy's party (with the exception of one horse drowned while swimming it ashore) was safely landed, and his first camp was formed on some open forest land behind the beach, at a small fresh water creek.

The object of Mr. Kennedy's expedition, was to explore the country to the eastward of the dividing range running along the N.E. coast of Australia at a variable distance from the shore, and terminating at Cape York, where a vessel with supplies was to meet the party in October, after which they were to start on their return to Sydney; proceeding at first down the western side of the peninsula to the Gulf of Carpentaria, and then shape such a course as was best calculated to bring them to the settled districts of New South Wales.

Of the disastrous results of this unfortunate expedition, I need not here speak; I shall afterwards have to allude to the melancholy death of its gallant leader, within a day's journey almost of the goal which he was struggling with desperate energy to reach—the nearest place where assistance could be procured for the few remaining survivors

T. Burley, delt.   stalbmandel & Walton, lithog.

CUTTING THROUGH THE SCRUB.

T. & W. Boone, Publishers, London 1852.

of his party, of whom, eventually, only three were saved. I last saw poor Kennedy on the evening before he broke up his camp; he was then in high spirits and confident of success. The party, of thirteen men and twenty-eight horses (with carts, a flock of sheep for food, &c.), appeared to be furnished with every requisite for their intended journey, and the arrangements and appointments seemed to me to be perfect. Nor did I, despite the forebodings of others, argue anything but a successful result to an undertaking, the blame of failure of which was *afterwards* attempted to be thrown upon those who had planned it.

The small granite island (one of the Family Group) off which we were anchored, afforded little of interest to us. Fresh water was found in small quantities, not available, however, for the use of vessels. The most curious production of the island is an undescribed plant of the singular family *Balanophoraceæ*, not before known as Australian, which was found here in abundance in the gloomy brushes, parasitic upon the roots of the tallest trees. We also met with here—in probably its southern limit upon the coast—a species of rattan (*Calamus Australis*), with long prickly shoots, well illustrated in the annexed drawing by Mr. Huxley, representing the process of " cutting through the scrub," during an excursion made with Mr. Kennedy, for the purpose of searching for a way out from the low swampy district of Rockingham Bay.

May 26th.—During the forenoon, the ship was moved over to an anchorage under the lee (N.W. side) of Dunk Island, where we remained for ten days. The survey of the coast line and Inner Passage to the northward was here commenced, and afterwards continued up to Torres Strait, by an unbroken series of triangulation; it included a space varying in width from 5 to 15 miles, extending through 7½ degrees of latitude and 4½ of longitude, with a coast line of upwards of 600 miles.

The programme of the survey may be briefly given as follows:— at the principal stations— chiefly islands off the coast—the various observations for determining astronomical positions and theodolite angles, were made by Captain Stanley and Mr. W. H. Obree, and the ship remained there at anchor for several days. Meanwhile, Lieut. Dayman, in the Asp, laid down the coast line and neighbourhood as far as the next station twenty or thirty miles in advance.—Lieut. Simpson with the pinnace continued the soundings several miles further out, both working in conjunction, and often assisted by another boat in charge of Mr. Heath, while the outside soundings devolved upon Lieut. Yule in the tender. The Rattlesnake in shifting from place to place, aided by boats in company, sounded the centre of the channel, usually following one of the lines run by Captain P. P. King, and marked upon his charts. The available boats permanently attached to the ship, were employed under various officers in the neighbourhood of the different anchorages, cutting up the ground, and filling up any gaps which might otherwise have been left in the new charts.

The summit of a very small rocky island, near the anchorage, named by Captain Stanley, Mouna Islet, formed the first station. Dunk Island, eight or nine miles in circumference, is well wooded,— it has two conspicuous peaks, one of which (the N.W. one), is 857 feet in height. Our excursions were confined to the vicinity of the watering place and the bay in which it is situated. The shores are rocky on one side and sandy on the other, where a low point runs out to the westward. At their junction, and under a sloping hill with large patches of brush, a small stream of fresh water, running out over the beach, furnished a supply for the ship, although the boats could approach the place closely only at high water.

Among the most interesting objects of natural history, are two birds, one a new and handsome fly-catcher, *Monarcha leucotis*, the other a swallow, which Mr. Gould informs me is also an Indian species. Great numbers of butterflies frequent the neighbourhood of the watering place,—one of these (*Papilio Urvillianus*) is of great size and splendour, with dark purple wings, broadly margined with ultramarine, but from its habit of flying high among the trees I did not succeed in catching one. An enormous spider, beautifully variegated with black and gold, is plentiful in the woods, watching for its prey in the centre of a large net stretched horizontally between the trees.

The seine was frequently hauled upon the beach with great success,—one evening, through its means, in addition to plenty of fish, no less than five kinds of star-fishes, and twelve of crustacea, several of which are quite new, were brought on shore.

Among the plants of the island the most important is a wild species of plantain or banana, afterwards found to range along the N.E. coast and its islands as far as Cape York. Here I saw for the first time a species of *Sciadophyllum*, one of the most singular trees of the eastern coast line of tropical Australia; a slender stem, about thirty feet in height, gives off a few branches with immense digitate dark and glossy leaves and long spike-like racemes of small scarlet flowers, a great resort for insects and insect-feeding birds.

Soon after the ship had come to an anchor, some natives came off in their canoes and paid us a visit, bringing with them a quantity of shell-fish, (*Sanguinolaria rugosa*), which they eagerly exchanged for biscuit. For a few days afterwards we occasionally met them on the beach, but at length they disappeared altogether, in consequence of having been fired at with shot by one of two of the " young gentlemen" of the Bramble, on a shooting excursion, whom they wished to prevent from approaching too closely a small village, where they had their wives and children. Immediate steps were taken, in consequence, to prevent the recurrence of such collisions, when thoughtless curiosity on one side is apt to be promptly resented on the other, if numerically superior in force. I saw nothing in the appearance of these natives to distinguish them from those of Goold Island, and the canoes are the same. The men had large prominent cicatrices on the shoulders, and across the breast and belly, the septum of the nose was perforated, and none of the teeth had been removed. I saw no weapons, and some rude armlets were their only ornaments.

On June 6th we ran to the northward 15½ miles, and anchored at noon under No. III. of the Barnard Isles, a group consisting of six high rocky wooded isles, the two southernmost of which are separated from the rest by an interval of four miles. I landed upon the two largest, (I. and III. of the charts), on the first only once. I there found nothing of much interest, except some very thick beds of conglomerate superimposed upon a compact basaltic looking rock. No. III., on the other hand, consists of mica slate, much contorted, and altered from its usual appearance, and containing lead ore (*galena*), with several veins of quartz, one of which, about two feet in thickness, traverses the island from side to side.

The islands of the N. E. coast of Australia, hitherto and subsequently visited during the survey, afford all the gradations between the simplest form of a sand bank upon a coral reef scantily covered with grass, a few creeping plants and stunted bushes on one hand,—and on the other a high, rocky, well-wooded island with an undulating succession of hills and valleys. In those of the latter class, to a certain extent only in the islands of Rockingham Bay, but in a very striking degree in those to the northward, there is so great a similarity in the vegetation, that an illustration of the botany may be taken from one of the Barnard Isles, No. III.—exhibiting what may be termed an Indo-Australian Flora.

The upper margin of the coral beach is overrun with *Ipomœa maritima*, a large purple-flowered *Bossiæa*, and some other leguminous plants, of which the handsomest is *Canvallia Baueriana*, a runner with large rose-coloured flowers. To these succeeds a row of bushes of *Scævola Kœnigii*, and *Tournefortia argentea*, with an occasional *Guettarda speciosa*, or *Morinda citrifolia*, backed by thickets of *Paritium Tiliaceum*, and other shrubs supporting large *Convolvulaceæ*, vine-like species of *Cissus;* *Guilandina Bonduc*, a prickly *Cæsalpinia, Deeringia Cœlosioides*, and a variety of other climbers. Penetrating this shrubby border, one finds himself in what in New South Wales would be called a *brush* or *scrub*, and in India a jungle, extending over the greater part of the island. Overhead are trees of moderate size, whose general character is constituted by a nearly straight stem, seldom branching except near the top, and furnished with glossy dark green leaves. Interspersed with them there are many which attain an enormous size, as in the case of a *Hernanda*, a *Castanospermum*, two fabaceous trees, and others of which neither flowers nor fruit were observed. Two palms, *Seaforthia elegans*, and *Livistona inermis*, also occur here. By far the most remarkable vegetable productions are the larger kinds of climbers. The principal of these, with a leafless and almost branchless cable-like stem, sometimes two or three hundred yards in length, rises over the summits of the tallest trees, and connects one with another in its powerful folds, occasionally descending to the ground. Another climber, *Lestibudesia arborescens*, rises by its slender stems to the tops of the trees, hiding them in its cascade-like masses · and graceful festoons of exuberant foliage. Besides several other exogenous woody climbers, of which a very remarkable one is a *Bauhinia*, with a compressed stem spirally twisted round its axis — the most interesting is *Calamus Australis*, rising in a clump, then arching along the ground and from tree to tree in a similar maner to *Flagellaria Indica*, here also abundant. Among the other plants of these brushes, are the curious *Dracontium polyphyllum*, with large simple and pinnatifid leaves, creeping like ivy up the trunks and lower branches of the trees—parasitical *Loranthaceæ*, with long dependant tufts of rush-like leaves—enormous masses of *Acrosticum alcicorne* and *A. grande*, with an occasional *Hoya carnosa*, *Dendrobium*, or other epiphyte. When the soil is

rich *Caladium macrorhizon* grows gregariously in
shady places, and *Hellenia cœrulea* on their margins,—and among stones and sometimes on trees,
tufts of *Grammitis Australis* spread out their large
and handsome undivided fronds.

Two species of rat occur here—one is the large
bandicoot of India, *Mus giganteus*, doubtless
introduced by some wrecked vessel, the other is
the pretty little *Mus Indicus*, found on all the
islands of the north-east coast and Torres Strait.
Among the birds, we found numbers of the Megapodius, always a welcome addition to our bill of
fare ; but our greatest prize was a new and splendid
rifle-bird, which Mr. Gould has since described
from my specimens and named *Ptiloris Victoriæ*,
as a mark of respect and gratitude for the patronage
bestowed upon his great work on the Birds of
Australia, in the forthcoming supplement to which
it will be figured along with some other novelties of
the Voyage of the Rattlesnake.

Before taking leave of the natural history of the
Barnard Group, I must not omit a pretty butterfly
inhabiting the densest parts of the brush ; it is the
Hamadryas Zoilus of the Voyage of the Astrolabe,
erroneously supposed in that work to be a native of
New Zealand.

One day I crossed over to the mainland in a boat
sent for the purpose of examining a small river
seen there to open upon a long sandy beach.   We
found a depth of four feet on the bar at low water,

so had no difficulty in entering—at a quarter of a mile from the mouth the water was quite fresh. We ascended about two miles and a half, when it became necessary to return on account of the shoalness of the stream, the boat* having grounded repeatedly. A party of about twenty natives made their appearance as soon as we entered the river, and after making ineffectual and repeated attempts to induce us to land, two or three of their number followed us along the bank, while the others made a straight course so as to cut off the windings and meet us at our turning place. The current here ran one and a half knots, but the quantity of water was trifling and the channel throughout very narrow, at times sweeping under the bank, so as not to allow room for the oars. At first the river was fringed with mangroves, afterwards with dense brush. The natives followed us down until we anchored for dinner in one of the reaches, when they all left on hearing the report of my gun while shooting on shore. They were painted with red and white, two of them being smeared all over with the former colour, mixed up with some greasy substance. They seemed peaceably disposed, as we saw no arms among them, and they approached close enough to take biscuit from our hands.

Near the mouth we again landed for half an

* Our first cutter, very serviceable on such occasions from her light draught; with fourteen men, arms, provisions, and stove for cooking, &c. she drew only a foot of water.

hour, and found a cluster of three or four dome-shaped huts, large and roomy, of neat construction, covered with sheets of melaleuca bark, and having one, sometimes two entrances. Some fishing nets, similar to those used at Moreton Bay, were seen. The men retired into the bush when we landed, nor would they come out to me when I advanced alone towards them, in order to look at the huts. We anchored for the night under No. I. of the Barnard Isles. Megapodii were here very plentiful, and about daylight very noisy, running about in all directions, repeating their loud call of *chro-co—chro-co*. Some of the bushes presented a fine show of the scarlet flowers of *Disemma coccinea*, a kind of passion-flower, before only found at Endeavour River by Sir Joseph Banks, during Cook's second voyage. In the morning we returned to the ship.

On June 12th, while passing a small opening in the land, a little to the northward of Double Point, the Asp was observed on shore with a signal for assistance, which was immediately sent, when she was got off without damage. At this place, as Lieut. Simpson informed me, a boomerang was obtained from the natives; we had not before observed this singular weapon upon the north-east coast, and its use is quite unknown on the north coast from Cape York to Port Essington. This one too was painted green, a colour which I never heard of elsewhere among the Australians, whose pigments are black, white, yellow, and red.

Near this place, while tacking close in shore, a

native dog was seen by Lieut. Simpson, in chace
of a small kangaroo, which, on being close pressed,
plunged into the water and swam out to sea, when
it was picked up by the boat, leaving its pursuer
standing on a rock gazing wistfully at its intended
prey, until a musket ball, which went very near its
mark, sent it off at a trot. The kangaroo lived on
board for a few days, and proved to constitute quite
a new kind, closely allied to *Halmaturus Thetidis*.

We anchored in the evening off the northern
extreme of Frankland Isle, No. IV. about three-
quarters of a mile off shore. At night a party was
sent on shore to look for turtle, but, after remaining
there for three hours, having walked several times
round the island, they returned without having seen
the slightest trace of these animals.

The Frankland Group consists of four islands,
two of which are very small, and each of the other
two (I and IV.) about a mile in length. To these
may or may not be added another high and much
larger detached island situated about five miles to
the N.W., about midway between the remainder of
the group and the main land. No. IV. is formed
of two wooded rocky eminences at its extremes,
connected by level ground, consisting of dead coral
and sand, thickly covered with trees at one part,
and scattered bushes at another. The low woody
portion of this island is strewed with flat blocks of
the same kind of recent coral conglomerate that
occurs in situ on the beach, also with quantities of

pumice twelve feet above high water mark of spring tides. There is little underwood, the trees overhead forming a shady grove. Herbaceous plants are few in number—of the others I shall only mention a wild nutmeg, *Myristica cimicifera,* not, however, of any commercial importance.

The Torres Strait rat was exceedingly plentiful here, in hollow trees and logs, also about the roots of the pandanus trees and under blocks of coral. Our dogs caught many, as they do not shew so much agility as is usual in the genus. The principal bird is the megapodius,—a gecko, and another small lizard are abundant,—of land shells we found a new *Scarabus* and a small brown *Helix,* in great abundance under blocks of coral, and on the trunks and branches of trees, a pretty *Cyclostoma* (*C. vitreum*) formerly found by the French in New Caledonia, also a new and pretty *Helix,* remarkable for its angular sinuated mouth and conical spire,—this last has been named *H. Macgillivrayi* by Professor E. Forbes. The reef furnished many radiata and crustacea, and as usual the shell collectors—consisting of about one-half the ship's company, reaped a rich harvest of cowries, cones, and spider shells, amounting to several hundred weight. One day I was much amused when, on hailing one of our men whom I observed perched up among the top branches of a tree, and asking whether it was a nest that he had found, the answer returned was—" Oh no, Sir, its these *geotrochuses* that I am after."

The southernmost island of the group differs from
No. IV. in being higher and more rocky. Many
of the trees here were very large, straight, and
branching only near the top. It appeared to me
that they would be highly useful as timber, and so
regretted being unable to procure specimens, on
account of their great height. With the exception
of a low sandy portion, overgrown with shrubs and
small trees, the remainder of the island is quite free
from underwood. Two small clumps of cocoa-nut
trees, loaded with fruit, were found on the eastern
side of the island, within reach of the spray, in a
place where they might have originated from a
floating nut or two thrown upon the beach. This
is the only instance in which I have seen this useful
plant growing wild in any part of Australia, or the
islands strictly belonging to it. We succeeded in
shooting down a number, and I know no more
grateful beverage than the milk of a young cocoa-
nut, especially under the influence of tropical noonday heat, on an island where there was not a drop
of fresh water to be found. As usual the megapodius
was plentiful, and one of our party killed six in a
few hours. I also shot a fine large crested pigeon,
of a species hitherto considered peculiar to the
settled parts of New South Wales, and to which
the singularly inappropriate specific name of *Antarc-
ticus* is applied; it thus ranges 380 miles within the
tropics.

June 20th.—Fitzroy Island. After anchoring for

a short time to form a station, we finally came to
under Fitzroy Island, half a mile from the shore.
This island is about five miles in circumference, high
and well-wooded, with two peaks, one of which is 861
feet in height.   The rock, when exposed, is granitic.
The small bay on the western side of the island,
where the ship lay, has a steep beach of fragments
of dead coral, through which oozes the water of two
streamlets, at one of which the ship completed her
stock with great facility.   Following upwards one
of the two branches of the principal stream through
a narrow gully, one reaches a small basin-like
valley, filled with dense brush, through which it is
difficult to pass, on account of the unusual quantity
of the prickly Calamus palm.   Several trees of the
pomegranate (*Punica Granatum*) were met with
bearing fruit; as this plant is found wild in India,
and here occurred in the centre of a thick brush not
likely to have been visited by Europeans, it is
probably indigenous.   A kind of yam (*Dioscorea
bulbifera*) was found here, and proved good eating.
In consequence of this, a party from the ship was
sent to dig for more, but, having mistaken the plant,
they expended all their time and trouble in rooting
up a convolvulus, with small, inedible, and probably
cathartic tubers.

A new species of large fruit-eating bat, or " flying-
fox," (*Pteropus conspicillatus*), making the third
Australian member of the genus, was discovered
here.   On the wooded slope of a hill I one day fell

in with this bat in prodigious numbers, presenting the appearance, while flying along in the bright sunshine, so unusual in a nocturnal animal, of a large flock of rooks. On close approach a strong musky odour became apparent, and a loud incessant chattering was heard. Many of the branches were bending under their loads of bats, some in a state of inactivity, suspended by their hind claws, others scrambling along among the boughs, and taking to wing when disturbed. In a very short time I procured as many specimens as I wished, three or four at a shot, for they hung in clusters, — but, unless killed outright, they remained suspended for some time, — when wounded they are to be handled with difficulty, as they bite severely, and on such occasions their cry reminds one of the squalling of a child. The flesh of these large bats is reported excellent; it is a favourite food with the natives, and more than once furnished a welcome meal to Leichhardt and his little party, during their adventurous journey to Port Essington.

One day we were surprised to see a small vessel approaching the anchorage from the southward. She proved to be a cutter of twenty-five tons, called the Will o' the Wisp, fitted out by a merchant in Sydney, and sent in a somewhat mysterious way (so as to ensure secrecy) to search for sandal, wood upon the north-east coast of Australia. If found in sufficient quantity, a party was to be left to cut it, while the vessel returned to Moreton Bay with the news, and communicated with the owner, who was to send a larger vessel to pick it up and convey it at once to the China market.* An inferior kind of sandal wood, the produce of *Exocarpos latifolia* (but which afterwards turned out to be useless), was met with in several localities,—as the Percy Isles, Repulse Bay, Cape Upstart, Palm Islands, &c. At this last place they had much friendly intercourse with the natives, who were liberally treated with presents. It is supposed that the sight of so many valuable articles had excited the cupidity of these savages, for, one morning, at half-past three o'clock, a party came off in "large canoes with outriggers," and boarded the cutter when all hands were below. Their first act was to throw into the cabin and down the fore hatchway some lighted bark, and when the master and one of the crew rushed on deck in a state of confusion, they were instantly knocked on the head with boomerangs and rendered insensible. At this crisis, had it not been for the successful courage of the mate, who cleared the deck with a sword, and allowed the remainder of the crew to come up to his assistance, the natives would probably have obtained possession of the

---

* In 1847 nearly 1000 tons of this wood, procured chiefly from New Caledonia, the New Hebrides, &c. were exported from Sydney to China, where it is burnt with other incense in the temples. The sandal-wood trade in these islands gives employment to about six small vessels, belonging to Sydney. In China it realizes about £30 per ton.

vessel; as it was the survivors retired in confusion, which was further increased by the discharge among them of a swivel gun, mounted on a pivot amidships.

At Goold Island, where the Will o'the Wisp next went in search of water, they had another affray with the natives, of whom several were shot, but whether justifiably, or from revengeful motives, is known to themselves only. Knowing that the Rattlesnake was upon the coast they proceeded in search of her to obtain surgical and other assistance, and, meeting two of the surveying boats, they were directed to Fitzroy Island.

Some parts of this account appeared so extraordinary, and others so improbable, that Captain Stanley felt it his duty to report it to the Colonial Government, along with the depositions of the men. Some days afterwards, the master, whose skull had been fractured, being pronounced to be in as fair a way to recovery as was possible under the circumstances the Will o' the Wisp sailed for Moreton Bay, which we afterwards learned she reached in safety.

July 26th.—A party left before daylight in the pinnace and first galley, to examine an opening in Trinity Bay, marked upon King's chart. We found it to present the appearance of a wide creek running through low mangrove swamps, and with the eye could trace its windings for the distance of two or three miles. In all probability this is the embouchure of a considerable fresh water stream, but the shallowness of the head of the bay and the usual bar off the mouth of the supposed river, determined Captain Stanley to return to the ship, as the time which would otherwise have been spent in exploring an useless creek might be devoted to some better purpose.

June 29th.—Left Fitzroy Island for an anchorage under Cape Grafton, where we remained for the three following days. While running down to the anchorage we entered a large patch of discoloured water, with a perfectly defined margin, yet the lead shewed no difference in the depth or nature of the bottom. It would also appear that since Captain King's survey the water has been shoaling hereabouts. On a small island inshore, the skull of a crocodile was found upon the beach, and this reminds me that several of these animals were seen in one of the rivers of Rockingham Bay. The Australian "alligator," as it is usually called, is a true crocodile, identical, according to Mr. Gray, with the common Indian species.

July 3rd.—Ran to the north-west fifteen miles, and, after having anchored midway to form a surveying station, brought up finally under a small unnamed islet in Trinity Bay. This island, viewed from our anchorage on its north-west side, presents the appearance of a ridge connecting two rounded eminences, with a sharp sea face exposing the stratification of the rock. This is a micaceous rock, assuming at one place the appearance of mica slate, and at another being a conglomerate, with frequent veins of quartz. The strata, which are often flexuous, or slightly contorted, have a westerly dip of 60°, and the strike is N.N.W. and S.S.E. On the windward side there is a long gradual slope, covered with tall coarse grass, among which many quail were found. The shore is fringed with the usual maritime trees and bushes, and an extensive mangrove bed runs out upon the reef in one place. This reef is of great extent, stretching out to windward upwards of a mile, as far as a small rocky isle like a hay-cock.

On July 7th we anchored to leeward of the Low Isles, in the northern part of Trinity Bay, in eight fathoms, mud, half a mile from the shore, and remained there for the four succeeding days. This small group may be said to consist of three islets. One is low, sandy, and well wooded, about 300 yards in diameter, and is situated at the north-west extremity of a horse-shoe reef, with its concavity to leeward; the other two may be looked upon as merely groves of mangroves on the reef, the roots of which are washed at high water, except in a few places, where narrow ridges of dead coral have afforded footing for the growth of a samphire-looking plant (*Salicornia Indica*). The sandy islet presents no remarkable feature. The remains of burnt turtle bones indicate the occasional visits of natives from the mainland. A solitary megapodius was shot, but the only other land-birds are a little yellow Zosterops, and the larger ground-dove (*Geopelia humeralis*).

During our stay we were fortunate in having fine weather, light winds, and low tides, which enabled such as were inclined to look for shells upon the reef to do so under the most favourable circumstances. This reef is of great extent, with all the varieties of coral, mud, and sand, and proved a most productive one. A sketch of the distribution of the principal of its productions may be of interest to some. Many kinds of fishes, *Murœna, Diodon, Balistes, Serranus,* &c. are found in the pools among the coral blocks; the first of these, of bright colours variously striped and spotted, resemble water-snakes, and are exceedingly active, gliding through the interstices in the coral and hiding in its hollows,—they bite savagely at a stick presented to them, and are by no means pleasant neighbours while wading about knee-deep and with bare arms turning over the coral which they frequent. On a former occasion I had been laid hold of by the thumb, and the wound was a long time in healing. Crustacea are also numerous; blue and green *Gonodactyli* leap about with a sharp clicking noise—legions of *Mycteris subverrucata* traverse the dry sands at low water—and in the shallow muddy pools, dull green *Thalamitœ* and *Lupeœ* swim off rapidly, and smooth *Calappœ* seek refuge by burrowing under the surface.

Of mollusca, two species of olive (*O. erythrostoma* and *O. leucophœa*) were found on the sandy margin of the islet—several *Cerithia* and *Subulœ* (*S. maculata* and *S. occulata*) creep along the sand flats, and, with some fine *Naticæ*, and a *Pyramidella*, may be found by tracing the marks of their long burrows. Several *Strombi* and *Nassa coronata* inhabit the shallow sandy pools; the egg-shell and many *Cyprææ* occur under coral blocks, which, when over sand, often harbour different kinds of cones—of which the handsome *C. Textile* is the commonest. A delicate white *Lima* (*L. fragilis*) is abundant here, merrily swimming away in the pool under an upturned stone, and leaving its fringe-like tentacles adhering to the hand when seized. Lastly, it would be improper to omit mentioning the very fine oysters adhering to the roots of the mangroves. But these are only a small portion of the shell-fish collected here. Among radiate animals, several *Ophiuræ* and *Ophiocomæ* and other *Asteriadæ*, with two kinds of *Echinus*, are also plentiful under blocks of coral (*Astræa* and *Meandrina*) in the pools; one of the last, remarkable for its very long, slender, black spines, has the power of giving an exceedingly painful puncture, if carelessly handled—for a few minutes the sensation is similar to that caused by the sting of a wasp; of the others, a fine *Ophiura* is remarkable for its great size and grass-green colour, and an *Ophiocoma* for the prodigious length of its arms.

July 19th.—Six days ago we anchored under the lee of the reef on which the Hope Islands are situated, but in a position which afforded little shelter. While off Cape Tribulation, a remarkable hill in the back-ground so strongly reminded us of the Peter Botte at Mauritius, that it was so named upon our chart,—it is 3311 feet in height, the Cape itself being 1454 feet. For about six days lately the weather has been very boisterous, blowing hard from E.S.E. with a considerable sea.

The weather having at length moderated, I yesterday and to-day visited the islands composing the group. A deep and clear channel of a mile in width separates these islands, the larger of which is surrounded completely, and the smaller partially, by an extensive reef. The former, or western one, is merely a long strip of heaped up coral and shells, with a little sand and some drift wood running parallel to the outer edge of the reef, in the direction of the prevailing wind. It is over-run with low bushes, and a few other plants, such as the large purple-flowered *Bossiœa*, and *Ipomœa maritima*. A long bank of dead coral only a few feet above high-water mark, with an intervening ditch-like hollow, separates it from the sea to the eastward; while on the other side, towards the reef, it is margined with tall mangroves. Small and barren though this spot be, it is yet inhabited by lizards and a species of rat. Besides the usual waders on the reef, I found great numbers of doves and honeysuckers, and, among the mangroves, fell in with and procured specimens of a very rare kingfisher, *Halcyon sordidus*. Among the mangroves a rare shell, a species of *Quoyia*, occurred.

The eastern and northern islet is nearly circular, half a mile in circumference—formed of coral and shell-sand, covered with bushes and small trees. The most conspicuous plant is the prickly *Guilandina Bonduc,* the long briar-like trailing and climbing shoots of which impede one while traversing the thickets. A pair of white-headed sea-eagles had established their aërie in a tree not more than twenty feet from the ground, and I could not resist the temptation of robbing them of their eggs.

July 28*th.*--Anchored under the Three Isles, between Capes Bedford and Flattery. The principal one of the group, situated to leeward of an extensive reef, is margined towards the reef by beds of coral—conglomerate, and elsewhere by a sandy beach—it is half a mile in length, composed of coral sand, the highest part not more than twelve feet above high-water mark, with several groves of low trees, and is over-run with tall sedge-like grass; the second is composed of a strip of heaped-up fragments of coral, to windward covered with bushes, and to leeward separated from the reef by a belt of mangroves; the third is a mere clump of mangroves not deserving of further notice. The botany of an island of this class, of which there are many on the N.E. coast of Australia, may serve as a specimen, as the plants are few. *Mimusops Kaukii* constituted the principal part of the arboreal vegetation, *Clerodendrum inerme* and *Premna obtusifolia* form low straggling thickets, — scattered bushes of *Suriana maritima* and *Pemphis acida* fringe the sandy margin of the island, and behind these the beautiful *Josephinia grandiflora,* a large white-flowered *Calyptranthus, Vitex ovata* and a *Tribulus* creep along the sand, or spread out their procumbent branches.

Traces of natives, but not very recent, were met with in a dried-up well dug to a great depth, and several low, dome-shaped huts, and numerous fireplaces, around which remains of shell-fish and turtle were profusely scattered. Many of the heads of these last animals were here and elsewhere seen stuck upon branches of trees, sometimes a dozen together.

July 31*st.*—I landed this morning with Mr. Obree, on one of the Two Isles off Cape Flattery, and we were picked up by the ship in passing. It is well-wooded, chiefly with the *Mimusops Kaukii,* trees of which are here often 60 feet high and 3 in diameter. Under the bark I found two new land-shells (to be described in the Appendix), one of them a flattish *Helix,* in prodigious numbers,— and this more than ever satisfied me that even the smallest islands and detached reefs of the north-east coast may have species peculiar to themselves, nor did I ever return from any one of the 37 upon which I landed without some acquisitions to the collection.

We remained a fortnight at Lizard Island, at the

usual anchorage, off a sandy beach on its north-western side.   Lizard Island is conspicuous from a distance, on account of its peak,*—the central part of a mountainous ridge running across the island, and dividing it into two portions, of which the eastern is hilly and the western low, and intersected by small ridges of slight elevation.   The island is about 2½ miles in greatest diameter ; the rock is a coarse grey granite, easily decomposable.   A large grassy plain extends westward from the central ridge,—a portion of this, half a mile from the beach, densely covered with coarse grass and reeds and scattered over with Pandanus trees, is usually a marsh.   At present it is dry, with a few pools of fresh water, connected below with a mangrove swamp opening upon the beach by a narrow creek. Formerly boats could ascend this a little way, but now the entrance dries across at low water,—nor could the fresh water conveniently be conducted to the beach by the hose and engine, as I had seen done in the Fly in the month of May.   Fortunately, however, we found a small stream in a valley on the northern corner of the island, which supplied our wants.

Although the dry barren nature of the soil—

* Capt. Stanley's azimuth and altitude observations, taken at two stations at the base, the distance between having been measured by the micrometer, give its height as 1161 feet ; and Lieut. Dayman's barometrical measurement makes it 1151 feet, above the sea level.

varying from coarse quartzose sand (from the disintegrated granite) to reddish clay—is not favourable to the growth of luxuriant vegetation, still several interesting plants were added to the herbarium. Of these the finest is a new *Cochlospermum*, a low spreading tree, nearly leafless at this time, but covered with clusters of very large and showy golden blossoms. A heath-like shrub, (*Chamælaucium*) common here, was remarkable for existing on the open plains as a weak prostrate plant, while in the scrub it formed a handsome bush 10 feet high, with a stem 6 inches in diameter.

Of quail, which in 1844 were very abundant, I saw not more than one or two,—probably the burning of the grass during the breeding season had effected this partial clearance. Snakes appear to be numerous,—two out of three which I examined were poisonous—the other was the diamond snake of New South Wales. A very fine land shell, *Helix bipartita*, was found in colonies at the roots of the trees and bushes. A large and handsome cowrie, *Cypræa Mauritiana*, generally distributed among the islands of the Pacific, was here found for the first time in Australia.

Aug. 1st.—I crossed over to Eagle Island with Mr. Brown, and spent a day and night there. This place was so named by Cook, who states in explanation of the name,—" We found here the nest of some other bird, we knew not what, of a most enormous size. It was built with sticks upon the ground, and was no less than 26 feet in circumference, and two feet eight inches high."[*] An American professor[†] conjectures the above nest to have possibly been that of the *Dinornis*, the gigantic New Zealand bird, known only by its fossil remains. A very slight knowledge, however, of ornithology, would be sufficient to confute the notion of any struthious bird constructing a nest of this kind, or of a wingless land bird of great size inhabiting an islet only a quarter of a mile in length. Both Mr. Gould and myself have seen nests of the same construction, the work of the large fishing-eagle of Australia.

This island is low and sandy, with a few casuarinas, or "she-oaks," a fringe of *Suriana maritima*, some *Tournefortiæ*, and thickets of *Clerodendrum inerme*. Land rail and other birds were numerous. The reef, which is very extensive, did not dry throughout at low water, but some sand banks along its lee margin were exposed, and upon them I found the greatest assemblage of "pretty" shells that I ever met with at one place. What would not many an amateur collector have given to spend an hour here? There were fine *Terebræ* in abundance, orange-spotted mitres, minutely-dotted cones, red-mouthed *Strombi*, glossy olives, and magnificent *Naticæ*, all ploughing up the wet sand in every

---

[*] Hawkesworth's Voyages, vol. ii. p. 599.
[†] In Silliman's Journal for July, 1844.

direction,—yet, with two exceptions, they are to be seen in every collection in Europe.

As usual we found plentiful remains of recent turtle feasts. One of the boat's crew, not over-stocked with brains, during his rambles picked up a human skull with portions of the flesh adhering. Accidentally learning this from the conversation of the men at our bivouac during supper, inquiry was made, when we found that he had foolishly thrown it into the sea, nor could it be found during a subsequent search. I was anxious to determine whether it was aboriginal or not. On the one hand, the natives of all parts of Australia usually evince the strongest desire to bury or conceal their own dead; on the other, there might have been some connexion between the skull and the remains of a hut of European construction, portions of clothing, a pair of shoes, some tobacco, and fragments of a whale boat seen here.—But all is mere conjecture.

August 14th.—After leaving Lizard Island, we passed to the southward of No. III. of the Howick Isles, and anchored off the N.W. extremity of No. I. in 6½ fathoms, mud. This is the largest of a group of about ten islands, which agree in being low, and covered for the most part with mangroves. No. I., however, is distinguished by having three bare hillocks at its south-eastern end, the central one of which forms a rather conspicuous peak. A party of natives was there seen watching our move-ments, but no communication with them was attempted. Opposite the ship we landed on a small sandy, bushy portion of the island, slightly elevated, fronted by the reef, and backed by mangroves. We found here the usual indications of occasional visits of the natives in a pit dug as a well, and numerous remains of turtle and fish about the fire-places. A few quails, doves, and other common birds were met with.

On August 18th we removed to an anchorage under No. VI., the second largest of the group. With the exception of a sandy, grassy plain, half a mile in length, the whole of the island is densely covered with mangroves, and fringed with a reef of coral, chiefly dead. Great numbers of large turtle-shells were scattered about, shewing the periodical abundance of these animals. Another large "vam-pyre-bat," *Pteropus funereus*, differing from that of Fitzroy Island, was met with in great numbers among the mangroves,—a very large assemblage of these animals on the wing, seen from the ship while approaching the island, quite resembled a flock of rooks. Here, as elsewhere on the mangrove-clad islands, a large honeysucker (*Ptilotis chrysotis*) filled the air with its loud and almost incessant, but varied and pleasing notes,—I mention it, because it is the only bird we ever met with on the north-east coast of Australia which produced anything like a song.

Aug. 21st.—We ran to the N.E. about twenty-eight miles, and anchored off Cape Melville, a remarkable granitic promontory; here the Great Barrier Reef closely approaches the coast, being distant only ten miles, and visible from the ship. A few miles to the south some pine-trees were seen on the ridges, as had previously been noticed by Cunningham, during King's Voyage. They appeared to be the same kind as that formerly alluded to at the Percy Isles, in which case this useful tree has a range on the north-east coast of 500 miles of latitude, being found as far south as Port Bowen.

Next day we shifted our berth to a more secure anchorage under the neighbouring Pipon Islets, where the Bramble joined us in the evening. The schooner had been sent on in advance of the ship to the northward nearly a month before, in order to be at the head of Princess Charlotte's Bay during the first week in August, according to an arrangement made by Captain Stanley with Mr. Kennedy, but no signs of the overland expedition were met with during ten days spent at the rendezvous.*

While at this anchorage, the Bramble, being in want of water, filled up at a small stream, inside of Cape Melville, assisted by some of our boats and people. The party so employed was one day attacked by a number of natives, but, the usual precaution of having sentries posted and a guard

---

* We afterwards learned that it was not until the middle of October (or two months afterwards) that Kennedy's party reached the latitude of Princess Charlotte Bay, at a considerable distance too, from the coast.

of marines close at hand prevented the loss of life on our part.

Aug. 28*th.*—After a run of 45 miles, we reached Pelican Island, the survey of the space thus rapidly gone over being left to Lieutenant Yule and the Bramble. The island is rather more than a quarter of a mile in length, with a large reef to windward; it is low and sandy, covered with coarse grass, and a bushy yellow-flowered *Sida.* Great numbers of birds frequent this place; of these the pelicans (*Pelecanus conspicillatus*) are the most remarkable, but, incubation having ceased, they were so wary that it was not without some trouble that two were killed out of probably a hundred or more. A pair of sea-eagles had their nest here, placed on a low bush, an anomaly in the habits of the bird to be accounted for by the disappearance of the "two clumps of trees," mentioned by King as formerly existing on the island, and the unwillingness of the birds to abandon the place. The shell collectors picked up nothing of consequence, but the sportsmen met with great success. On the 29th, about twenty brace of quail and as many land-rail were shot, in addition to many oyster-catchers, plovers, godwits, and sand-pipers. Shooting for the pot is engaged in with a degree of eagerness commensurate with its importance, now that our live stock has been exhausted, and we have little besides ship's provisions to live upon. Three turtle, averaging 250 pounds weight, were caught by a party sent for the purpose of searching for them, and it was supposed that one or two others which had come up to lay escaped detection from the darkness of the night.

On August 31st, we removed to an anchorage under No. V. of the Claremont group, and remained there during the following day. The island is about two-thirds of a mile in circumference, low and sandy, with a large reef extending to windward. The island is thinly covered with coarse grass and straggling bushes, with one large thicket containing a few trees, of which the tallest is a solitary Mimusops. We found quail here in great plenty, and they afforded good sport to a " First of September" shooting party, provided with a setter. At length the poor quail had their quarters so thoroughly beaten up, that several, in attempting to escape from the island, were observed to fall into the water from sheer exhaustion. Nor did the birds receive all the benefit of the shot, for Captain Stanley, while observing with the theodolite, became unwittingly a target for a juvenile shooter; but, fortunately, no damage was done. Some turtle were seen at night, but they were too wary to be taken. I found several nests with eggs, by probing in all the likely places near their tracks with my ramrod; in passing through an egg, the end of the rod becomes smeared with the contents, and comes up with a little sand adhering to it, directing one where to dig.

No. VI. of the Claremont group was next visited.

This, which is only a quarter of a mile in length, is situated on the lee side of an extensive reef. It is quite low, being composed of heaped-up fragments of shells and coral, overrun with a suffruticose *Sida*, and stunted bushes of *Clerodendrum* and *Premna*, with a glossy-leaved euphorbiaceous plant occasionally forming small thickets. Sea fowl and waders were very numerous, but the breeding season was over. Land-rail existed in such great numbers that upwards of fifty were shot.

I cannot see the propriety of considering the sand bank, marked No. VII., as a member of the Claremont group; as, at high water, it is a mere strip of sand 200 yards in length, with a few plants of *Salsola* on the highest part.

On September 8th, we anchored to the westward of the north end of Night Island, a mile off shore, and remained there for the two succeeding days. This island is two miles in length, and half a mile in breadth, surrounded by a narrow reef of dead coral and mud. With the exception of a very narrow portion fronted by a sandy beach, the place is densely covered with mangroves. A sandy portion, of about five acres in extent, is thickly covered with bushes and small trees, of which the most conspicuous is a Bombax or cotton-tree, 20 to 30 feet in height, with leafless horizontal branches bearing both flowers and fruit. Numbers of the Torres Strait Pigeon (*Carpophaga luctuosa*) crossed over from the main land towards evening to roost;

and at that time, and early in the morning, great havoc was usually made among them. Even this small spot produced a fine white, brown-banded *Helix*, not found elsewhere,—it occurred on the branches of the cotton trees.

Three days afterwards we ran to the northward ten miles, and anchored under the Sherrard Isles, where our stay was protracted until the 16th by blowing weather. These islets are two in number, a quarter of a mile apart, surrounded and connected by a reef. One is 120 yards in length, sandy, and thinly covered with coarse grass and maritime plants, with a few bushes; the other is only 30 yards across, and is covered by a clump of small trees of *Pemphis acida* and *Suriana maritima*, appearing at a distance like mangroves.

A small low wooded islet off Cape Direction, where I landed for a few hours, was found to be composed entirely of dead coral with thickets of mangrove and other bushes, and presented no feature worthy of further notice. We were detained at an anchorage near Cape Weymouth for seven days by the haziness of the weather, which obscured distant points essential to the connexion of the survey. After having anchored once for the night under the lee of reef " e" of King's chart—one of the most extensive we had hitherto seen, being fourteen miles in length,—on September 26th, the ship anchored under the largest of the Piper Islets.

This group consists of four low bushy and wooded

islets, situated on two reefs separated by a deep channel. The larger of the two on the south-eastern reef, off which the ship lay, is about half a mile in circumference. The trees are chiefly a kind of *Erythrina*, conspicuous from its light coloured trunk and leafless branches; one of the most abundant plants is a *Capparis*, with long drooping branches, occasionally assisted by a *Cissus* and a *Melotria*, in forming small shady harbours. In the evening, vast numbers of white pigeons came over from the mainland to roost, and of course, all the fowling-pieces were put in requisition. Some deep pits dug in the centre of the island were perfectly dry, and are probably so during the latter half of the dry season, or after the month of July. On this island we observed the remains of a small establishment for curing trepang—a large sea slug found on the reefs and in shoal water, constituting a valuable article of commerce in the China market, where in a dried state it fetches, according to quality, from £5 to £200 a ton. This establishment had been put up by the crew of a small vessel from Sydney, and several such have at various times made voyages along this coast and in Torres Strait, collecting trepang and tortoiseshell, the latter procured from the natives by barter.

Sept. 28*th.*—On our way to the northward to-day, we passed Young Island, of King, which had been previously examined in one of our boats, and found to be merely a reef covered at high water.

Twenty-nine years before it was an embryo islet with two small trees upon it.   And as the subject of the rate of increase of a coral reef, and of the formation of an island upon it, is a subject of interest and of great practical importance, I give below in a note* two records of the former appearance of Young Island.

Sept. 29th.—Passing inside of Haggerstone Island, we rounded Sir Everard Home's group and anchored under Sunday Island, where the Bramble joined us after a month's absence.   This is a small, high, rocky island, of flesh-coloured compact felspar. On one side is a large patch of brush with some mangroves and a coral reef.

A few days afterwards we ran down to the Bird Isles, and anchored.   They are three low, wooded islets, one detached from the other two, which are situated on the margin of a circular reef.   On the north-west island we saw a small party of natives from the mainland, consisting of two men and a

* * * " Passed at about three-quarters of a mile to the northward of a small rocky shoal, on which were two small trees. This particular is recorded as it may be interesting at some future time, to watch the progress of this islet, which is now in an infant state ; it was named on the occasion Young Island."—Narrative of a Survey of the Intertropical and Western Coasts of Australia, performed between the years 1818 and 1822, by Captain P. P. King, R.N., vol. i. p. 226.   Its appearance in 1839 is described as " an elevated reef, with one small mangrove growing on the highest part."—Stokes' Voyage of the Beagle, vol. i. p. 57.

boy, in great distress from want of water, until
Lieut. Yule kindly supplied their wants. They had
been wind-bound here for several days, the weather
for some time previously having been too boisterous
to admit of attempting to reach the shore, although
only a few miles distant, in their split and patched-
up canoe. This was of small size, the hollowed out
trunk of a tree, with a double outrigger, and altogether a poor imitation of that used by the islanders
of Torres Strait ; the paddles were of rude workmanship, shaped like a long-handled cricket-bat.
Their spears and throwing sticks were of the same
kind as those in use at Cape York, to be afterwards
described. These people were wretched specimens
of their race, lean and lanky, and one was suffering
from ophthalmia, looking quite a miserable object ;
they had come here in search of turtle,—as I understood. Each of the men had lost a front tooth, and
one had the oval cicatrix on the right shoulder, characteristic of the northern natives, an imitation of that
of the islanders. They shewed little curiosity, and
trembled with fear, as if suspicious of our intentions.
I made a fruitless attempt to pick up some scraps of
their language ; they understood the word *powd* or
" peace" of Torres Strait.

On this island the principal trees are the leafless
Erythrina, with waxy, pink flowers. Great numbers of pigeons resorted here to roost. I found here
a large colony of that rare and beautiful tern,

Sterna melanauchen, and mixed up with them a few individuals of the still rarer *Sterna gracilis.*

We anchored under Cairncross Island, on the afternoon of Sept. 3rd, and remained during the following day. The island is about a quarter of a mile in length, low and sandy, covered in the centre with tall trees, and on the outskirts with smaller ones and bushes. These large trees (*Pisonia grandis*) form very conspicuous objects from their great dimensions, their smooth, light bark, and leaf-less, dead appearance. Some are from eighty to one hundred feet in height, with a circumference at the base of twenty feet. The wood, however, is too soft to be useful as timber. Nowhere had we seen the Torres Strait pigeon in such prodigious numbers as here, crossing over in small flocks to roost, and returning in the morning ; yet many remained all day feeding on the red, plum-like fruit of *Mimusops Kaukii.* In the first evening not less than one hundred and fifty-nine pigeons were brought off after an hour's work by seven shooters, and next day a still greater number were procured. Being large and well flavoured birds, they formed no inconsiderable addition to our bill of fare, and appeared on the table at every meal, subjected to every possible variety of cooking. Some megapodii also were shot, and many eggs of a fine tern, *Onychoprion Panaya,* were picked up.

CHAPTER IV.

At length, on October 7th, we reached Cape
York, and anchored in the northern entrance to
Port Albany. At daylight next morning two
parties were sent in various directions in search of
water. I found no traces of natives in Evans'
Bay, but at another place, while digging in the bed
of a watercourse, we were joined by a small party of
them, one of whom turned out to be an old acquaintance. They seemed to be quite at home in
our company, asking for pipes, tobacco, and biscuit,
with which I was fortunately able to supply them.
Indeed, a day or two before, some of them had
communicated with the Asp in a most confident
and friendly manner. Had water been found near
the best anchorage in Port Albany, it was Captain
Stanley's intention to have taken the ship there,
but, as it appeared from the various reports,
that Evans' Bay was preferable at this time for

watering, both as affording the largest supply, and the greatest facilities for obtaining it, the ship was accordingly removed to an anchorage off the south part of the bay, and moored, being in the strength of the tide running round Robúmo Island.

Shortly after our arrival at Cape York, the two sets of old wells, dug by the Fly, were cleared out, and we completed water to seventy-five tons. These wells are situated immediately behind the sandy beach,—they are merely pits into which the fresh water, with which the ground had become saturated during the rainy season, oozes through the sand, having undergone a kind of filtration. At times a little surf gets up on the shore, but never, during our stay of three weeks, was it sufficient to inter- rupt the watering.

While the ship remained at Cape York, the Bramble, Asp, pinnace, and our second cutter, were engaged, under their respective officers, in the survey of Endeavour Strait and the Prince of Wales Channel, which they finished before we left, thus completing the survey of the Inner Route between Dunk and Booby Islands. Previous to leaving for that purpose, the pinnace had been sent to Booby Island, for letters in the "post office" there, and some of us had the good fortune to receive commu- nications from our friends in Sydney, which had been left by vessels passing through. Most passing vessels heave-to off the island for an hour, the dangers of Torres Strait having been passed, and record their names, &c. in the log book kept there, and by it we found, that with one exception, all this season had taken the Outer Passage, and most of them had entered at Raine's Islet, guided by the beacon erected there in 1844, by Captain F. P. Blackwood, of H.M.S. Fly, thus demonstrating the superior merits of this passage over the other openings in the Barrier Reef, and the accuracy of the Fly's survey.

On October 21st, the long and anxiously looked for vessel from Sydney arrived, bringing our supplies, and the letters and news of the last five months. We had for a short time been completely out of bread, peas, and lime juice, and two cases of scurvy had appeared among the crew.

It had been arranged that Mr. Kennedy with his expedition should, if possible, be at Cape York in the beginning of October to communicate with us, and receive such supplies and assistance as might be required; but the month passed away without bringing any signs of his being in the neighbourhood. During our progress along the coast a good look out had been kept for his preconcerted signal —three fires in a line, the central one largest—and bush-fires which on two occasions at night assumed somewhat of that appearance had been answered, as agreed on, by rockets sent up at 8 P.M., none of which however were returned. A schooner from Sydney arrived on the 27th with two additions to his party, including a surgeon, also supplies, consisting chiefly of sheep, with instructions from the Colonial Government to await at Port Albany the arrival of the expedition. The live stock were landed by our boats on Albany Island, where a sheep pen was constructed, and a well dug,—but the water was too brackish for use. A sufficient supply however had previously been found in a small cave not far off, where the schooner's boat could easily reach it.

I shall now proceed to give an account of the neighbourhood of Cape York, derived from the present and previous visits, as a place which must eventually become of considerable importance—and first of the aborigines :—

On the day of our arrival at Cape York, a large party of natives crossed over in five canoes under sail from Mount Adolphus Island, and subsequently their numbers increased until at one time no less than 150 men, women, and children, were assembled at Evans' Bay. But their stay was short, probably on account of the difficulty of procuring food for so large an assemblage, and the greater part dispersed along the coast to the southward. While collecting materials for a vocabulary,* I found that several

---

* In illustration of the difficulty of framing so apparently simple a document as a vocabulary, and particularly to shew how one must not fall into the too common mistake of putting down as certain every word he gets from a savage, however clearly he may suppose he is understood, I may mention that on going over the different parts of the human body, to get their names by pointing to them, I got at different times and from different

dialects were spoken, but I failed then to connect them with particular tribes or even find out which, if any, were the resident ones. Among these were two or three of the Papuan race, from some of the islands of Torres Strait. It appeared to me that a constant friendly intercourse exists between the natives of the southern portion of Torres Strait and those of the main land about Cape York, which last, from its central position, is much frequented during their occasional, perhaps periodical migrations. This free communication between the races would account for the existence in the vocabulary I then procured at Cape York of a considerable number of words (at least 31 out of 248) identical with those given by Jukes in his vocabularies of Darnley Island and Masseed, especially the latter.

The physical characteristics of these Australians seen at Cape York differ in no respect from those of the same race which I have seen elsewhere. The absence of one or more of the upper incisors was not observed here, nor had circumcision or any similar rite been practised, as is the case in some parts of the continent. Among these undoubted Australians were, as already mentioned, two or three Papuans. They differed in appearance from the others in having the skin of a much lighter colour — yellowish brown instead of nearly black — the hair on

individuals — for the *shin-bone*, words which in the course of time I found to mean respectively, *the leg—the shin-bone—the skin—* and *bone* in general.

the body woolly and growing in scattered tufts, and that of the head also woolly and twisted into long strands like those of a mop. On the right shoulder, and occasionally the left also, they had a large complicated, oval scar, only slightly prominent, and very neatly made.

The custom of smoking, so general throughout Torres Strait, has been introduced at Cape York. Those most addicted to it were the Papuans above mentioned, but many of the Australians joined them, and were equally clamourous for tobacco. Still it was singular to notice that although *choka* (tobacco) was in great demand, biscuit, which they had corrupted to *bĭshĭkar*, was much more prized. Their mode of smoking having elsewhere* been described, I need not allude to it further than that the pipe, which is a piece of bamboo as thick as the arm and two or three feet long, is first filled with tobacco-smoke, and then handed round the company seated on the ground in a ring—each takes a long inhalation, and passes the pipe to his neighbour, slowly allowing the smoke to exhale. On several occasions at Cape York, I have seen a native so affected by a single inhalation, as to be rendered nearly senseless, with the perspiration bursting out at every pore, and require a draught of water to restore him; and, although myself a smoker, yet on the only occasion when I tried this mode of using

* Jukes' Voyage of the Fly, Vol. i. p. 165.

tobacco, the sensations of nausea and faintness were produced.

These people appeared to repose the most perfect confidence in us—they repeatedly visited the ship in their own canoes or the watering boats, and were always well treated ; nor did any circumstance occur during our intimacy to give either party cause of complaint. We saw few weapons among them. The islanders had their bows and arrows, and the others their spears and throwing-sticks. As the weather was fine, at least as regarded the absence of rain, no huts of any kind were constructed ; at night the natives slept round their fires without any covering. During our stay the food of the natives consisted chiefly of two kinds of fruit, the first (a *Wallrothia*) like a large yellow plum, mealy and insipid ; the second, the produce of a kind of mangrove (*Candelia*) the vegetating sprouts of which are prepared for food by a process between baking and steaming. At low water the women usually dispersed in search of shell-fish on the mud-flats and among the mangroves, and the men occasionally went out to fish, either with the spear, or the hook and line.

The country in the immediate vicinity of Evans' and Cape York Bays consists of low wooded hills alternating with small valleys and plains of greater extent. The coast line, when not consisting of rocky headlands, is either a sandy beach, or is fringed with mangroves. Behind this, where the country is flat, there is usually a narrow belt of dense brush or jungle. In the valleys, one finds what in the colony of New South Wales would be termed open forest land, characterized by scattered eucalypti and other trees, and a scanty covering of coarse sedge-like grass growing in tufts on a red clayey soil, covered with nodules of ironstone and coarse quartzose sand. As characteristics of this poor soil, the first objects to attract the attention are the enormous pinnacled ant-hills of red clay and sand, often with supporting buttresses. These singular structures, which are sometimes twelve feet in height, are of great strength and toughness —on breaking off a piece, they appear to be honeycombed inside, the numerous galleries beiug then displayed. The ants themselves are of a pale brown colour, a quarter of an inch in length. In sailing along the coast, these ant-hills may be distinctly seen from the distance of two or three miles.

The rock in the immediate neighbourhood of Cape York is a porphyry with soft felspathic base, containing numerous moderately sized crystals of amber-coloured quartz, and a few larger ones of flesh-coloured felspar. It often appears in large tabular masses split horizontally and vertically into blocks of all sizes. At times when the vertical fissures predominate and run chiefly in one direction, the porphyry assumes a slaty character, and large thin masses may be detached.

One of the most interesting features in the botany

of Cape York, is the occurrence of a palm, not hitherto mentioned as Australian. It is the *Caryota urens* (found also in India and the Indian archipelago), one of the noblest of the family, combining the foliage of the tree-fern with a trunk a foot in diameter, and sixty in height. It is found in the dense brushes along with three other palms, *Seaforthia, Corypha,* and *Calamus.* Another very striking tree, not found elsewhere by us, is the fine *Wormia alata,* abundant on the margin of the brushes, where it is very conspicuous from its large yellow blossoms, handsome dark-green foliage, and ragged, papery bark of a red colour.

One day I explored some caves in the sandstone cliffs at Port Albany in quest of bats, and was fortunate enough to get quite a new *Rhinolophus* or horse-shoe bat. In one of the caves, which only admitted of entry on the hands and knees, these bats were so numerous, and in such large clusters, that I secured no less than eleven at one time, by using both hands. Small kangaroos appeared to be plentiful enough, but we were not so fortunate as to shoot one. The natives one day brought down to us a live opossum, quite tame, and very gentle ; this turned out to be new, and has since been described by Mr. Gould under the name of *Pseudocheirus nudicaudatus.*

In the brushes the sportsman may find the megapodius, brush-turkey, and white pigeon, and in the forest flocks of white cockatoos, and various parrots

and parrakeets, besides thrushes, orioles, leather-
heads, &c., but I shall not now enter upon the
ornithology of the district. A very large lizard
(*Monitor Gouldii*) is common at Cape York,—it
climbs trees with great agility, and is very swift,
scampering over the dead leaves in the scrubs, with
nearly as much noise as a kangaroo. Snakes,
although apparently not very plentiful, yet require to
be carefully looked for in order to be avoided ; one
day I killed single individuals of two kinds,—one a
slender, very active green whip-snake, four feet in
length,—the other, the brown snake of New South
Wales, where its bite is considered fatal. Fish are
plentiful at Cape York ; they may be caught with the
hook and line from the rocks, or at a little distance
off, and the sandy beach of Evans' Bay is well-
adapted for hauling the seine upon. A curious
fresh-water fish (*Megalops setipinnis*) is found in the
lagoon here, and even in the wells dug by the Fly,
there were some full grown individuals ; it much
resembles the herring, in shape, colour, and size.
The shells may be very briefly dismissed. The
principal landshell is a very large variety of *Helix
bipartita*, here attaining its greatest size. The most
striking shell of the sand-flats is a handsome olive
(*O. ispidula*), remarkable for its extraordinary varia-
tions in colour, size, and even form.

In viewing Cape York as the probable site of a
future settlement or military post, an important
feature to be noticed is the comparative abundance

of fresh water at the very close of the dry season. In Evans' Bay it may always be procured by digging behind the beach, especially at the foot of some low wooded hillocks, towards its western end. Native wells were met with in most of the smaller bays, and the size of the dried up watercourses indicates that during the wet season, a considerable body is carried off by them from the flats and temporary lagoons.

Were one inclined, from interested motives, to extol the natural capabilities of the immediate neighbourhood of Cape York, it would be very easy to speculate upon, and at once presume its peculiar fitness for the growth of tropical produce. Thus, any swampy land might at once be pronounced peculiarly adapted for paddy fields, and the remainder as admirably suited to the growth of cotton, coffee, indigo, &c. With the exception of a piece of rich soil, several acres in extent, on the eastern margin of a watercourse, leading from the small lagoon behind Evans' Bay, and which would be a good site for a large garden, I did not see much ground that was fit for cultivation. Very fine rich patches occur here and there in the brushes removed from the coast, but in the belts of brush along the beaches the soil, despite the accumulation of vegetable matter, is essentially poor and sandy. It may be added that the value of the garden land above alluded to, is much enhanced by its proximity to a constant supply of water, to be procured by digging in the bed of the lagoon. Nearly all the grass is of a coarse sedge-like description, mixed, however, in places with grasses of a finer kind. Towards the end of the dry season, the grass, when not burnt off by the natives, presents a most uninviting, withered appearance, being so dry as almost to crumble into dust if rubbed between the palms of the hand.

As one of the more immediate beneficial results of our survey of the Inner Passage, would be to facilitate its use by steamers, should arrangements at present contemplated for the continuance of the "overland" communication between Great Britain and India, from Singapore to the Australian colonies, by way of Torres Strait, ever be carried into effect, so it was of importance to find some place in the neighbourhood of Cape York, convenient as a coaling station during either monsoon. An eligible spot for this purpose was found in Port Albany, the name given by Lieut. Yule, who surveyed it in 1846, to the narrow channel separating Albany Island from the main land. Here a small sandy bay with a sufficient depth of water close inshore, was, after a minute examination by Captain Stanley, considered to be well adapted to the running out of a jetty, alongside of which the largest steamer could lie in perfect safety. This little bay has anchorage close inshore for three or four vessels only, as a little further out they would be in the stream of tide which runs with great strength, especially in the neighbourhood of the various points; however, it is completely sheltered from any wind which may be experienced on this part of the coast.

On several occasions I landed on Albany Island, and walked over the place. It is three miles in length, and one in greatest breadth, its outline irregular from the number of bays and small rocky headlands. On its western side the bays are small, and the · shores generally steep and rocky, with sandy intervals, the banks being covered with brush of the usual Australian intertropical character. The rock here is either a stratum of ironstone in irregular masses and nodules cemented together by a ferruginous base, or a very coarse sandstone, almost a quartzose conglomerate, forming cliffs, occasionally thirty feet or more in height. The latter stone is suitable for rough building purposes, such as the construction of a pier, but is much acted on by the weather. On the northern and eastern sides the bays are large and generally sandy, with the land sloping down towards them from the low undulating hills, which compose the rest of the island. These hills are either sandy or covered with ironstone gravel* over red clay. They

---

* A sample of this ironstone picked up from the surface has furnished materials for the following remarks, for which I am indebted to the politeness of Warrington W. Smyth, Esq., of the Museum of Practical Geology.

"On examining the specimens which you presented to our Museum, I see that they consist for the most part of the red or

are thinly covered with a sprinkling of *Grevillea*, *Boronia*, and *Leucopogon* bushes, with occasional tufts of the coarsest grass.   There must always be, however, sufficient pasturage for such cattle and sheep as a small party in charge of a coaling depot would require.   There is also sufficient water in the island for their support, and by digging wells, no doubt the quantity would be greatly increased. In addition there are several small spots where the soil is suitable for gardening purposes, thus ensuring a supply of vegetables during the greater part, perhaps the whole of the year.

On November 2nd we sailed from Cape York on our way to Port Essington and Sydney, but owing to the prevalence of light airs, chiefly from the eastward, and calms, we did not reach Booby Island until the 4th, having passed out of Torres

anhydrous peroxide of iron,—similar in chemical character to the celebrated hœmatite ore of Ulverstone and Whitehaven.   It is, however, less rich in iron than would be inferred from its outward appearance, since the pebbles on being broken, exhibit interiorly a loose and cellular structure, where grains of quartz and plates of mica are interspersed with the ore, and of course reduce its specific gravity and value.

"Such an ore, if occurring in great quantity, and at no great distance from abundant fuel and from a supply of limestone for flux, may prove to be very valuable; but I should fear that your suggestion of employing the coral and shells of the coast, for the last mentioned purpose, might impair the quality of an iron thus produced, for the phosphoric acid present in them would give one of the constituents most troublesome to the iron-master, who wishes to produce a strong and tough iron."

Strait by the Prince of Wales Channel. The Bramble was left to perform some work in Endeavour Strait* and elsewhere along the Inner Passage, and after its completion to make the best of her way to Sydney down the eastern coast of Australia against the trade-wind, before successfully accomplished by only two other vessels besides herself. Of course a considerable degree of interest has been excited by this intended procedure, as the two vessels start under pretty equal circumstances to reach the same place by two very different routes, of the merits of one of which comparatively little is known.

November 9th.—Since leaving Booby Island, the weather has been fine with light easterly winds, the westerly monsoon in these seas not usually setting in until the month of December. We first made the land in the neighbourhood of Cape Croker, and soon afterwards saw the beacon on Point Smith. Entering Port Essington we ran up the harbour, and anchored off the settlement of Victoria early in the afternoon.

On landing and walking over the place after an

---

* Since the survey of Endeavour Strait in 1844 by Lieutenant Yule in the Bramble (then attached to the Fly under Captain F. P. Blackwood), several sunken rocks have been discovered, thereby lessening the value of the passage through the Strait, as others, yet undetected, to be found only by " sweeping" for them, may be presumed to exist. Captain Stanley was strongly of opinion that the Prince of Wales' Channel was far preferable, especially for large ships, to Endeavour Strait.

absence of more than three years, I might naturally have looked for some signs of improvement in the appearance of the settlement and condition of the unfortunate residents, had I not been aware of the non-progressive nature of the system which had long been established there. I saw no such indications of prosperity except in the flourishing and improved appearance of the cocoa-nut trees now in full bearing, as if nature boldly asserted her rights in opposition to the dormant or even retrograde condition of everything else in the place.

We found the settlement in a ruinous condition. Even the hospital, the best building in the place, had the roof in such a state that when rain came on some of the patients' beds had to be shifted, and the surgeon found it necessary to protect his own bed by a tent-like canopy. With few exceptions, every one was dissatisfied, and anxiously looked forward to the happy time when the party should be relieved, or the settlement finally abandoned. The unhealthiness* of the place, so often denied,

* As illustration of this point, I would direct attention to the following tabular view of the Detachment of Marines at Port Essington, from the time of the arrival of the *second* party to their final departure, embracing a period of five years. I have not been able to procure any authentic statement of the mortality among the *first* party.

Found there	1	officer	0 men	}Nov. 19th, 1844.
Arrived by Cadet	3	do.	52 do.	
Do. by Freak	2	do.	6 do.	1847.
	6		58	

had now shewn itself in an unequivocal manner; every one had suffered from repeated attacks of intermittent fever, and another fever of a more deadly character had occasionally made its appearance, and, operating upon previously debilitated constitutions, frequently proved fatal.

There can, I think, be little doubt that much of the unhealthiness of the garrison depended upon local influences. The situation of Victoria, at the distance of sixteen miles from the open sea on the shores of an almost land-locked harbour, was unfavourable for salubrity, although in other respects judiciously chosen. Occasionally for days together the sea breeze has not reached as far up as the settlement, and the heat has been almost stifling; usually however the sea breeze set in during the forenoon, and after blowing for some hours was succeeded by a calm, often interrupted by a gentle

Died	1 officer	12 men	
Were invalided	1	do. 13 do.	
Were taken away by Mœander	4	do. 33 do.	Nov. 30th, 1849.
	6	58	

I may remark that, although it would obviously be unjust to suppose that all the cases of death and invaliding are to be attributed to the effects of the climate, yet the loss of the services of twenty-seven men out of fifty-eight in five years by these means, clearly proves the unhealthiness of the place. Another may be added to the list, for Captain Macarthur was shortly afterwards invalided in Sydney, a victim to the climate of Port Essington.

land-wind. Within 400 yards of the hospital a great extent of mud overgrown with mangroves, dry at low water, must have exercised a prejudicial influence; at times while crossing this swamp, the putrid exhalations have induced a feeling almost amounting to nausea. And if anything more than another shews the comparative unhealthiness of the site of the settlement, it is the fact, that invalids sent to Point Smith (at the entrance of the harbour) or Coral Bay,—both of which places are within the full influence of the sea breeze,—speedily recovered, although relapses on their return to Victoria were not unfrequent.

Even in the important article of food—setting aside other secondary stores—the Port Essington garrison have almost always been badly supplied. I have seen them obliged to use bread which was not fit for human food — the refuse of the stock on hand at the close of the war in China, and yet there was none better to be got. In short, I believe, as I stated some years ago in a Colonial paper, that there is probably no vessel in Her Majesty's navy, no matter where serving, the men of which are not better supplied with all the necessaries and comforts of life than are the residents at Port Essington. All these have volunteered for the place, but their preconceived ideas formed in England almost always on reaching the place gave way to feelings of regret at the step they had taken; I well remember the excitement in the settlement, and the feelings of joy everywhere expressed, when in October 1845, the first party learned that their relief had arrived.

I shall now proceed to make some remarks upon Port Essington, ere the subject becomes a matter of history, as I fervently hope the abandonment of the place will render it ere many years have gone by ;* but before doing so I may premise a brief account of the former British settlements on the north coast of Australia.†

The British Government having determined to form an establishment on the northern coast of Australia, Captain J. J. Gordon Bremer, with H.M.S. Tamar, sailed from Sydney in August 1824, in company with two store ships and a party of mili-

* Port Essington was finally abandoned on November 30th, 1849, when the garrison and stores were removed to Sydney by H.M.S. Mœander, Captain the Hon. H. Keppel. I may mention that most of the remarks in this chapter relative to Port Essington appear as they were originally written in my journal soon after leaving the place in the Rattlesnake ; they are mostly a combination of the observations made during three visits, at intervals of various lengths, including a residence in 1844, of upwards of four months. I am also anxious to place on record a somewhat connected but brief account of the Aborigines, as I have seen many injudicious remarks and erroneous statements regarding them, and as it is only at Port Essington, for the whole extent of coast line between Swan River and Cape York, that we were able to have sufficient intercourse with them to arrive at even a moderate degree of acquaintance with their manners, customs, and language.

† See Voyage round the World, by T. B. Wilson, M.D.

tary and convicts, the latter chiefly mechanics. On September 20th, they arrived at Port Essington, when formal possession was taken of the whole of the coast between the 129th and 135th meridians of east longitude. A sufficiency of fresh water not being found at this place it was determined to proceed to Melville Island, where they arrived on the 30th, and commenced forming the settlement of Fort Dundas in Apsley Strait. This settlement, however, after an existence of four years, was abandoned on March 31st, 1829, in consequence of the continued unfavourable accounts transmitted to the Home Government. Hostilities with the natives had early commenced, and several lives were lost on either side.

Meanwhile in anticipation of the abandonment of Melville Island, it had been resolved to found a second settlement upon the north coast of Australia. For this purpose, H.M.S. Success, Captain Stirling, with a convoy of three vessels conveying troops, convicts, stores, and provisions, sailed from Sydney, and arrived at Raffles' Bay on June 17th, 1827. Next day the new settlement of Fort Wellington was formed. A grand error was made in the very beginning, for the site was chosen behind a mud-bank, dry at low tides, in order to secure proximity to a lagoon of fresh water, which after all disappeared towards the close of the dry season. At first the natives committed many depredations, chiefly during the night. About a month after the founding of the settlement, it was thought necessary to order the sentries to fire upon the natives whenever they approached, and on one occasion they were greeted with a discharge of grape-shot. At length one of the soldiers was speared, and in reprisal a party was sent out, which, coming unexpectedly upon a camp of natives, killed and wounded several, including a woman and two children. When the Bugis paid their annual visit to the coast several prahus remained to fish for trepang under the protection of the settlement. Of the healthiness of the place the medical officer states, " There is no endemic disease here. The climate of the place surpasses every other as far as I know, which is equally as near the equator; and were it not for the great height of atmospheric temperature, I should consider this one of the best in the world." However, two years after the foundation of the settlement, when hostilities with the natives had ceased, and a friendly intercourse been established—when the Bugis had already taken advantage of the protection of Europeans to carry on the trepang fishery in the bay—when the reported unhealthiness of the climate had never exhibited itself-- in short when the settlement had been brought into a flourishing state, orders were suddenly received for its entire abandonment, which were carried into effect on August 29th, 1829.

Eight years afterwards, Government resolved for the fourth time to establish a settlement on the north coast of Australia, with the double view of affording shelter to the crews of vessels wrecked in Torres Strait, and of endeavouring to throw open to British enterprise the neighbouring islands of the Indian Archipelago. For this purpose, H.M.S. Alligator, under the command of Captain J. J. Gordon Bremer, and H.M.S. Britomart (Lieut. Owen Stanley), were sent out, and left Sydney for Port Essington in September 1837. Another vessel with stores accompanied the Alligator, and both arrived at Port Essington on October 27th of the same year. Soon afterwards, upon a site for the settlement being chosen, the necessary operations were commenced, and by the end of May in the following year, the preliminary arrangements having been completed, the Alligator left, and Captain John Macarthur, R.M., with a subaltern, assistant-surgeon, storekeeper, and a linguist, together with a detachment of forty marines, remained in charge of the new settlement. The Britomart remained behind for several years as a tender to this naval station, or military post,—for either term is equally applicable, and was afterwards succeeded in her charge by H.M.S. Royalist. In October, 1845, the remains of the original party which had been there for seven years (including also a small detachment sent down from China), were relieved by a draft from England of two subalterns, an assistant-surgeon, and fifty-two rank and file of the Royal Marines, Captain Macarthur still remaining as commandant.

The Port Essington experiment I am afraid is to

be regarded as a complete failure.   Yet it could not
well have been otherwise.   It was never more than a
mere military post, and the smallness of the
party, almost always further lessened by sickness,
was such that, even if judiciously managed, little
more could be expected than that they should be
employed merely in rendering their own condition
more comfortable.   And now after the settlement
has been established for eleven years, they are not
even able to keep themselves in fresh vegetables,
much less efficiently to supply any of Her Majesty's
vessels which may happen to call there.

In order to develope the resources of a colony,
always provided it possesses any such, surely something more is required than the mere presence of a
party of soldiers, but it appears throughout, that
Government were opposed to giving encouragement
to the permanent settlement at Port Essington, of
any of her Majesty's subjects.   It is well perhaps
that such has been the case, as I can conceive few
positions more distressing than that which a settler
would soon find himself placed in were he tempted
by erroneous and highly coloured reports of the
productiveness of the place—and such are not wanting,—to come there with the vain hopes of being
able to raise tropical productions* for export, even

* I need not here enlarge upon the unfitness of Port Essington for agricultural pursuits—even that point has long ago been
given up. The quantity of land which might be made productive
is exceedingly small, and although cotton, sugar cane, and other

with the assistance of Chinese or Malay labourers.
Wool, the staple commodity of Australia, would
not grow there, and the country is not adapted for
the support of cattle to any great extent.

Yet the little settlement at Port Essington has
not been altogether useless. The knowledge of
the existence of such a military post, within a few
days' sail of the islands in question, together with
the visits of Commander Stanley in the Britomart,
had completely prevented a repetition of the outrages formerly committed upon European trading
vessels at the various islands of the group extending
between Timor and New Guinea. The crews and
passengers of various vessels wrecked in Torres
Strait had frequently found in Port Essington a
place of shelter, after six hundred miles and more
of boat navigation, combined with the difficulty of
determining the entrance, owing to the lowness of
the land thereabouts, which might easily be passed
in the night, or even during the day, if distant more
than ten or twelve miles. I have myself been a
witness to the providential relief and extreme hospitality afforded there to such unfortunates. Still,
as a harbour of refuge, it is obvious that Cape York
is the most suitable place, situated as it is within a
short distance of the spot where disasters by ship-
wreck in Torres Strait and its approaches have been
most frequent.

tropical productions thrive well in one of the two gardens, there
is no field for their growth upon a remunerative scale.

Port Essington has sometimes been alluded to as being admirably adapted for a depot from which European goods can be introduced among the neighbouring islands of the Indian Archipelago, but on this subject I would perfectly coincide with Mr. Jukes, who states—" Now, the best plan for a vessel wishing to trade with the independent islands, obviously, is to go to them at once ; while she has just as good an opportunity to smuggle her goods into the Dutch islands, if that be her object, as the natives would have if they were to come and fetch them from Port Essington."

The natives of the Cobourg Peninsula are divided into four tribes, named respectively the Bijenelumbo, Limbakarajia, Limbapyu, and Terrutong. The first of these occupies the head of the harbour (including the ground on which the settlement is built), and the country as far back as the isthmus,—the second, both sides of the port lower down,—the third, the north-west portion of the peninsula,—and the last have possession of Croker's Island, and the adjacent coasts of the mainland. From the constant intercourse which takes place between these tribes, their affinity of language, and similarity in physical character, manners, and customs, they may be spoken of as one.

The Aborigines of Port Essington scarcely differ from those of the other parts of Australia,—I mean, there is no striking peculiarity. The septum of the nose is invariably perforated, and the right central incisor — rarely the left, is knocked out during childhood. Both sexes are more or less ornamented with large raised cicatrices on the shoulders and across the chest, abdomen, and buttocks, and outside of the thighs. No clothing is at any time worn by these people, and their ornaments are few in number. These last consist chiefly of wristlets of the fibres of a plant — and armlets of the same, wound round with cordage, are in nearly universal use. Necklaces of fragments of reed strung on a thread, or of cordage passing under the arms and crossed over the back, and girdles of finely twisted human hair, are occasionally worn by both sexes, and the men sometimes add a tassel of the hair of the opossum or flying squirrel, suspended in front. A piece of stick or bone thrust into the perforation in the nose completes the costume. Like the other Australians, the Port Essington blacks are fond of painting themselves with red, yellow, white, and black, in different styles, considered appropriate to dancing, fighting, mourning, &c.

These people construct no huts except during the rainy season, when they put up a rude and temporary structure of bark. Their utensils are few in number, consisting merely of fine baskets of the stems of a rush-like plant, and others of the base of the leaf of the *Seaforthia* palm, the latter principally used for containing water. Formerly bark canoes were in general use, but they are now completely superseded by others, hollowed out of the trunk of a tree, which they procure ready-made from the Malays, in exchange for tortoise-shell, and in return for assistance in collecting trepang.

The aboriginal weapons are clubs and spears,—of the latter the variety is very great, there being at least fourteen distinct kinds. Their clubs are three in number, made of the tough heavy wood called *wallăru*, a kind of gum-tree, the iron-bark of New South Wales; one is cylindrical, four feet long, tapering at each extremity; the other two, of similar length, are compressed, with sharp edges,— one narrow, the other about four inches in greatest width, and resembling a cricket-bat in shape. These weapons on account of their great weight are used only at close quarters, and are never thrown like the waddy of New South Wales. The spears of the Port Essington natives may be divided into two classes, —1st, those thrown with the hand alone, and 2nd, those propelled by the additional powerful leverage afforded by the throwing-stick. The hand-spears are made entirely of wood, generally the wallaroo, in one or two pieces, plain at the point or variously toothed and barbed; a small light spear of the latter description is sometimes thrown with a short cylindrical stick ornamented at one end with a large bunch of twisted human hair. The spears of the second class are shafted with reed. The smallest, which is no bigger than an arrow, is propelled by a large flat and supple throwing-stick to a great distance, but not with much precision. Of the larger ones (from eight to twelve feet in length), the two most remarkable are headed with a pointed, sharp-edged, flatly-triangular piece of quartz or fine grained basalt, procured from the mountains beyond the isthmus. These large reed-shafted spears are thrown with a stiff flat throwing-stick a yard long, and with pretty certain effect within sixty paces.

The food of the aborigines consists chiefly of fish and shell-fish, to which as subsidiary articles may be added lizards, snakes, opossums, various birds, and an occasional kangaroo, turtle, dugong, or porpoise. Several roots (one of which is a true yam), together with various fruits in their seasons, — especially a cashew-nut or Anacardium, also the base of the undeveloped central leaves of the cabbage-palm, are much prized. The digging up of roots and collecting of shell-fish are duties which devolve upon the females.

Before the arrival of Europeans, in cases of remarkable disease or accident, certain old men known by the name of *bilbo* (by which cognomen the medical officers of the settlement have also been distinguished) were applied to for advice. I know of no popular remedies, however, with the exception of tight ligatures near a wound, bruise or sore, the object of which is to prevent the malady from passing into the body. In like manner for a head-ache, a fillet is bound tightly across the forehead. These people, like most other savages, recover in a most surprising manner from wounds and other injuries which would probably prove fatal to an European. The chief complaint to which they are subject is a mild form of ophthalmia, with which I once saw three-fourths of the natives about the settlement affected in one or both eyes; they themselves attributed this affection to the *lúrgala*, or cashew-nut, then in season, the acrid oil in the husk of which had reached their eyes.

On the death of any one of the natives, the relatives give utterance to their grief in loud cries, sobs, and shrieks, continued to exhaustion. Some cut their bodies and tear their hair, and the women paint their faces with broad white bands. The body is watched by night, and the appearance of the first falling star is hailed with loud shouts and waving of fire-brands, to drive off the *yúmburbar*, an evil spirit which is the cause of all deaths and other calamities, and feeds on the entrails of the newly dead. When decomposition has gone on sufficiently far, the bones are carefully removed, painted red, wrapped up in bark, and carried about with the tribe for some time ; after which they are finally deposited, either in a hollow tree or a shallow grave, over which a low mound of earth and stones is raised, occasionally ornamented with posts at the corners. I was unable to find out what circumstances determine the mode of burial in each case ; neither differences of sex, age, or class are sufficient, as several natives whom I questioned told me which of the two kinds of burial his or her body would receive, without being able to assign any reason. Their reverence for the dead is probably not very great, as even a relative of the deceased will sell the skull or skeleton for a small consideration, on condition of the matter being kept a secret. Like other Australians they carefully refrain from mentioning the name of any one who is dead, and like them, believe in the transmigration of souls,—after death they become Malays (the first strangers they had come in contact with), in precisely the same way as in New South Wales, &c. "when black-fellow die, he jump up white-fellow."

In addition to the *yúmburbar* above mentioned, there is another supernatural being, which has a corporeal existence. It appears in the shape of a man, and loves to grapple with stragglers in the dark, and carry them off. So much is the *arlak* an object of dread, that a native will not willingly go alone in the dark, even a very short distance from his fire, without carrying a light. Some have assured me that they had seen this *arlak*, and one man shewed me wounds said to have been inflicted by its teeth, and I have no doubt of his having firmly believed that they were produced in this manner.

Although in each tribe there are three distinct classes, possibly ranks, or perhaps something analogous to the division in other countries into castes, yet there does not appear to be anything approaching to chieftainship. There are a few elderly men, however, in each tribe, who, having acquired a reputation for sagacity and energy, exercise a certain degree of authority over the younger members, and generally manage important matters in their own way. Yet very few of these principal men are of the highest class, the *manjerojelle*,—the middle is termed *manjerawúle*,— and the lowest *manbulget*, but I could not succeed in making out what privileges, if any, are enjoyed by the superior classes. The members of all three appeared to be upon a perfect equality.

Polygamy, although one of their institutions, is little practised, as few men have more than one wife at a time. The betrothal of a female takes place in infancy, and often even before birth. A few half-caste children have been born, but they do not appear to thrive, although this does not imply any want of attention on the part of the mothers.

These natives are fond of social enjoyment. Their evenings are passed away round the fires, with songs generally of a low, plaintive, and not unpleasing character, time being kept by beating one bone or stick upon another. They have besides what may be called a musical instrument—the *ibero*—a piece of bamboo, three feet in length, which, by blowing into it, is made to produce an interrupted, drumming, monotonous noise. In their dances I observed nothing peculiar.

In illustration of their laws relative to punish ments, and to shew their identity with those of other Australian tribes, I may mention a circumstance which came under my own knowledge. One night about ten o'clock, hearing an uproar at a native encampment near the hospital, I ran out and found that a young man, named Munjerrijo, having excited the jealousy of another, of the name of Yungun, on account of some improper conduct towards the wife of the latter, had been severely wounded, his arm being broken with a club, and his head laid open with an iron-headed fishing spear. As the punish ment was considered too severe for the offence, it was finally determined, that, upon Munjerrijo's re covery, the two natives who had wounded him should offer their heads to him to be struck with a club, the usual way, it would appear, of settling such matters.

Like the other Australian tribes, those of Port Essington are frequently at feud with their neigh bours, and quarrels sometimes last for years, or, if settled, are apt to break out afresh. In these cases the *lex talionis* is the only recognised one. I may give an example. A Monobar native (inhabitant of the country to the westward of the isthmus) was shot by a marine in the execution of his duty, for attempting to escape while in custody, charged with robbery. When his tribe heard of it, as they could not lay their hands upon a white man, they enticed into their territory a Bijenelumbo man, called Nein mal, who was a friend of the whites, having lived with them for years, and on that account he was selected as a victim and killed. When the news of Neinmal's death reached the settlement, some other Bijenelumbo people took revenge by killing a Monobar native within a few hundred yards of the houses. Thus the matter rests at present, but more deaths will probably follow before the feud is ended. Both these murders were committed under circumstances of the utmost atrocity, the victims being surprised asleep unconscious of danger and perfectly defenceless, then aroused to find themselves treacherously attacked by numbers, who, after spearing them in many places, fearfully mangled the bodies with clubs.

In some of the settled districts of Australia missionaries have been established for many years back, still it must be confessed that the results of their labours are far from being encouraging. Indeed no less an authority than Mr. Eyre, writing in 1848, unhesitatingly states as follows: " Nor is it in my recollection," says he, " that throughout the whole length and breadth of New Holland, a single real and permanent convert to Christianity has yet been made amongst them."* From what I myself have seen or heard, in the colony of New South Wales, I have reason to believe the missionary efforts there, while proving a complete failure so far as regards the Christianising of the blacks, have yet been produc-

* Journals of Expeditions of Discovery into Central Australia, &c. by E. J. Eyre, vol. ii. p. 420.

tive of much good in rendering them less dangerous and more useful to their white neighbours, without however permanently reclaiming more than a few from their former wandering and savage mode of life, and enabling them and their families to live contentedly on the produce of their own labour.   I am not one of those who consider that the Australian is not susceptible of anything like such permanent improvement as may be termed civilization, although it appears to have been sufficiently proved that his intellectual capacity is of a very low order.

Many of the Port Essington natives have shewn a remarkable degree of intelligence, far above the average of Europeans, uneducated, and living in remote districts,—among others I may mention the name of Neinmal (the same alluded to in the preceding paragraph), of whose character I had good opportunities of judging, for he lived with me for ten months.   During my stay at Port Essington, he became much attached to me, and latterly accompanied me in all my wanderings in the bush, while investigating the natural history of the district, following up the researches of my late and much lamented friend Gilbert.*   One day, while detained by rainy weather at my camp, I was busy in skinning a fish,—Neinmal watched me attentively for some time and then withdrew, but returned in half an hour afterwards, with the skin of another fish in

* See Journal of an Overland Expedition in Australia, &c. by Dr. Ludwig Leichhardt, p. 309, for an account of his death.

his hand prepared by himself, and so well done too, that it was added to the collection.   I could give many other instances of his sagacity, his docility, and even his acute perception of character,—latterly, he seemed even to read my very thoughts.   He accompanied me in the Fly to Torres Strait and New Guinea, and on our return to Port Essington begged so hard to continue with me that I could not refuse him.   He went with us to Singapore, Java, and Sydney, and from his great good humour became a favourite with all on board, picking up the English language with facility, and readily conforming himself to our habits, and the discipline of the ship.   He was very cleanly in his personal habits, and paid much attention to his dress, which was always kept neat and tidy.   I was often much amused and surprised by the oddity and justness of his remarks upon the many strange sights which a voyage of this kind brought before him.   The Nemesis steamer under weigh puzzled him at first—he then thought it was "all same big cart, only got him shingles* on wheels!"   He always expressed great contempt for the dulness of comprehension of his countrymen, "big fools they," he used often to say, "black fellow no good."   Even Malays, Chinamen, and the natives of India, he counted as nothing in his increasing admiration of Europeans, until he saw some sepoys, when he altered his opinion a little, and thought that he too, if only big enough, would

* Wooden "tiles" generally used for covering the roofs of houses in Australia.

like to be a soldier.   The poor fellow suffered much
from cold during the passage round Cape Leeuwin
and was ill when landed at Sydney, but soon recovered.   Although his thoughts were always cen-
tred in his native home, and a girl to whom he was
much attached, he yet volunteered to accompany
me to England, when the Fly was about to sail, but
as I had then no immediate prospect of returning
to Australia, I could not undertake the responsi-
bility of having to provide for him for the future.
I was glad then when Lieut. Yule, who was about
to revisit Port Essington, generously offered to take
him there—while in the Bramble he made himself
useful in assisting the steward, and, under the
tuition of Dr. MacClatchie, made some proficiency
in acquiring the rudiments of reading and writing.
At Port Essington, the older members of his family
evinced much jealousy on account of the attention
shewn him, and his determination to remain with
Mr. Tilston, the assistant-surgeon, then in charge,
and endeavoured to dissuade him from his purpose.
While upon a visit to his tribe he met his death in
the manner already recorded.   His natural courage
and presence of mind did not desert him even at the
last extremity, when he was roused from sleep to
find himself surrounded by a host of savages thirst-
ing for his blood.   They told him to rise, but he
merely raised himself upon his elbow, and said— "If
you want to kill me do so where I am, I won't get
up—give me a spear and club, and I'll fight you all
one by one!"   He had scarcely spoken when a man

named Alerk speared him from behind, spear after spear followed, and as he lay writhing on the ground his savage murderers literally dashed him to pieces with their clubs. The account of the manner in which Neinmal met his death was given me by a very intelligent native who had it from an eye-witness, and I have every reason to believe it true, corroborated as it was by the testimony of others.

Even Port Essington was destined to become the scene of missionary labours. A party of three persons, sent out by the " Society for the Propaga-tion of the Faith," one an Italian Roman Catholic priest, the others lay brothers of his order, em-barked at Sydney, sometime in 1847. The vessel conveying them unfortunately struck on a reef near the Northumberland Isles during the night, and Father Anjello was the only one of his party saved, and reached Port Essington in a most destitute condition. Nothing daunted, however, he com-menced his labours among the blacks, by first acquiring the native language,* in which he ulti-mately became so proficient as to understand it thoroughly. A hut was built for him at a place called Black Rock, near the entrance of the harbour, at the distance of 14 miles from the settlement.

* I regret that the arrangements for this work will not admit of my publishing in the Appendix a Port Essington vocabulary, consisting of about 650 words, in four dialects, formed in 1844, and corrected and improved in 1848 ; the MSS. will be deposited in the library of the British Museum.

Here he collected together as many of the children of the Limbakarajia tribe as he could induce to remain in the neighbourhood. He endeavoured to instruct them in the elements of his religion, and taught them to repeat prayers in Latin, and follow him in some of the ceremonious observances of the Roman Catholic Church. Like other children this amused them, and so long as they were well fed and supplied with tobacco, everything went on as he could desire. Meanwhile he was supported chiefly by the contributions of the officers of the garrison, themselves not well able to spare much. While leading this lonely life he seems gradually to have given way to gloomy despondency. I recollect one passage in his diary (which I once saw for an hour), where he expresses himself thus : "Another year has gone by, and with it all signs of the promised vessel. Oh! God, even hope seems to have deserted me." At length a vessel from Sydney arrived, bringing a large supply of stores of every kind for the mission, but it was too late, for Father Anjello and his sorrows were alike resting in the tomb. One day news came that he was ill; a boat was sent immediately for him, and found him dying. He was removed to the settlement and next day he breathed his last—another, but not the last victim to the climate. His death-bed was described to me as having been a fearful scene. He exhibited the greatest horror of death, and in his last extremity blasphemously denied that there was a God!

In concluding the subject of the Aborigines, I may add that at present the natives of Port Essington have little to thank the white man for. The advantage of being provided with regular food and other comforts enjoyed by such as are in service are merely temporary, and, like the means of gratifying two new habits—the use of tobacco and spirits—to which they have become passionately addicted, will cease when the settlement is abandoned. The last importation of the whites was syphilis, and by it they will probably be remembered for years to come.

During our stay at Port Essington, I made an excursion in the decked boat of the settlement (which Capt. Macarthur kindly allowed me the use of) to Coral Bay, a station for invalids, very pleasantly situated on the western side of the harbour, twelve miles from Victoria. We found there my old friend Mr. Tilston,* the assistant-surgeon, with some convalescents under his charge. This is a much cooler and pleasanter locality than the neighbourhood of the settlement, still the heat was at times very great. I had here pointed out to me a kind of tea-tree, or Melaleuca, which had a short time before been

---

* In addition to zealous attention to his medical duties, Mr. Tilston's great mechanical skill was often of service to the settlement. He was much attached to Natural History pursuits, made large collections, and many drawings. His gentleness of disposition endeared him to all. He died of fever in the following year.

recognized by a Malay as that producing the valuable cajeput oil, and on trial, the oil procured from the leaves by distillation, was found to be scarcely inferior in pungency to that of the *Mela-leuca Cajeputi* of the Moluccas. Here, too, we saw some of the play-houses of the greater bower-bird (*Chlamydera nuchalis*), and had the pleasure of witnessing the male bird playing his strange antics as he flew up to the spot and alighted with a dead shell in his mouth, laid it down, ran through the bower, returned, picked up the shell, and rearranged the heap among which it was placed, flew off again and soon returned with another,—and so on.

On November 16th we got under weigh at day-light, but the wind died away in the afternoon, and we anchored half way down the harbour. Next day we got out to sea on our voyage to Sydney. We were all glad to leave Port Essington,—it was like escaping from an oven. During our stay the sky was generally overcast, with heavy cumuli, and distant lightning at night, but no rain fell, and the heat was excessive. These were indications of the approaching change of the monsoon ;—the rainy season, with the wind more or less westerly, usually commencing in December and continuing until March.

December 3rd.—Lat. 11° 2′ S. long. 123° 11′ E. To-day we may be said to have cleared the land after a dead beat to the westward, between the Sahul Bank and the islands of Timor and Rottee. It took us eleven days to make good less than 300 miles. The land was in sight during the greater portion of this time, and we had a good view of the noble mountain-range of Timor, also of Rottee and the Strait of Semao, which last we entered with the intention of passing through, but the wind headed us and we had to pass to the southward of Rottee. For a few days after leaving Port Essington we experienced very light and variable winds, which gradually settled into south-westerly, with occasional gloomy blowing weather and frequent squalls at night.

At length on January 24th, 1849, a long and monotonous passage of sixty-eight days brought us to Sydney, from which we had been absent for nine months.

CHAPTER V.

THE most eventful occurrence during our stay
in Sydney, was the arrival of the schooner which
we had left at Port Albany, awaiting the arrival of
Mr. Kennedy. She brought the sad news of the
disastrous failure of his expedition, and of the death
of all but three composing the overland party,
including their brave but ill-fated leader. I was
present at the judicial investigation which shortly
afterwards took place, and shall briefly relate the
particulars. I shall not easily forget the appearance
which the survivors presented on this occasion,—

pale and emaciated, with haggard looks attesting the misery and privations they had undergone, and with low trembling voices, they gave their evidence.

It would appear that their difficulties commenced at the outset, as many weeks passed before they got clear of Rockingham Bay, its rivers, swamps, and dense scrubs, fenced in by a mountain chain. Six weeks elapsed before they were enabled to pursue a northerly course, the scrubs or dense brushes still continuing, requiring the party to cut their way. The carts were abandoned on July 18th, and the horses were packed. Sickness early made its appearance, the stock of provisions was getting low, the horses long failing in strength were dying of weakness, and their flesh was used as food.

On November 10th, or upwards of five months after leaving Rockingham Bay, having made less than 400 miles in a direct line towards their destination, and three of the party having been completely knocked up, and the remainder in a feeble state; nineteen of their horses dead, and their provisions reduced to one sheep, forty-six pounds of flour, and less than one pound of tea,—Mr. Kennedy resolved to form a light party consisting of himself, three men, and the aboriginal Jackey Jackey, and push on for Cape York, distant about 150 miles, to procure assistance for the remainder, and save them from impending death by the combined influences of sickness, exhaustion, and starvation.

On November 13th Kennedy started, leaving eight men at the camp at Weymouth Bay. Near Shelburne Bay one of the party accidentally shot himself, and another was too ill to proceed; consequently, it was determined to leave them behind in charge of the third man, with a horse for food, while Kennedy and the black pushed on for Port Albany. At length near Escape River, within twenty miles of Cape York, a tribe of natives with whom they had had some apparently friendly intercourse, tempted by their forlorn condition and a savage thirst for plunder, attacked them in a scrub and with too fatal success, as the gallant leader of this unfortunate expedition breathed his last after receiving no less than three spear wounds. The affecting narrative of what passed during his last moments as related by his faithful companion, is simply as follows.—"Mr. Kennedy, are you going to leave me?" "Yes, my boy, I am going to leave you," was the reply of the dying man, "I am very bad, Jackey; you take the books, Jackey, to the Captain, but not the big ones, the Governor will give anything for them." "I then tied up the papers;" he then said, "Jackey, give me paper and I will write." "I gave him paper and pencil, and he tried to write; and he then fell back and died, and I caught him as he fell back and held him, and I then turned round myself and cried; I was crying a good while until I got well; that was about an hour, and then I buried him; I dug up the ground with a tomahawk, and covered him over with logs, then grass, and my shirt and trowsers; that night I left him near dark."

About eight days after, Jackey Jackey, having with wonderful ingenuity succeeded in escaping from his pursuers, contrived to reach Port Albany, and was received on board the vessel, which immediately proceeded to Shelburne Bay to endeavour to rescue the three men left there. The attempt to find the place was unsuccessful, and from the evidence furnished by clothes said by Jackey to belong to them, found in a canoe upon the beach, little doubt seemed to exist as to their fate. They then proceeded to Weymouth Bay, where they arrived just in time to save Mr. Carron, the botanical collector, and another man, the remaining six having perished. In the words of one of the survivors, " the men did not seem to suffer pain, but withered into perfect skeletons, and died from utter exhaustion."

Such was the fate of Kennedy's expedition, and in conclusion, to use the words of the Sydney Morning Herald, " it would appear that as far as earnestness of purpose, unshrinking endurance of pain and fatigue, and most disinterested self-sacrifice, go, the gallant leader of the party exhibited a model for his subordinates. But the great natural difficulties they had to encounter at the outset of the expedition so severely affected the resources of the adventurers, that they sunk under an accumulation of sufferings, which have rarely, if ever been equalled, in the most extreme perils of the wilderness."

Our stay in Sydney was protracted to the unusual period of three months and a half, affording ample time for refreshing the crews after their long and arduous labours, thoroughly refitting both vessels, and completing the charts. The object of our next cruize, which was expected to be of equal duration with the last, was to undertake the survey of a portion of the Louisiade Archipelago, and the south-east coast of New Guinea. For this purpose we sailed from Sydney on May 8th, deeply laden, with six months provisions on board, arrangements having also been made for receiving a further supply at Cape York in October following.

The Bramble joined us at Moreton Bay, where we did not arrive until May 17th, our passage having been protracted beyond the usual time by the prevalence during the early part of light northerly winds and a strong adverse current, which on one occasion set us fifty-one miles to the southward in twenty-four hours. We took up our former anchorage under Moreton Island and remained there for nine days, occupied in completing our stock of water, and obtaining a rate for the chronometers—so as to ensure a good meridian distance between this and the Louisiade. Since our last visit, the pilot station had been shifted to this place from Amity Point, the northern entrance to

Moreton Bay being now preferred to that formerly in use.

One night while returning from an excursion, I saw some fires behind the beach near Cumboyooro Point, and on walking up was glad to find an encampment of about thirty natives, collected there for the purpose of fishing, this being the spawning season of the mullet, which now frequent the coast in prodigious shoals. Finding among the party an old friend of mine, usually known by the name of Funny-eye, I obtained with some difficulty permission to sleep at his fire, and he gave me a roasted mullet for supper. The party at our bivouac, consisted of my host, his wife and two children, an old man and two wretched dogs. We lay down with our feet towards a large fire of drift wood, partially sheltered from the wind by a semicircular line of branches, stuck in the sand behind us; still, while one part of the body was nearly roasted, the rest shivered with cold. The woman appeared to be busy all night long in scaling and roasting fish, of which, before morning, she had a large pile ready cooked; neither did the men sleep much—for they awoke every hour or so, gorged themselves still further with mullet, took a copious draught of water, and wound up by lighting their pipes before lying down again.

At daylight every one was up and stirring, and soon afterwards the men and boys went down to the beach to fish. The rollers coming in from seaward broke about one hundred yards from the shore, and in the advancing wave one might see thousands of large mullet keeping together in a shoal with numbers of porpoises playing about, making frequent rushes among the dense masses and scattering them in every direction. Such of the men as were furnished with the scoop-net waded out in line, and, waiting until the porpoises had driven the mullet close in shore, rushed among the shoal, and, closing round in a circle with the nets nearly touching, secured a number of fine fish, averaging two and a half pounds weight. This was repeated at intervals until enough had been procured. Meanwhile others, chiefly boys, were at work with their spears, darting them in every direction among the fish, and on the best possible terms with the porpoises, which were dashing about among their legs, as if fully aware that they would not be molested.

On May 26th, we sailed from Moreton Bay;—but, before entering into the details of this, the most interesting portion of the Voyage of the Rattlesnake, a brief but connected account of the progress of discovery on the south-east coast of New Guinea, and the Louisiade Archipelago, will enable the reader more clearly to perceive the necessity then existing for as complete a survey of these shores and the adjacent seas as would enable the voyager to approach them with safety. A glance at any of the published charts will show a vague outline of coast and islands and reefs, with numerous blanks—a compilation from various sources, some utterly unworthy of credit; and of the inhabitants and productions of these regions, nothing was known beyond that portion at least of them were peopled by a savage and warlike race.

The first navigator who saw the shores in question, appears to have been Luiz Vaez de Torres, in the Spanish frigate La Almiranta, coming from the eastward, in August 1606.   In lat. 11½° S., Torres came upon what he calls the *beginning of New Guinea,* which, however, appears to have been a portion of what is now known as the Louisiade Archipelago.   Being unable to weather the easternmost point of this land (Cape Deliverance), he bore away to the westward along its southern shores. " All this land of *New Guinea,*" says he, in his long forgotten letter to the king of Spain (a copy of which was found in the Archives at Manila, after the capture of that city by the British, in 1762), " is peopled with Indians, not very white, much painted, and naked, except a cloth made of the bark of trees. They fight with darts, targets, and some stone clubs, which are made fine with plumage.   Along the coast are many islands and habitations.   All the coast has many ports, very large, with very large rivers, and many plains.   Without these islands there runs a reef of shoals, and between them [the shoals] and the mainland are the islands. There is a channel within.   In these parts I took possession for your Majesty.

" We went along 300 leagues of coast, as I have mentioned, and diminished the latitude $2\frac{1}{2}°$, which brought us into 9°. From hence we fell in with a bank of from three to nine fathoms, which extends along the coast above 180 leagues. We went over it along the coast to $7\frac{1}{2}$ S. latitude, and the end of it is in 5°. We could not go further on for the many shoals and great currents, so we were obliged to sail out S.W. in that depth to 11° S. latitude."

By this time Torres had reached the Strait which now bears his name, and which he was the first to pass through. He continues, ... " We caught in all this land twenty persons of different nations, that with them we might be able to give a better account to your Majesty. They give much notice of other people, although as yet they do not make themselves well understood."*

M. de Bougainville, in June, 1768, with two vessels, La Boudeuse and L'Etoile, was proceeding to the eastward towards the coast of Australia, when the unexpected discovery of some detached reefs (Bougainville's reefs of the charts) induced him to alter course and stand to the northward. No land was seen for three days. "On the 10th, at daybreak," says he, " the land was discovered, bearing from east to N.W. Long before dawn a deli-

---

* Burney's Chronological History of Voyages and Discoveries in the South Sea or Pacific Ocean. Vol. II. (Appendix) p. 475.

cious odour informed us of the vicinity of this land, which formed a great gulph open to the south-east. I have seldom seen a country which presented so beautiful a prospect; a low land, divided into plains and groves, extended along the sea shore, and afterwards rose like an amphitheatre up to the mountains, whose summits were lost in the clouds. There were three ranges of mountains, and the highest chain was distant upwards of twenty-five leagues from the shore. The melancholy condition to which we were reduced* neither allowed us to spend some time in visiting this beautiful country, which by all appearances was rich and fertile, nor to stand to the westward in search of a passage to the south of New Guinea, which might open to us a new and short route to the Moluccas by way of the Gulph of Carpentaria. Nothing, indeed, was more probable than the existence of such a passage."† Bougainville, it may be mentioned, was not aware of the previous discovery of Torres, which indeed was not published to the world until after our illustrious navigator Cook, in August, 1770, had

* They were beginning to run short of provisions, and the salt meat was so bad that the men preferred such *rats* as they could catch. It even became necessary to prevent the crew from eating the *leather* about the rigging and elsewhere in the ship.

† Voyage autour du Mond par la Fregate du Roi La Boudeuse et la Flûte l'Etoile en 1766-1769, p. 258. See also the chart of the Louisiade given there, which, however, does not correspond very closely with the text.

confirmed the existence of such a strait by passing
from east to west between the shores of Australia
and New Guinea.

The Boudeuse and Etoile were engaged in working to windward along this new land (as it was
thought to be) until the 26th, when, having doubled
its eastern point, to which the significant name of
Cape Deliverance was given, they were enabled to
bear away to the N.N.E. The name of Gulph of
the Louisiade was bestowed by Bougainville upon
the whole of the space thus traversed by him,
extending between Cape Deliverance and that portion of (what has since been determined to be) the
coast of New Guinea of which he gives so glowing a
description, and calls the Cul de Sac de l'Orangerie
upon his chart.

The next addition to our knowledge of these shores
was made in August, 1791, by Captain Edwards in
H.M.S. Pandora, shortly before the wreck of that
vessel in Torres Strait, when returning from Tahiti
with the mutineers of the Bounty. In the published
narrative of that voyage the following brief account
is given. " On the 23rd, saw land, which we supposed to be the Louisiade, a cape bearing north-east
and by east. We called it Cape Rodney. Another
contiguous to it was called Cape Hood : and a mountain between them, we named Mount Clarence.
After passing Cape Hood, the land appears lower,
and to trench away about north-west, forming a
deep bay, and it may be doubted whether it joins

New Guinea or not."[*] The positions assigned to two of these places, which subsequent experience has shewn it is difficult to identify, are

Cape Rodney . Lat. 10° 3′ 32″ S. . Long. 147° 45′ 45″ E.
Cape Hood . Lat. 9° 58′ 6″ S. . Long. 147° 22′ 50″ E.[†]

In the following year, Captains Bligh and Portlock, in the Providence and Assistance, conveying bread-fruit plants from Tahiti to the West Indies, saw a portion of the south-east coast of New Guinea, when on their way to pass through Torres Strait. A line of coast extending from Cape Rodney to the westward and northward about eighty miles, the latter half with a continuous line of reef running parallel with the coast, is laid down in a chart by Flinders,[‡] as having been "seen from the Providence's masthead, Aug. 30th, 1792."

The northern portion of the Louisiade Archipelago was yet unknown to Europeans, and for almost all the knowledge which we even now possess regarding it, we are indebted to the expedition under the command of Rear-Admiral Bruny d'Entrecasteaux, who, on June 11th, 1793, with La Recherche and

[*] Voyage round the world in His Majesty's frigate Pandora, performed under the direction of Capt. Edwards, in the years 1790, 1791, and 1792. By Mr. G. Hamilton, late surgeon of the Pandora, p. 100.

[†] Ibid. p. 164. Krusenstern assumes these longitudes to be 45′ too far to the westward, adopting Flinders' longitude of Murray's Islands, which differs by that amount from Captain Edwards'.

[‡] Flinders' Voyage to Terra Australis.—Atlas. Pl. 13.

L'Esperance, during his voyage in search of the unfortunate La Perouse, came in sight of Rossel Island. The hills of that island were enveloped in clouds, and the lower parts appeared to be thickly wooded with verdant interspaces. A harbour was supposed to exist in the deep bay on the north coast of Rossel Island, but access to it was found to be prevented by a line of breakers extending to the westward as far as the eye could reach. D'Entrecasteaux passed Piron's Island, which he named, as well as various others, and on St. Aignan's observed several huts, and the first inhabitants of the Louisiade whom they had seen, for, at Renard's Isles, a boat sent close in to sound, had observed no indications of natives, although smoke was afterwards seen rising from the largest of the group. At the Bonvouloir Islands, they had the first communication with the natives, who came off in a very large canoe and several others which approached near enough for one of the officers of L'Esperance to swim off to them. The natives shewed much timidity and could not be induced to come on board the frigate. Some sweet potatoes and bananas were given in return for various presents. No arms were seen among them, and these people did not appear to understand the use of iron.* The remainder of the voyage does not require further

* Voyage de [Bruny] d'Entrecasteaux envoyé a la recherche de la Perouse. Redigé par M. de Rossel, ancien Capitaine de Vaisseau, tom. i. p. 405, et seq. See also Atlas.

notice here, as the Dentrecasteaux Isles of the charts belong to the north-east coast of New Guinea.

In June 1793, Messrs. Bampton and Alt, in the English merchant ships Hormuzeer and Chesterfield, got embayed on the south-east coast of New Guinea, and after in vain seeking a passage out to the north-east, were forced to abandon the attempt and make their way to the westward, through Torres Strait, which they were no less than seventy-three days in clearing. Among other hydrographical results, was the discovery of large portions of the land forming the north-west shores of this bay, extending from Bristow Island to the northward and eastward for a distance of 120 miles.

In 1804, M. Rualt Coutance, commanding the French privateer L'Adèle, made several discoveries on the south-east coast of New Guinea which were recorded by Freycinet, from the MS. journal of Coutance, in the history of Baudin's voyage.* A portion of this is unquestionably the land seen by Captain Bligh in 1792,—but in addition detached portions of the shores of the great bight of the south-east coast were seen, as in the neighbourhood of Freshwater Bay and elsewhere.

Mr. Bristow, the master of an English merchant

* Voyage de découvertes aux Terres Australes, exécuté sur les corvettes Le Geographe, Le Naturaliste, et la goëlette La Casuarina—pendant les annees 1801-4, sous le commandement du Capitaine de vaisseau N. Baudin. Redige par M. Louis Freycinet. Navigation et Geographie, p. 462, and Atlas, pl. 1.

vessel, visited the northern part of the Louisiade Archipelago in 1806, but added nothing of consequence to our knowledge of the group, although various islands were named anew, as if discoveries of his own. His Satisfaction Island is clearly Rossel's, and Eruption Island is St. Aignan's of D'Entrecasteaux.*

Since Bougainville's voyage the southern shores of the Louisiade remained unvisited until the year 1840, when Captain Dumont d'Urville, with the French corvettes L'Astrolabe and La Zelée, during his last voyage round the world, determined upon attempting their exploration. On May 23rd, the expedition (coming from the eastward), rounded Adèle Island and Cape Deliverance, at the distance of about twenty miles. Next morning, the thickness of the weather prevented them from clearly distinguishing the features of the land. They steered towards South-east Island, but found close approach prevented by an immense continuous reef, supposed to be part of that seen on the previous day to the southward of Rossel Island. On Conde's Peninsula, some natives and a small village were observed. In the evening a long line of islands (the Calvados group), appeared to the north, and the reef, which before had been continuous, with the exception of some small openings, now existed only as a few isolated patches. D'Urville stood off to

* See Krusenstern's Recueil de Memoires Hydrographiques, &c. p. 154.

sea for the night, and next morning passed close to some low woody islets (Montemont), enclosed by a reef stretching to the eastward, and supporting upon it many scattered islands covered with verdure. Bougainville's chart was found of very little assistance; in the evening, however, they recognized the low wooded isle which he had called Ushant. Several high rocks (Teste Isles) in sight when they stood off for the night served next morning as a connecting point.

On the 26th, a crowd of small islands, mostly inhabited, were seen at a short distance off, and in the back ground some high mountain summits were visible. Approaching more closely, D'Urville observed numerous channels intersecting the coast which they appeared to divide into a multitude of islands, and it seemed doubtful whether the land seen belonged to the Louisiade or to New Guinea. On the 27th, the two ships reached the Cul de sac de l'Orangerie,— the appearance of the land at this place was considered to "agree perfectly with the pompous description" of Bougainville. D'Urville would willingly have searched for an anchorage here, but sickness prevented him from delaying much longer on this coast. Many canoes had been seen during the day, and one with six men at length came off, followed by some smaller ones, each carrying two or three people. The natives could not be induced to venture on board, and for a long time hesitated to receive some presents conveyed to them on a plank, in return for cocoa-nuts, a stone axe, and some shells. These natives appeared to be unarmed; by signs they invited the Frenchmen to visit them on shore. D'Urville was now anxious to determine whether, as represented by his charts,* a passage existed between this portion of the "Louisiade of Bougainville," and what was then considered to be the south-east extremity of New Guinea, in the neighbourhood of Cape Rodney. Next day, however (28th), a high chain of mountains was seen to occupy the space assigned to the supposed passage. On the 29th, a barrier reef was found extending to the eastward in the direction of the coast line; they were unable clearly to identify Cape Rodney and Point Hood, of the English charts. In the evening D'Urville saw a chain of high mountains which he named Mount Astrolabe, and a well marked headland (Cape Passy) beyond which the coast appeared to trend to the northward. The expedition now shaped a course for Torres Strait, having in seven days made a "running survey" extending over a space of 450 miles in length, without anchoring or communicating with the inhabitants.†

---

* This matter had been discussed by the Russian Admiral Krusenstern; see "Recueil de Mémoires Hydrographiques pour servir d'analyse et d'explication a l'Atlas de l'Ocean Pacifique," p. 60. Also in his Atlas, a general chart of the Pacific Ocean, and two others of New Guinea, and the Louisiade Archipelago, published in 1824.

† Voyage au Pole Sud et dans l'Oceanie sur les corvettes

During his survey of the northern and eastern entrances of Torres Strait, Captain F. P. Blackwood, in H.M.S. Fly, spent two months in 1845, upon the south-east coast of New Guinea, 140 miles of which, including that part seen by Bampton and Alt in 1793, was surveyed as completely as the time and means would permit. This country presented a great sameness of aspect; low muddy shores covered at first with mangroves, and, further back, with dense forests, were found to be intersected by numerous channels of fresh water, the mouths, there is reason to suppose, of one or more large rivers, of which this great extent of country is the delta. Great mud banks, extending from ten to twenty miles out to sea, prevented approach except in the boats. Several of these channels were entered by the surveying parties, and one (Aird River), was ascended by Captain Blackwood to the distance of twenty miles from its mouth. Many villages were seen scattered along the coast and on the river banks. The natives, apparently closely resembling the Torres Strait Islanders, appeared to be a savage and warlike race, and refused to have any friendly intercourse with the white men, whose boats they attempted to cut off on various occasions. They seemed to be perfectly naked, and their principal

L'Astrolabe et la Zelée pendant les années 1837-1840. Sous le commandement de M. J. Dumont d'Urville. Histoire du Voyage, tom. ix. p. 208—215. Atlas Hydrographique, Pl. 1.

weapons were observed to be bows and arrows and wooden sword-like clubs.*

In the following year, a further addition to the survey of the south-east coast of New Guinea was made by Lieut. C. B. Yule, while in command of H.M. schooners Bramble and Castlereagh. This survey was commenced at Cape Possession, and continued to the westward and northward as far as Cape Blackwood, where the Fly's work ended, a distance equal to two degrees of longitude.† Many large river mouths were observed, the fresh water on one occasion extending two or three miles out to sea. The country had ceased to present the low monotonous appearance shewn to the westward, and had become more broken with wooded hills, and on the extreme east, ranges of lofty mountains were seen in the distance; one of these (Mount Yule) attains an elevation of 10,046 feet. Landing was attempted only once, on which occasion the whole party,—their two boats having been capsized in the surf, and their ammunition destroyed,—were set upon by a large body of natives and plundered of everything, even to their clothes, but not otherwise injured, although completely at the mercy of these savages.

In company with the Bramble we sailed from

* Narrative of the Surveying Voyage of H.M.S. Fly, commanded by Captain F. P. Blackwood, R.N. by J. B. Jukes, Naturalist to the Expedition, vol. i. p. 282, &c.

† See Admiralty Chart, No. 1914.

Moreton Bay for the Louisiade on May 26th. Next day it began to blow fresh, commencing at south-east and coming up to east, and on the 28th the wind had increased to a heavy gale from E.S.E. to E. On the following morning the gale broke, the wind having suddenly fallen and shifted round from E. to N.E. and N.W. by W. until it became variable, and at night died away altogether. On June 3rd we picked up the south-east trade-wind in lat. 20° 8' S.; and next day and those following until we made the land, having left the beaten track from Sydney to the outer passages leading to Torres Strait,* we hauled on a wind at night so as to avoid going over unexplored ground. No reefs, however, were seen between Moreton Bay and the Louisiade.

On June 10th (our noon position of that day being lat. 11° 38' S. and long. 154° 17' E.), at daylight, high land was seen extending from N. to N.W., distant about twenty-five miles. It proved to be the largest Ile du Sud Est of D'Urville's chart, and Rossel Island, the latter forming the eastern termination of the Louisiade Archipelago. Next day we fell in with the Bramble in the neighbourhood of Cape Deliverance of the English chart (by Laurie), her rendezvous in case of separation; we had parted company during the late gale, in which she lost her jib-boom and stern-boat. The whole of

---

* See a very useful chart of the Coral Sea, constructed by Mr. J. O. Evans, formerly master of H.M.S. Fly.

June 12th was spent in working to windward to weather the eastern end of Rossel Island,—Cape Deliverance of Bougainville,—the barrier reef to the southward of the two large islands in sight preventing us from closely approaching the land from that quarter.

June 13th.—Having gained a good offing, we bore up at daylight, and stood in for Rossel Island with the Bramble a-head.   We passed at a distance Adèle Island (so named after Coutance's ship), low and woody, situated at the eastern extreme of the barrier reef surrounding Rossel Island, at a variable distance from the land.   The southern portion of this great coral reef here makes a sharp turn round the islet, and runs back ten miles to connect it with Rossel Island, where it loses the character of a barrier, becomes narrow and fringing and almost disappears for a time.   Passing Cape Deliverance* and getting into smooth water on the northern side of Rossel Island, we ran along it at a distance from the shore of about two miles and a half.

Rossel Island (named after one of D'Entrecasteaux' officers) is 22 miles in length from east to west, and 10½ in greatest width; it is high and

---

* As the longitude of Cape Deliverance varies considerably in different charts, its determination by the three best authorities may here be given :—

D'Entrecasteaux places it in long. 154° 26' E. of Greenwich.

D'Urville   154° 26'   do.

Owen Stanley   154° 20'   do.

mountainous, and thickly wooded, with occasional large, clear, grassy patches. Towards the western end the hills become lower and more detached, but present the same features. The mountain ridges, one of which, but not the highest elevation (which was obscured by clouds), is 2522 feet in height— form sharp narrow crests and occasional peaks, but the outline is smooth and the rock nowhere exposed, even the steepest ridges being covered with vegetation. Some of the trees appeared to be of great dimensions, others were tall and straight, branching only near the top, and many, probably *Melaleuca leucodendrum*—were conspicuous from the whiteness of their trunks. Large groves of cocoa-palms scattered about from the water's edge to half way up the hills, formed a pleasing break in the sombre green of the forest scenery. The shores are either bordered with mangroves with an occasional sandy beach, or clothed with the usual jungle of the island.

As we advanced to the westward the reef gradually extended out from the island with a short space inside, and this appearance continued for several miles, until, upon the land trending away to the south-west, the line of reef left it and ran out to the westward as far as the eye could reach, in an apparently unbroken line of surf. This is Rossel Reef of the charts along which we ran for* 35

* It extends 17 miles beyond the westernmost point of Rossel Island.

miles, sounding occasionally, but although within a mile of its edge, no bottom was got with upwards of 100 fathoms of line. From the mast-head we could see the surf of the southern border of this great reef, the space between being a lagoon of apparently navigable water. At the western extremity of the reef there appeared to be a clear opening, but the day was too far advanced to admit of entering it to search for an anchorage, and the ship was hove to for the night.

Rossel Island, judging from the little we saw of it, appears to be well inhabited. The first natives seen were a party of five men, apparently naked, who came out upon the beach from a grove of cocoa-nut trees, and stood gazing at the unusual sight to them of two vessels passing by. Opposite a pretty creek-like harbour, the windings of which we could trace back a little way among the hills, several canoes of various sizes were seen, each with an outrigger on one side, and one of them furnished with a large mat-sail of an oblong shape, rounded at the ends. The people, of whom there were usually about six or seven in each canoe, appeared to be engaged in fishing in the shoal water. One man in a very small canoe was bailing it out with a large melon-shell so intently that he appeared to take no notice whatever of the ship which passed within a quarter of a mile of him. We saw many huts close to the beach, usually three or four together, forming small villages. They appeared to be long and low, resting on the ground, with an opening at each end, and an arched roof thatched with palm-leaves. The most picturesque situations were chosen for these hamlets in the shade of the cocoa-nut trees, and about them we could see numbers of children, but no women were made out, and most of the men were fishing on the reef. At one place we observed what appeared to be a portion of cultivated ground; a cleared sloping bank above the shore exhibited a succession of small terraces, with a bush-like plant growing in regular rows.

June 14th.—In the morning we found ourselves so far to leeward of the opening seen last night, with a strong breeze and a considerable head sea, that the attempt to work up for it was abandoned, and we kept away to the westward to look for an anchorage. We then ran along the northern side of Piron* Island, which is five miles in length, and one and a half in breadth, of moderate elevation, and sloping gently towards each extreme. It exhibits a range of low grassy hills, with smooth rounded outline, a straggling belt of wood—often mangroves — along the shore, patches of brush here and there in the hollows, and on the hill tops, scattered along the ridge, a few solitary tall bushy trees with silvery-looking foliage. The bright green of the tall grass gave a pleasing aspect to the whole island, large tracts of which

---

* Piron was draughtsman to D'Entrecasteaux's Expedition.

appeared like fields of unripe grain. We saw few
natives, the opposite, or southern shore, being probably that chiefly inhabited. Close approach to
Piron Island was prevented by a second barrier
reef, which we followed to the N.N.W. for several
miles beyond the end of the island, anxiously looking
out for an opening into the fine expanse of pale blue
water seen to extend to the southward as far as the
large south-east island.*   At length an opening in
the reef was observed, and the ship hauled off and
hove to, while Lieut. Yule examined it in one of his
boats.   In the afternoon the Bramble having made
the signal "passage clear but narrow," was directed
to enter, and we followed her through a fine opening
400 yards wide, and were immediately in soundings,
which 111 fathoms of line had failed to procure
only a short distance outside.   After standing to
the southward for two miles we anchored in 15
fathoms water. The name of Coral Haven was
bestowed upon this new harbour. We remained
here all next day, during which the natives in their
canoes came off to the Bramble, and one or two of
the boats away sounding, but would not venture to
approach the ship.

June 16th.—The ship was moved in one and a
half miles to the southward, towards the land, and
anchored in ten fathoms, close to a reef covered at
high water, and about a mile distant from a small
bank of dead coral and sand; the former of these

* This is 41 miles long, and 10¼ in greatest width.

was selected by Capt. Stanley as the starting point of the survey, and on the latter magnetical observations were made by Lieutenant Dayman.

In the afternoon I took a passage in a boat sent with a party to Pig Island—the name afterwards given to that nearest us—to search for water, and endeavour to communicate with the natives. A party of eight men, fishing upon the reef surrounding a small islet, allowed us to approach within a short distance, but upon our attempting to leave the boat they became alarmed and retreated to their canoe in which they paddled off in great haste to the landing place under a small village in sight of the ship. This consisted of three or four long barn-like huts, raised from the ground on posts. A large village was also seen on Joannet Island, situated, like the other, on the brow of a hill in a commanding position. Five of our party landed about half a mile from where the canoe had disappeared, apparently in some creek of a mangrove swamp; while walking along the muddy shore we were met by about a dozen natives, who gradually fell back as we approached. Seeing them apparently afraid of our number and weapons,—they themselves being unarmed, — I left my gun behind, and, advancing alone, holding up a green branch in each hand, was allowed to come up to them. They were apparently in a state of great agitation, and very suspicious of our intentions. The spokesman of the party was much lighter in colour than the others, and I at first

fancied he spoke some Malay dialect from the similarity in sound and intonation of his words, nor was
it until I had used some of the commonest and least
changeable Malay words—as those meaning fire,
water, &c.—without being understood, that I was
convinced of my mistake. Two others of our party
were allowed to come up one by one, and some
trifling articles were exchanged for various ornaments. Still they would not suffer any one with a
gun to approach, although anxious to entice us
singly and unarmed to their village towards which
they were gradually leading us, and where they
could be reinforced by another party, whom we saw
watching us on the edge of the mangroves.

But it was not considered expedient to waste more
time upon the natives, so we turned back and
walked along the eastern side of the island one and a
half miles, with the boat in company outside. A
small stream of fresh water was found, not sufficient,
however, for our wants, nor was the place suitable
for the approach of boats. The rock on Pig Island,
where exposed at some of the points, is mica slate,
soft and splintery in many places, with frequent
veins of quartz. The hills,* although often running
in ridges, have a rounded outline, and the soil on the
smooth grassy places—comprising three-fourths of
the island—is composed of disintegrated rock mixed
with pieces of undecomposed quartz, any considerable

* The highest part of the island, measured up to the tops of
the trees, is 479 feet.

accumulation of vegetable mould being probably prevented by the heavy rains. The grass is very luxuriant without being rank; it was not known to me, for, unlike most of the other plants, I had not met with it in Australia. Indeed the frequency of the cocoa-nut palm was the only non-Malayo-Australian feature in the vegetation. As no botanist had previously visited the Louisiade, a few of the principal plants may be mentioned. These are *Guilandina Bonduc, Tournefortia argentea, Morinda citrifolia, Paritium Tiliaceum, Casuarina equisetifolia,* and *Clerodendrum inerme,** among the trees and shrubs, which were often overgrown with *Lygodium microphyllum,* and *Disemma coccinea.* The only birds seen were the sacred kingfisher, the sulphur-crested cockatoo, and the Australian crow. The shells on the reef were all Australian likewise, but under some decaying logs, on the beach, I found single species of *Auricula, Truncatella, Scarabus,* and *Melampus.*

The men we saw to-day were dark copper coloured, with the exception of the spokesman, whose skin was of a light brownish yellow hue. The hair in nearly all was frizzled out into a mop, in some instances of prodigious size; the light coloured man, however, had his head closely shaved.† The physiognomy

* These are all common to Polynesia, the Indian Archipelago, and tropical Australia.

† This allowed us to observe its contour, which was remarkable. The forehead was narrow and receding, appearing as if artificially

varied much; some had a savage, even ferocious
aspect. The nose was narrower and more prominent, the mouth smaller, the lips thinner, the eyes
more distant, the eyebrows less overhanging, the
forehead higher, but not broader, than in the
Australian, with whom I naturally compared them
as the only dark savage race which I had seen much
of. They used the betel, or something like it, judging from the effect in discolouring the teeth and
giving a bloody appearance to the saliva; each man

carried his chewing
materials in a small
basket, the lime, in
fine powder, being
contained in a neat
calabash with a stop-
per, and a carved
piece of tortoise-
shell like a paper-
cutter was used to
convey it to the
mouth.

None had the artificial prominent scars on the
body peculiar to the Australians, or wanted any of

flattened, thereby giving great prominence and width to the
hinder part of the skull. Altogether this man appeared so
different from the rest, that for some time he was supposed to
belong to a different class of people, but I afterwards often
observed the same configuration of head combined with dark
coloured skin and diminutive stature.

the front teeth, but the septum of the nose was perforated to admit an ornament of polished shell, pointed and slightly turned up at each end.   The lobe of the ear was slit, the hole being either kept distended by a large plug of rolled up leaf, apparently of the banana, or hung with thin circular earrings made of the ground down end of a cone-shell (*Conus millepunctatus*) one and a half inches in diameter, with a central hole and a slit leading to the edge.   A piece of cloth-like substance, the dried leaf of the Pandanus or some palm was used by all as a breech cloth,—it passes between the legs and is secured in front and behind to a narrow waist-band.

June 17th.—I formed one of the party in the second cutter, sent in command of Lieut. Simpson, on a similar mission to that of yesterday.   As we passed along the north side of Pig Island we saw small groups of natives upon the grassy ridges watching the boat, and, upon our closely approaching the north-west point of the island, one of them, whom we recognised as our light-coloured acquaintance of yesterday, came running down to the top of a bank inviting us by gestures to land.

Four of our party got on shore with difficulty after a long wade upon the reef, up to the waist in water, but, on ascending the bank, the " red man," as we provisionally named him, retired to a small group of natives who were coming up.   Following them as they gradually fell back in the direction of

the village, in a short time the two foremost, Messrs.
Huxley and Brierly,* the latter having laid down
his rifle, were allowed to approach and parley.
Meanwhile, Lieut. Simpson and I remained behind
watching the natives who quickly surrounded the
two others, offering tortoise-shell, green plantains,
and other things for barter, and hustling them in no
very ceremonious way while intent upon sketch-
ing, and having to keep their subjects in good
humour by treating them to sundry scraps of
extempore melo-dramatic performance. New comers
were continually making their appearance, and all
the party were now suddenly observed to have furnished themselves with spears, none of which had
been seen at first, and which had probably been
concealed among the long grass at the spot to which
they had led us. These weapons are made of
polished cocoa-nut wood, eight to ten feet long,
sharp at each end, and beautifully balanced, the
thickest part being two-fifths of the distance from
the point ; one end was usually ornamented with a
narrow strip of palm leaf, fluttering in the breeze
like a pennon as usually carried. One man was
furnished with a two-edged carved and painted instrument like a sword. Most of these people had
their face daubed over with broad streaks of charcoal down the centre and round the eyes, occasionally
variegated with white, giving them a most forbid-

* A talented marine artist who accompanied us upon this and
the preceding cruise, as Captain Stanley's guest.

Interview with the Natives of Pedvar Bay.

ding aspect.   At length a live pig was brought down from the village, slung on a pole, and was purchased for a knife and a handkerchief.   This was a master stroke of policy, as the natives well knew that it would take two of us to bear off our prize to the boat, thus rendering our little party less formidable. The number of men had been gradually increasing until it amounted to about thirty, all with spears. They were also becoming more rude and insolent in their behaviour, and seeing this I left my post on a hillock, and joined Simpson to take part in the expected fray.   The natives were now evidently bent on mischief, and we fully expected they would not much longer delay making an attack, with the advantage of a commanding position on a hillock which we must descend to return to the boat.   At this crisis one of our party discovered that he had lost a pistol from his belt, and attempted to recover it by shewing another and making signs evincing great anxiety to recover the lost weapon.   On this there was a general movement among the natives, who began drawing back into a cluster, balancing their spears and talking to each other very earnestly. It being evident that the pistol had been stolen, and not dropped accidentally among the grass, it was also apparent that by attaching undue importance to its loss our safety might be supposed to depend upon its possession.   We then slowly commenced our retreat, two in advance carrying the pig, and the remainder covering the retreat.   Being the last of our party, as I slowly descended the hillock sideways, watching every motion of what we might fairly consider as the enemy, with spare caps between my teeth, and a couple of cartridges in one hand, I was in momentary expectation of receiving a spear or two, which probably would have been the case, had I stumbled or turned my back to them for a moment. As we drew back along the ridge and dipped into the first hollow a party of the natives detached themselves from the rest as if to come round upon our flank, but this fortunately was formed by a steep ascent covered with dense jungle which would have occupied them some time to get through. Arriving at the bank above the boat, the pig carriers with their burthen speedily reached the bottom, all three rolling down together. When they were well clear we followed, keeping a sharp look out behind in case of any advantage being taken of our position. The boat had grounded upon the reef with the falling tide, but with some difficulty was got afloat, when we left the place.

After rounding the point we opened a large bay on the west side of the island where we saw the mouth of a small stream pointed out by the natives during our last interview, but, on approaching within 300 yards, it was found that boats could not get any closer in at low water, the shore being everywhere fringed by a reef. This is the most beautiful and sheltered portion of the island, well wooded, with a sandy beach, clumps of cocoa-nut trees, and a village of four or five huts. We landed on a small islet connected with the south-west point of Pig Island by a reef, and strolled about with our guns while the boat's crew were having their dinners. Several *Megapodii* were seen and one was shot,—it afterwards proved to be the *M. Duper-reyi*, previously known as a native of Port Dorey on the north-west coast of New Guinea. While holding on to the reef a party of natives, apparently from Brierly Island, paddled up in a canoe, and, after some hesitation at first, came alongside calling out *kelumai—kelumai*, which we conjectured to be their word for iron. For a few trifling articles we obtained a spear or two, and some cooked yams, and parted good friends, after which we returned to the ship, having completed the circuit of the island without finding a practicable watering place.

June 18*th.*—Five canoes came off this morning with seven or eight natives in each, but apparently not with the intention of bartering, although they remained for a short time near the Bramble; it was thought that some allusions were made by them to the pistol stolen yesterday, but this did not appear to be certain. After a while they crossed over to the ship, and from a respectful distance—as if afraid to come closer—used many violent gesti-culations, talking vehemently all the while, and repeatedly pointed to the break in the reef by which we had entered Coral Haven, waving us off at the same time. Our red friend from Pig Island made himself as conspicuous as on former occasions, and none shouted more loudly or wished to attract more attention to himself. Unfortunately his eloquence was quite thrown away upon us, nor had his threatening gestures the desired effect of inducing us to leave the place and proceed to sea.

June 20*th*. — I returned to the ship after a short cruize in the pinnace sent away with Lieutenant Simpson to ascertain whether a passage for the ship to the eastward existed between Piron Island and South-east Island. Independently of numerous detached coral patches, the channel was found to be completely blocked up by a reef stretching across from one island to the other, beyond which, separated by an extensive tract of shoal water, a heavy surf was breaking on what is probably an outer barrier. Many snakes were seen on the surface of the water, and large shoals of skipjacks (*Caranx*) playing about in long extended lines occasionally presented the appearance of a breaking reef. The fish were attended by flocks of terns and noddies, the former the beautiful *Sterna melanauchen*.

June 21*st*. — Landed on the neighbouring Observation Reef, and spent some hours there searching for shells, but nearly all were Torres Strait species. The reef is margined with blocks of coral, but the centre is mostly smooth and covered with sand part of which dries at low water; the rise and fall, ascertained by a tide-pole set up here, was only four feet. I had a good opportunity of witnessing the mode of fishing with the seine practised by the natives of the Louisiade. One of these nets, apparently of the usual dimensions, measured 130 feet in length, with a depth of a yard only. The upper border is supported, when in the water, by numerous small thin triangular floats of light wood, and the lower margin is strung with a series of perforated shells—chiefly single valves of *Arca scapha*— serving as sinkers. The cordage is of a white colour, very light, and neatly laid up, the meshes are an inch wide, and the centre of the net ends in a purse-like bag. A party of eight men poled along the shallow margin of the reef in their canoe, using the seine at intervals. When a shoal of fish is seen, three men lay hold of the net and jump out into the water,—it is run out into a semicircle, the men at the extremes moving onwards with one person in advance on each side splashing the water with long poles and stones to drive the fish towards the centre. The canoe now makes a sweep and comes up to the opening, when the net is closed in upon it, and hauled in-board with its contents. This mode of fishing would appear to be practised also at some of the islands of Polynesia, for similar seines are exhibited in the ethnological gallery of the British Museum from the Feejees and elsewhere. In addition to the seine, we had occasionally observed in canoes alongside the ship a small scoop-net with a very long handle, and once procured a

fishing hook of singular
construction. This last is
represented by the right-
hand figure of the accom-
panying woodcut. It is
seven inches in length,
made of some hard wood,
with an arm four and a half
inches long, turning up at
a sharp angle, and tipped
with a slightly curved barb

of tortoise-shell projecting horizontally inwards an
inch and a half.

During the afternoon one of the crew of a boat
upon the reef, while incautiously handling a frog-
fish (*Batrachus*) which he had found under a stone,
received two punctures at the base of the thumb
from the sharp dorsal spines partially concealed by
the skin. Immediately severe pain was produced
which quickly increased until it became intolerable,
and the man lay down and rolled about in agony.
He was taken on board the ship in a state of great
weakness. The hand was considerably swollen, with
the pain shooting up the arm to the axilla, but the
glands there did not become affected. The pulse fell
to as low as 40 beats in the minute, with a constant
desire to vomit. Large dozes of opium in the course
of time afforded relief, but a fortnight elapsed before
the man was again fit for duty.

June 23rd.—I accompanied Mr. Brown, the

master, who was sent to examine and report upon a watering place said to have been found a day or two ago on South-east Island, about four miles north from the ship. We found the coast thereabouts fringed with mangroves, a gap in which, margined by forest trees, indicated the place which we were in search of. The ebb tide was scarcely beginning to make, yet a narrow band of shingle off the entrance of the creek had barely water enough upon it to allow the boat to cross. Beyond the bar we got into deep water, and after pulling up for 300 yards found it only brackish. Our further progress, however, was impeded by the narrowing of the creek, which besides was blocked up with dead trees and some rocks in its bed a few yards ahead of us. The fresh water being thus unattainable without much trouble, and the bar at the entrance adding to the difficulty of watering the ship there, we turned back to search elsewhere. While standing along shore to the eastward, opposite an opening in the low hills behind the coast we observed another breach in the mangroves backed by trees of a different description, and thought it worthy of examination. Tacking inshore we found a small bight, with shoal water, on a bank of mud extending right across, beyond which the entrance of a creek fringed with mangroves was discovered. Our hopes were still further raised, when, ascending about 200 yards, with a depth of two and three fathoms, the surface water was found to be quite drinkable. While passing the entrance on our return a great lizard, about five feet in length, rushed out from an adjacent swamp across a narrow strip of sandy beach and plunged into the water after receiving an ineffectual charge of small shot. The boat's crew pronounced it confidently to have been a young alligator, but, although in a very likely haunt for these animals, it was probably only a monitor.

We then crossed over to Round Island, small, uninhabited, 230 feet in height, thickly covered with trees and underwood, and connected on the eastern side with the reef running across to Piron Island. The rock here is still mica slate, varying much in texture and composition, often highly ferruginous; the strata run E.S.E. and W.N.W. with a northerly dip of about 45°.

June 24th.—In the course of the day no less than seven canoes with natives, including several women and children, came off to the ship boldly and without hesitation, as if confidence were now established. At one time we had five canoes alongside, with a brisk and noisy traffic going on. The people parted very readily with their weapons and ornaments, also cocoa-nuts in abundance, and a few yams and bananas, for strips of calico and pieces of iron hoop. Axes, however, were more prized than any other article, and the exhibition of one was certain to produce great eagerness to procure it, amidst much shouting and cries of *kelumai!* The purpose to which they applied the iron hoop we found was to substitute it for the pieces of a hard green stone (nephrite) in the heads of their axes and adzes. The one figured on page 198 represents the usual form of these instruments. The V-shaped handle is a single piece of wood, and the stone, previously ground down to a fine edge, is fixed in a cleft at the end of the short arm, and firmly secured by cordage. This axe is usually carried by being hooked over the left shoulder with the handle crossing the breast diagonally.

Among our visitors to-day I noticed two who had large white patches on the skin, as if caused by some leprous complaint,—one man had lost his nose, and in addition was affected with elephantiasis of the left foot.

After leaving us two of the canoes paddled up to the tide pole on the neighbouring reef, and before a boat could reach them, the natives managed to secure the pigs of iron ballast with which it was moored. They communicated with two canoes, coming from the direction of Piron Island, which soon afterwards came under the stern. As one of the stolen pigs was seen partially concealed in the bow of one of the last comers the jolly boat was manned to recover it, when the canoes left in great haste with the boat in chase. As the boat approached a cocoa-nut was thrown overboard from the canoe, as if to cause delay by stopping to pick it up, but, the intended effect not being produced, the stolen ballast also was thrown out, when the boat of course returned.   By Captain Stanley's orders two musket shots were fired over the canoes, while about 800 yards distant, to shew that although in fancied security they were still within reach.   The splash of the first bullet caused them to paddle off in great haste, and, when they again stopped, a second shot, striking the water beyond the canoes, sent them off to the shore at their utmost speed.

With a single exception, to be afterwards noticed, the canoes seen by us in Coral Haven are of the following description.   The usual length is about twenty-five feet, and one of this size carries from seven to ten people.   The body is formed by the hollowed out trunk of a tree, tapering and rising at each end, short and rounded behind, but in front run out into a long beak.   A stout plank on each side raises the canoe a foot, forming a gunwale secured by knees, the seam at the junction being payed over with a black pitch-like substance.   This gunwale is open at the stern, the ends not being connected, but the bow is closed by a raised end-board fancifully carved and painted in front of which a crest-like wooden ornament fits into a groove running along the beak.   This figure head, called *tabúra*, is elaborately cut into various devices, painted red and white, and decorated with white egg-shells and feathers of the cassowary and bird of paradise.   The bow and stern also are more or less profusely ornamented with these shells, which besides are strung about other parts of the canoe, usually in pairs. An outrigger extends along nearly the whole length of the left or port side of the canoe. In its construction there are employed from six to eight poles, two inches in diameter, which rest against one side of the body of the canoe and are secured there, then passing out through the opposite side about five feet, inclining slightly upwards at the same time, are connected at the ends by lashing to a long stout pole completing the strong frame work required for the support of the float. This last is a long and narrow log of a soft and very light wood (probably a cotton tree) rising a little and pointed at each end so as to offer the least possible resistance to the water. Four sticks passing diagonally downwards from each of the transverse poles are sunk into the float and firmly secure it. A strip of the inner portion of the outrigger frame is converted into a platform by long sticks laid lengthways close to each other,—here the sails, masts, poles, spears, and other articles are laid when not in use. The paddles vary slightly in form but are usually about four feet in length, with a slender handle and a pointed lance-shaped blade. The number of men able to use the paddles is regulated in each canoe by that of supporting outrigger poles, the end of each of which, in conjunction with one of the knees supporting the gunwale, serves as a seat. One sitter at each end, being clear of the outrigger, is able to use his paddle on either side as requisite in steering, but

the others paddle on the right or starboard side only.
The man seated at the stern closes with his body
the opening between the ends of the raised gunwale
and thus keeps out the spray or wash of the sea.
Still they require to bail frequently, using for this
purpose the large shell of the *Melo Ethiopica*.   In
calms and light airs these canoes of Coral Haven
may be overtaken without difficulty by a fast-
pulling ship's boat, but on going to windward with
a moderate breeze and a little head sea they
appeared to have the advantage.   The sails are
from twelve to fifteen feet in length and a yard
wide—made of coarse matting of the leaf of the
cocoa-nut tree stretched between two slender poles.
The mast is stepped with an outward inclination
into one of three or four holes in a narrow shifting
board in the bottom of the canoe, and is secured near
the top to a slender stick of similar length made
fast to the outside part of the outrigger ; a second
pole is then erected stretching diagonally outwards
and secured to the outer one near its centre. Against
the framework thus formed the sails are stuck up
on end side by side to the number of three or four,
occasionally even five, and kept in their places by
long sticks placed transversely, their ends as well
as those of the mast being sharpened to serve as
skewers which in the first instance secure the sails.
While under sail either the bow or stern of the
canoe may be foremost, this being regulated by the
necessity of having the outrigger on the weather
side, unless in a very light wind.   From the sail

being placed so far forward these canoes do not lay
up close to the wind, but when going free considerable speed may be obtained.

Among the canoes which visited the ship one
was of a quite different construction from the rest
and resembled some of those which we had seen
while passing along the northern side of Rossel
Island.   It contained seven men, and came from

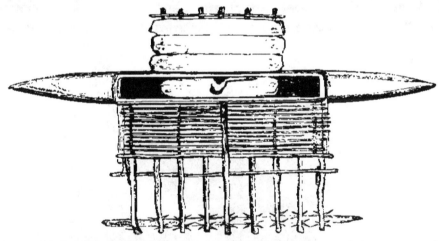

the eastward—probably from Piron Island.   The
body of a canoe of this class is formed like the
other, or more common kind, of the hollowed out
trunk of a large tree, tapering to a point and rising
slightly at the ends, which, however, are alike and
covered over by a close-fitting piece of wood, each end
being thus converted into a hollow cone.   The sides
are raised by a plank two feet high and end boards
forming a kind of long box, with the seams pitched
over.   One side is provided with an outrigger simi-

lar to that already described, and on the other is a
small stage, level with the gunwale, six feet long,
planked over, and projecting four feet or thereabouts.
The mast is a standing one stepped into a board in
the bottom,—it is lashed to a stout transverse
pole, and is further supported by two fore and aft
stays.   The halliards reeve through a hole in a projecting arm a foot long at the masthead.   But the
sail forms the most curious feature in the whole
affair.*   It measures about fifteen feet in width by

eight in depth and is made of rather fine matting

* The annexed illustration represents this kind of sail,—it was
not however taken from the canoe in question, but on a subsequent occasion, and at another part of the Louisiade Archipelago.

stretched between two yards and rounded at the sides. The sail when not in use is rolled up and laid along the platform—when hoisted it stretches obliquely upwards across the mast, confined by the stays, with the lower and foremost corner resting on the stage and the tack secured to the foot of the mast. Both ends being alike, the mast central, and the sail large and manageable, a canoe of this description is well adapted for working to windward. Tacking is simply and expeditiously performed by letting go the tack, hauling upon the sheet, and converting one into the other. The large steering paddles are eight or nine feet long, with an oblong rounded blade of half that length.

June 26th.—Yesterday afternoon the Rattlesnake was removed to the neighbourhood of the proposed watering-place on South-east Island, and anchored in seventeen fathoms, mud, a mile off shore. Soon after daylight I accompanied Captain Stanley and a party in two boats to ascend the neighbouring creek and determine whether a practicable watering-place existed there. For several hundred yards above the entrance we found the channel preserving a nearly uniform width of about fifteen yards, with low muddy shores covered with mangroves, some of which attained the unusual dimensions of 60 to 80 feet in height, with a circumference at the base of 6 to 8 feet. To this succeeded during our upward progress a low bank of red clay backed by rising ground and tangled brush, with very large trees at intervals, and others arching over the stream, their branches nearly touching the water. Gigantic climbers hung down in long festoons passing from branch to branch, and the more aged trunks supported clumps of ferns and parasitical plants. Here and there an areca palm shot up its slender stem surmounted by a cluster of pale-green feathery leaves, or the attention was arrested for a moment by a magnificent pandanus—its trunk raised high above the ground by the enormous supporting root-like shoots,—or some graceful tree-fern with dark widely-spreading foliage exceeding in delicacy the finest lace.

Meanwhile the creek had slightly narrowed, the dead trees in the water became more frequent and troublesome, and the thickets on the banks encroached more and more upon the channel so as not to allow room for the oars to pass, obliging the men to use them as poles. At every turn in the windings of the stream (still too brackish to be fit to drink) some beautiful glimpse of jungle scenery presented itself as we passed upwards—long vistas and stray bursts of sunshine alternating with the gloomy shadows of the surrounding woods. A deep silence pervaded the banks of this water never before visited by civilized man, its monotony broken only by the occasional brief word of command, the splash of the oars, or the shrill notes of some passing flights of parrots. The river, for now it might fairly be called one, retained the same character until we had

T. Huxley, delt.   Hullmandel & Walton, Lithog.

WATERING CREEK, LOUISIADE ARCHIPELAGO.

T. & W. Boone, Publishers, London. 1852.

gone up about a mile, when further progress was stopped by a ridge of rocks stretching across from side to side marking the limits of the tidal influence. Over this the rush of fresh water formed a strong rapid backed by a deep, sluggish, winding stream, draining a large basin-like valley bounded behind by the central ridge of the island, the principal hills of which attain an elevation of from 992 to 1421 feet, and one, Mount Rattlesnake, is 2689 feet in height. At times the body of water discharged here must be immense, judging from the quantity of drift wood and other detritus lodged in the trees twelve feet above the present level of the stream, probably during the inundations of the rainy season. These floods must also spread over the low land on the margin of the river to a considerable distance, the deep red clay there, evidently the washings of the hills, bearing the marks of having been under water. The jungle in places is very dense, but, with the exercise of a little patience and labour, it can be penetrated at almost every point. On rising ground it is often bordered by a thicket of creeping and climbing plants mixed up with bushes and patches of *Hellenia cærulea.* The low wooded hills are covered with tall grass growing on very poor soil—of partially decomposed mica-slate with lumps of quartz.

It being considered practicable to water the ship at this place, we returned on board. In the afternoon the first load of water was brought off, and in the course of the week we procured 78 tons with less trouble than had been anticipated. I afterwards repeatedly visited the watering creek, and a brief account of the productions of its neighbourhood may here be given as a popular contribution to the natural history of the little known Louisiade Archipelago.

The rock is scarcely ever exposed on the banks of the river except at the rapid before alluded to. Though still mica-slate, it is there of much greater hardness and denser texture than on Pig and Round Islands, and stretches across the stream like a dyke, running nearly north and south with a westerly dip of about 60°. Elsewhere, along the shores of Coral Haven, this mica-slate is of a leaden hue and glistening lustre, yielding to the nail, with a slight greasy feel, especially in some pieces of a shining ash-grey, acted upon by salt water. From hand specimens alone it is difficult to assign a name to this rock, as it partakes more or less of the characters of mica, chlorite, and talc-schists.

Among the botanical productions *Nepenthes destillatoria*, the famous pitcher-plant of the East, deserves mention. It grows abundantly among the tall grass on the skirts of the jungle, and the pitchers invariably contained a small quantity of limpid fluid of a slightly sweetish taste, with small insects floating on its surface. The finest of the tree-ferns (*Hemitelium*) grew alone near the watering-place, and was cut down to furnish specimens. The trunk measured fifteen feet in height, with a diameter at the base of eight inches.

No mammalia were procured on South-east Island—indeed the only one seen was a flyiug-squirrel which I caught a glimpse of one evening at the river-mouth as it sprung off among the mangroves from the summit of a dead tree —it appeared to be of the size of an ordinary rat, and was probably a *Petaurus*. Wild pigs must be very numerous—as indicated by fresh marks where they had been wallowing in the beds of the ditch-like rivulets, their footprints everywhere, and well beaten tracks through the jungle. But none of the animals themselves, probably from their extreme shyness and partially nocturnal habits, were ever encountered by our shooting parties. I was after-wards informed by Mr. Inskip that while in the Bramble, in the neighbourhood of Condé Peninsula, a native in a canoe alongside having his attention directed to a very large boar's tusk which he wore as an ornament, described, by pantomimic gestures, that the animal had cost much trouble in killing it, having repeatedly charged him, and received no less than eight spear wounds before it fell.

Birds were plentiful, but owing to the difficulty of seeing them among the thick foliage, few, com-paratively, were shot. The most interesting specimen procured was one of a very handsome scarlet Lory, closely allied to *Lorius domicellus*, a bird widely spread over the Indian Archipelago. It was usually seen in small flocks passing over the tops of the trees, uttering a loud sharp scream at intervals. Another parrakeet, not so big as a sparrow, of a green colour, was sometimes seen in flocks, but we could not succeed in getting one. The Torres Strait and Nicobar pigeons, also Duperrey's Mega-podius were common enough, as well as many other birds, twelve species of which are also found in Australia,—a most unlooked-for occurrence.

No snakes were seen during our rambles, but small lizards occurred everywhere. A large lizard, apparently *Monitor Gouldii*, was shot from a tree on the banks of the river. Although not troubled by mosquitoes, such of us as strolled about much in the bush were sadly tormented by sand-flies—a minute two-winged insect whose bite raises a small swelling followed by much itching. On going to bed one night, I counted no less than sixty-three of these marks on my left leg from the ankle to half way up the thigh, and the right one was equally studded with angry red pimples. Among many kinds of ants I may mention the green one, which is found chiefly on trees and bushes, of the leaves of which it makes its nest. Should one unconsciously disturb them by getting entangled among the branches in the neighbourhood of a nest, he may expect a whole swarm upon him before he can extricate himself, and is first made aware of their presence by feeling sharp stinging pains in various places, especially the neck, caused by their bites.

A small fire-fly (a species of *Lampyris*) is plentiful, showing out at night like a twinkling phosphorescent spark, slowly flitting about from tree to tree or resting on the leaves wet with dew. Nor must I omit a very splendid day-flying moth (*Cocytia D'Urvillei*) which is common on the skirts of the woods and thickets ; several even came on board the ship at various times.

Very few fish were caught at this anchorage, but on the mud-flat at the mouth of the creek, shoals of mullet and "guard-fish" were seen daily. In the fresh water I observed several small species of Cyprinidæ rising at flies, but, not being provided with the requisite tackle, none were caught.

The muddy mangrove-covered banks of the lower part of the creek furnished the collection with an *Auricula* and a very fine *Cyrena*, apparently the same as the Australian and New Guinea *C. Cyprinoides*. Many fresh-water shells were found in the neighbourhood of the watering-place — three kinds of *Melania*, a *Mytilus*, a *Navicella*, and five species of *Neritina*—but most of these have been already described as inhabitants of the Feejee Islands and other places in Polynesia, and elsewhere. One might reasonably have anticipated a rich harvest of land-shells in the damp forests of South-east Island, yet diligent search on the trunks of the trees and among the dead leaves about their roots produced only four species, all of which however are new. The finest of these is a *Pupina*, the giant of its race, of a glossy reddish pink colour with red mouth.

During our stay here the ship was daily visited by canoes from Pig Island and its vicinity, also from a village or two on South-east Island, a few miles to the eastward of our anchorage. They usually made their appearance in the morning and remained for an hour or so, bartering cocoa-nuts, yams, ornaments and weapons for iron hoop, knives, and axes. After leaving us, those coming from the eastward, as the wind was unfavourable for their return, landed at the mouth of the creek and waited for the flood tide. Our intercourse throughout was peaceful, which was fortunate for both parties, for, if inclined to be hostile, the natives might frequently have attacked our watering-boats while passing up and down the river, impeded occasionally by dead trees and shoals, with a dense forest on each side. Latterly, however, as if suspicious of our intentions or tired of our protracted stay, they fired the grass on the hill at the entrance of the creek, possibly to deter us from entering. Still we thought this might have been done without reference to us, but afterwards two or three men with spears were seen by passing boats skulking along the banks of the river on their way to the rapid, where they again set fire to the grass as if to smoke us out or prevent our return. But the grassy tracts along the tops of the low hills in the vicinity being intersected by lines and patches of brush the fire did not extend far, as had also been the case lower down, so caused us no inconvenience.

Among our numerous visitors we occasionally saw a woman or two, but none were favourable specimens of their kind. Unlike the men, whose only covering was the breech-cloth formerly described, the women wore a short petticoat of grass-like stuff, probably the pandanus leaf divided into fine shreds, —worked into a narrow band which ties round the waist. They usually, when alongside the ship, held a small piece of matting over the head with one hand, either to protect them from the sun or partially to secure themselves from observation, as in their manners they were much more reserved than the men.

At Coral Haven we have already seen considerable variety displayed in the various styles of painting the body. Pounded charcoal mixed up with cocoa-nut oil, and lime obtained from burnt shells similarly treated, are the pigments made use of. The most common fashion of painting is with a broad streak down the forehead, and a circle round each eye. Occasionally the entire body is blackened, but often the face only—with daubs of paint on the temples, cheek, and round the mouth and one or both eyes, rendering a forbidding countenance inexpressibly hideous in our sight.

The ornaments worn by these savages are very numerous, besides which they are fond of decorating the person with flowers and strong-scented plants.

In what may be considered as full dress, with the face and body painted, they are often decked out with large white cowries appended to the waist, elbows and ankles, together with streamers of pandanus leaf.   Among many kinds of bracelets or armlets the most common is a broad woven one of grass, fitting very tightly on the upper arm. There are others of shell,—one solid, formed by grinding down a large shell (*Trochus Niloticus*) so as to obtain a well polished transverse section, and another in two or three pieces tied together, making a round smooth ring ; of the former of these five or six are sometimes worn on one arm.   But the most curious bracelet, and by no means an uncommon

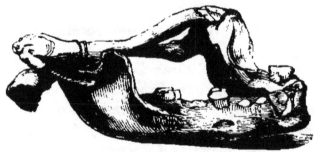

one, is that made of a human lower jaw with one or more collar bones closing the upper side crossing from one angle to the other.   Whether these are the jaws of former friends or enemies we had no means of ascertaining; no great value appeared to be attached to them ; and it was observed, as a curious circumstance, that none of these jaws had the teeth discoloured by the practice of betel chewing.

We procured various sorts of necklaces,—strings of shells, black seeds, and dogs teeth.   As the canine teeth alone are used in making one of the last description, the number of dogs required to complete a single necklace must be considerable. A round thin, concave piece of shell (*Melo Ethiopica*), with a central black portion, is often worn suspended by a string round the neck, and similar ornaments, but much smaller, are attached to the hips and elbows. The long nose-stick of shell is only occasionally worn, although every one, of either sex, has the septum of the nose pierced for its reception,—an operation most likely performed during infancy, as I once saw that it had been done to a child about a year old.

Nearly all the men carried in their hair a comb projecting in front or on one side. This article is usually made of wood, but occasionally of tortoise-shell, a foot in length, thin, flat, and narrow, with about six very long, slightly diverging, needle-shaped teeth, but it admits of much variety of size and shape, and frequently has various ornaments attached to it. The spatula used by betel chewers to introduce the lime to the mouth, although often made of tortoise-shell and resembling that figured on a preceding page, is more commonly made of cocoa-nut wood, with a massive handle, deeply divided by a slit, and when struck upon the knee it is made to produce a loud clicking noise like that of castanets.

CHAPTER VI.

July 2nd.—THE Bramble having returned from
an exploration to the westward with the report that
there was a passage out of Coral Haven in that
direction, the ship left her anchorage off the
watering place this morning, with boats ahead and
on each side of her, repeating the soundings by
signal; she ran along the land to the westward
seven or eight miles, passed between Pig and South-
east Islands, rounded the north-west end of the
latter, stood between it and Joannet Island to the
W.S.W. for about five miles, and anchored early in
the forenoon in 15 fathoms, water, under a small
detached reef and dry sand-bank. Several very fine
red snappers were caught with hook and line soon

after anchoring, and smaller fish of many kinds were caught in abundance,—they were mostly species of *Pentapus, Diacope,* and *Mesoprion.*

While passing a small island—afterwards named in honour of Mr. Brierly—distant from our anchorage about two miles N.W. by W., several women and dogs were seen on shore, and soon afterwards two canoes, which had followed us from the anchorage, were seen to put in there. In the afternoon two boats were sent to this island, to communicate with the natives, and search for an anchorage near it. We landed upon a sandy beach, after wading over the fringing reef, and were met by some natives who had come round a neighbour- ing point from the windward or inhabited side. Although at first cautious of approach, yet in the course of a few minutes they came freely about us to the number of twenty, each carrying two or three spears—not the beautifully polished and well- balanced ones we had seen elsewhere, but merely slender, rudely-fashioned sticks sharpened at each end. About twelve women, dressed in the usual petticoat of grass-like stuff, followed at a distance, and kept close to the point for some time; but at length the natural curiosity of the sex (I suppose) overcame their fear, and although repeatedly ordered back by the men, they drew up closer and closer to have a peep at the strangers. Two of the youngest and most attractive of these ladies advanced to within twenty yards, and received with much apparent delight, and a great deal of capering and dancing about on the sand, some strips of a gaudy handkerchief conveyed to them by a lad decorated with streamers of pandanus leaf at the elbows and wrists—evidently the Adonis of the party. Some of the men had formerly been off to the ship, and one or two carried axes of the usual form, but headed with pieces of our iron hoop, neatly ground to a fine edge. A few cocoa-nuts were given us for a knife or two, and we saw their mode of climbing for them, which one man did with the agility of a monkey, ascending first by a few notches, made years ago, afterwards by clasping the trunk with his arms, arching his body with the feet against the tree, and then walking up precisely in the mode of the Torres Strait Islanders. Like these last people too, they open the nut with a sharp stick, and use a shell (a piece of mother-of-pearl oyster) for scraping out the pulp. After a stay of half an hour we returned to the boat leaving the natives in good humour. Our search for a safe anchorage for the ship was unsuccessful, so we returned on board.

July 3rd.—After the good understanding which appeared to have been established yesterday, I was rather surprised at observing the suspicious manner in which we were received to-day by the people on Brierly Island. In two boats we went round to a small sandy point on the northern side of the island where seven or eight canoes were hauled up on the beach, but some time elapsed before any of the natives came close up—even to a single unarmed man of our party who waded ashore—the others remaining in the boats—although tempted by the display of pieces of iron hoop and strips of calico. One of the natives, carrying a wooden sword, and apparently a leading man among them, made some signs and used gesticulations expressive of sleep or death with reference to a part of Joannet Island which he repeatedly pointed to. This we could not understand.* After a certain degree of confidence had been restored, five or six of us remained on shore, and great harmony appeared to prevail throughout the combined party. In one place the sergeant of marines was seated on the sand with a ring of people round him whom he was drilling into the mode of singing a Port Essington aboriginal song, occasionally rising to vary his lesson with a dance,—in another, a group of natives were being initiated in the mysteries of the Jew's harp, or kept amused by the performance of various antics. Mr. Huxley as usual, was at work with his sketch-book, and I employed myself in procuring words for an incipient vocabulary. My principal informant was called Wadai, a little withered old man with shaved

* Although not understood at the time, he referred to an affray between two boats detached from the ship on surveying service and some Joannet Island canoes, which had occurred only a few hours before at the place indicated ; of this we had not yet heard, but the news had reached Brierly Island, and occasioned our strange reception. This is a remarkable instance of the rapidity with which intelligence may be conveyed from one island to another.

head, on which some one had stuck a red night-cap which greatly took his fancy.   Not being of so volatile a nature as the others he remained patiently with me for half an hour.   He shewed me the mode of using the betel, which, as practised by these people has this peculiarity, that the leaf of the siri or betel pepper is not employed, as is universally the case among the Malays.   A small portion of the green betelnut (the fruit of the *Areca Catechu*) which here curiously enough is named ērēka—is broken off with the teeth and placed in the mouth; then the spatula, formerly described, moistened with saliva, is dipped into a small calabash of lime in fine powder, with which the tongue and lips are smeared over by repeated applications.   The bolus is then kept in the mouth, and rolled over and over until it is thought requisite to renew it.   The practice of betel chewing is not confined to the men, for the few women whom we had seen alongside the ship in Coral Haven, had their teeth blackened by it.

One of the natives seen to-day exhibited a remarkable case of malformation of the teeth.   The lower incisors were wanting, and the upper ones had coalesced and grown downwards and outwards, forming an irregular dark protruding mass which I at first took to be a quid of betel.   Another man with a diseased leg had lost one hand at the wrist, and the long shrivelled arm presented a curious appearance.

Several dogs were also seen close to, for

T. Baxter, delt.

HUT ON BRIERLY ISLAND, LOUISIADE ARCHIPELAGO.

T. & W. Boone, Publisher, London, 1852.

Hullmandel & Walton, Lithog.

the first time—they were wretched half-starved objects of various colours, but agreed in being long-bodied, short-legged, and prick-eared, with sharp snout and long tail, slightly bushy, but tapering to a point. They do not bark, but have the long melancholy howl of the dingo or wild dog of Australia.

At length some of us found our way to the huts of the natives which were close at hand, and had thus an opportunity of examining one of them minutely, besides verifying what we had before seen only from a distance, and with the aid of the telescope. The distinctive characters of these huts consist in their being long and tunnel-like, drooping and overhanging at each end, raised from the ground upon posts, and thatched over. The four huts composing the village were placed in two adjacent clearings, fifty or sixty yards in length, screened from the beach by a belt of small trees and brush-wood. Behind is the usual jungle of the wooded islands of the Archipelago, with a path leading through it towards the centre of the island. A solitary hut stood perched upon the ridge near the summit shaded by cocoa-palms, and partially hid among the bushes and tall grass. It differed from those of the village in having the posts projecting through the roof, but whether used as a dwelling or not, is a matter of conjecture. It may possibly have been used for the reception of the dead. In the village an approximate measurement gave thirty feet as the length, nine the breadth, and thirteen the height in centre of one of these huts— the one figured in the accompanying plate ; the annexed woodcut gives an end view of another.

All four were built upon exactly the same plan. The supporting posts are four in number, and raise the floor about four and a half feet from the ground, leaving a clear space beneath.   Before entering the body of the hut each post passes through an oval disc of wood, a foot and a half in diameter, the object of which is probably to prevent the ingress into the dwelling of snakes, rats, or other vermin, most likely the *Mus Indicus*, with which all the islands to the westward are overrun. To the stout uprights are lashed transverse bars supporting three long parallel timbers running the whole length of the floor; on these seven or eight transverse poles are laid, crossed by about a dozen longitudinal and slighter ones, on which a flooring of long strips of the outer wood of the cocoa-nut tree is laid across. After penetrating the floor, the main posts rise five feet higher, where they are connected at top by others as tie-beams, which cross them, and project a little further to sustain the two lateral of the five longitudinal supports of the roof, which, at the gable ends, are further secured by other tie-beams. On the two central cross-bars also is laid a platform running one half the length of the hut, floored on one side, forming a partial upper

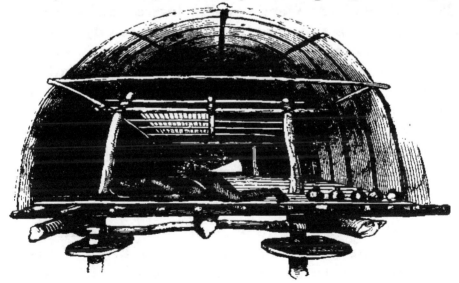

story, with a space of three feet between it and the ceiling. The sides and roof are formed of slender poles or rafters arching over from side to side, secured by lashings of rattan to five poles running lengthways; the whole forming a strong framework thatched over with coarse grass pulled up by the roots in large tufts, with a few cocoa-palm leaves laid over all. The lower part of the sides and upper portion of the ends under the overhanging gables are formed by strips of coarse matting. There are usually entrances at both ends, and the centre of one side, closed by a flap of matting finer than the rest. Opposite each door an inclined beam—one end of which rests on the ground, and the other leans against the fork of a short upright post—serves as a step for mounting by.

Near these huts were several large sheds, open at one side, where the cooking is performed,—judging from the remains of fires under them. On two small stages, planked over, we saw a number of thin and neatly carved earthen pots, blackened with smoke; these are usually a foot in diameter, but one was as much as eighteen inches. I was struck with a feature exhibiting the cleanly habits of these savages, from whom in this respect the inhabitants of many villages in the mother country might take a lesson,—it consisted in the well swept ground, where not a stray stone or leaf was suffered to remain, and the absence about the dwellings of everything offensive to the smell or sight. I could not help contrasting the condition of these people with that of the Australian blacks, a considerable portion of whose time, at certain periods of the year, is spent in shifting about from place to place, searching for food, living from hand to mouth, and leading a hard and precarious life. But here, on this little island, the cocoa-nut tree alone would be sufficient to supply many of the principal wants of man. The fruit serves both for food and drink,—the shell is used to carry about water in,*—the fibres of the husk are converted into cordage, and the leaves into matting, while the wood is fashioned into spears and other useful articles. The cultivation of bananas and yams—of the latter of which, and of two other edible roots, we saw large quantities in the huts,—costs him very little trouble,—he occasionally keeps a few pigs, and when inclined, can always catch plenty of fish, and occasionally a turtle upon the reefs at low water.

Before leaving the beach I presented old Wadai with an axe, as a recompence for his civility. The poor man looked quite bewildered at his unexpected good fortune, and for a little while was quite speechless,—not understanding the nature of a gift, or being taken with a sudden fit of generosity, he afterwards waded out to the boat with some cocoanuts to give me in return.

* Some of these are represented in the preceding woodcut,— the hole in the top is usually plugged with a portion of banana leaf.

Q 2

July 4th.—The first cutter was sent to Brierly Island to-day, for the double purpose of endeavouring to procure yams from the natives for the use of the ship's company, and enabling me to make additions to my vocabulary and collection. Mr. Brady took charge of the bartering, and drawing a number of lines upon the sandy beach, explained that when each was covered with a yam he would give an axe in return. At first some little difficulty occurred as the yams were brought down very slowly—two or three at a time,—but at length the first batch was completed and the axe handed over. The man who got it—the sword-bearer of yesterday—had been trembling with anxiety for some time back, holding Mr. Brady by the arm and watching the promised axe with eager eye. When he obtained possession of it he became quite wild with joy, laughing and screaming, and flourishing the axe over his head. After this commencement the bartering went on briskly amidst a great deal of uproar, the men passing between the village and the beach at full speed, with basketfuls of yams, and too intent upon getting the *kiram kelumai* (iron-axes), to think of anything else. Meanwhile Mr. Huxley and myself walked about unheeded by almost any one. The women kept themselves in the bush at a little distance, making a great noise, but avoided shewing themselves. Occasionally we caught a glimpse of these sable damsels, but only one female came near us,—a meagre old woman who darted past with an axe in her hand, and sprang up into one of the huts like a harlequin, shewing at the same time more of her long shrivelled shanks than was strictly decorous. Besides the usual petticoat reaching to the knee, made of a grass or some leaf—perhaps of the pandanus,—cut into long shreds, this dame wore a somewhat similar article round the neck, hanging over the breast and shoulders, leaving the arms free. An axe was offered to one of the men, who had previously sat for his portrait, to induce him to bring the woman to Mr. Huxley, who was anxious to get a sketch of a female, but in spite of the strong inducement we did not succeed, and any further notice taken of the woman seemed to give offence. While wandering about the place we came upon a path leading in to the adjacent brush, but blocked up by some cocoa-nut leaves recently thrown across. This led past an enclosure of about three-quarters of an acre, neatly and strongly fenced in, probably used as a pen for keeping pigs in, judging from the absence of anything like cultivation, and the trodden-down appearance, apparently made by these animals, a jaw bone of one of which was picked up close by.

At length the natives appeared anxious to get rid of us, after obtaining about seventeen axes and a few knives, in return for 368 pounds of yams, which cost us little more than a halfpenny per pound. After wading out to the boat, the natives assisted in shoving her off, and when we had got well clear of the beach, they treated us to what might have been one of their dances, dividing into two parties, and with wild pantomimic gesture, advancing and retiring, and going through the motion of throwing the spear, with one or two of which each was provided. Even during the height of the bartering very few of the natives had laid aside their weapons, and it was evident that they were influenced by no very friendly feeling towards us, and were glad to be relieved of our presence. They had latterly become more noisy than usual, and even insolent, and I believe that had we staid a little longer, hostilities would have commenced, as they probably regarded our forbearance to be the result of fear.

We landed on the opposite side of the island to give me an opportunity of procuring some specimens, as it was judged that our shooting there would not annoy the inhabitants. The boat remained off at anchor while some of us strolled along the beach, getting an occasional shot. Birds however were few. Among those seen were the fishing-eagle, osprey, and two smaller birds—all Australian. On the slope behind the beach we saw for the first time signs of cultivation,—in a small plantation of bananas and yams. There was no fence, but the ground had been partially cleared, leaving the stumps of the smaller trees and shrubs as posts for the yam plants (a *Dioscorea* with broad heart-shaped leaves) to train themselves upon. After a stay of nearly an hour, we were moving down towards the boat, when

the natives made their appearance round the point,
coming up in straggling order. One in advance of
the rest came along at a rapid pace with his spear
poised, and pointed it at the nearest of our party,
when within a few yards of him, with what intention
I do not presume to say,—but the natives were evidently in a state of great excitement. As they
might erroneously have supposed that we had been
making free with their cocoa-nuts and yams, some
grass which had been cut for the sheep on board
was taken out of the bag and shewn them as being
intended for our *bobo* (pigs)—which they appeared
to understand. The one among them who had
yesterday made the allusion to Joannet Island
pointed to our guns, talking at the same time with
great energy, and making signs as if wishing to see
the use of a weapon of whose wonderful effects he
had lately heard. As many swallows were flying
about, I told Wilcox,—probably the best shot of the
party—to shoot one, which was done cleverly, and
the bird fell at our feet. The indications of surprise
were not so great as I expected to have seen exhibited, but after several more shots had been fired,
some with ball along the water, a few of the natives
began to shew signs of uneasiness and sneaked
away. Old Wadai, however (perhaps feeling perfectly secure under the shelter of his perfect in-
significance), and one or two others sat down under
a tree beside us, apparently unconcerned, and some

of the rest remained on the beach until after our departure.

We did not afterwards land upon Brierly Island, so I may conclude with a short description. It is not more than half a mile in length, with a central ridge attaining the height of 347 feet, and sloping downwards at each end. It is well wooded with low trees and brushwood, and mixed up with them there is a profusion of cocoa-palms scattered about in clumps, from the margin of the beach to the shoulders of the hill; long coarse grass, at this time of a beautiful light green tint, covered the remainder. The usual fringing coral reef surrounds the island, running off to a great distance in one direction. The greater part of the shore and the projecting points are rocky (where the soft splintery mica slate has been exposed), with occasional sandy beaches. We saw no fresh water, but the declivities here and there shewed deep furrows in the red clayey soil, the effects of torrents after heavy rains.

To-day and yesterday I obtained in all about 130 words of the language of the Brierly Island people. The small vocabulary thus formed, the first ever obtained in the Louisiade Archipelago, leads to some interesting results, and fills up one of the gaps in the chain of philological affinities which may afterwards be brought to bear upon the perplexing question—Whence has Australia been peopled? Taking the numerals as affording in the present instance the most convenient materials for hasty comparison, I find words in common—not only with those of other divisions of the Pelagian Negroes,* as the inhabitants of the north coast of New Guinea on the one hand, and New Ireland on the other, but also with the Malay and the various Polynesian languages or dialects spoken from New Zealand to Tahiti.† This latter affinity between the woolly and straight-haired sections of oceanic blacks appears to me to render it more curious and unexpected that the language of the Louisiade should completely differ from that of the northern part of Torres Strait,‡ the inhabitants of both being connected by strong general similarity and occasionally identity in manners and customs, and having many physical characteristics common to both. Yet while the natives of the Louisiade use the decimal system of the Malays and Polynesians, the Torres Strait islanders have simple words to express the numerals *one* and *two* only, while *three* is represented by a compound.§

* Natural History of Man, by J. C. Pritchard, M.D. 2nd ed. p. 326.

† D'Urville's Voyage de l'Astrolabe. Philologie. Tom. ii.

‡ Jukes' Voyage of the Fly, vol. ii. p. 274.

§ These remarks I give as written in my journal, with the sole exception of the term Pelagian Negroes. The reader is referred to Dr. Latham's observations on my Vocabularies in the Appendix to this work.

July 6th.—Lieutenants Dayman and Simpson, with the pinnace and second galley, returned to the ship after an absence of several days. On the morning of the 4th, after having spent the night at anchor in one of the bays on the south side of Joannet Island, they were attacked by the natives under the following circumstances:—In the grey of the morning the look-outs reported the approach of three canoes, with about ten men in each. On two or three persons shewing themselves in the bow of the pinnace in front of the rain-awning, the natives ceased paddling, as if baulked in their design of surprising the large boat, but, after a short consultation, they came alongside in their usual noisy manner. After a stay of about five minutes only they pushed off to the galley, and some more sham bartering was attempted, but they had nothing to give in exchange for the *kelumai* so much coveted. In a short time the rudeness and overbearing insolence of the natives had risen to a pitch which left no doubt of their hostile intentions. The anchor was got up, when some of the blacks seized the painter, and others in trying to capsize the boat brought the gunwale down to the water's edge, at the same time grappling with the men to pull them out, and dragging the galley in-shore towards the shoal water. The bowman, with the anchor in his hand, was struck on the head with a stone-headed axe, the blow was repeated, but fortunately took effect only on the wash-streak; another of the crew was struck at with a similar weapon, but warded off the blow, although held fast by one arm, when, just as the savage was making another stroke, Lieutenant Dayman, who until now had exercised the utmost forbearance, fired at him with a musket. The man did not drop although wounded in the thigh; but even this, unquestionably their first experience of fire-arms, did not intimidate the natives, one of whom, standing on a block of coral, threw a spear which passed across the breast of one of the boat's crew and lodged in the bend of one arm, opening the vein. They raised a loud shout when the spear was seen to take effect, and threw several others which missed. Lieutenant Simpson, who had been watching what was going on then fired from the pinnace with buck shot and struck them, when, finding that the large boat, although at anchor, could assist the smaller one, the canoes were paddled in-shore in great haste and confusion. Some more musket shots were fired, and the galley went in chase endeavouring to turn the canoes, so as to bring them under the fire of the pinnace's 12-pounder howitzer, which was speedily mounted and fired. The shot either struck one of the canoes or went within a few inches of the mark, on which the natives instantly jumped overboard into the shallow water, making for the mangroves, which they succeeded in reaching, dragging their canoes with them. Two rounds of grape-shot crashing through the branches dispersed the party, but afterwards they moved two of the canoes out of sight. The remaining one was brought out after breakfast by the galley under cover of the pinnace, and was towed off to some distance. The paddles having been taken out and the spears broken and left in her, she was let go to drift down towards a village whence the attacking party were supposed to have come. Some blood in this canoe, although not the one most aimed at, shewed that the firing had not been ineffective.

This act of deliberate treachery was perpetrated by persons who had always been well-treated by us, for several of the natives present were recognised as having been alongside the ship in Coral Haven. This, their first act of positive hostility, affords, I think, conclusive evidence of the savage disposition of the natives of this part of the Louisiade when excited by the hope of plunder, and shews that no confidence should ever be reposed in them unless, perhaps, in the presence of a numerically superior force, or the close vicinity of the ship. At the same time the boldness of these savages in attacking, with thirty men in three canoes, two boats known to contain at least twenty persons—even in hopes of taking them by surprise—and in not being at once driven off upon feeling the novel and deadly effects of musketry, indicates no little amount of bravery. In the course of the same day, when Lieut. Dayman was close in-shore with the galley laying down the coast line, he had occasion to approach the native village before alluded to, and observed the men following the boat along the beach within gunshot, sharpening and poising their spears, violently gesticulating and calling out loudly, as if daring him to land. A favourable opportunity was now afforded for punishing the natives for their treachery; but from highly commendable motives of humanity, no steps were taken for this purpose by Lieut. Dayman, and they were treated with silent contempt.

July 10*th*.—The Bramble and two of our boats were sent to ascertain whether an easy passage to the westward existed in-shore near the islands (the Calvados Group) extending in that direction, while, at the same time, the ship stood to the southward and anchored in 28 fathoms, four miles inside the barrier-reef. On our way we passed numerous small coral patches, and others were afterwards found to the westward, running in irregular lines, and partially blocking up the passage inside the barrier, which it was expected would have been found clear. We remained here for five days, during which period we had much variety of weather—sometimes blowing hard from E.S.E. to E.N.E. with squalls and thick gloomy weather—at other times nearly a calm, the air disagreeably close and muggy, the temperature varying from 75° to 85°, with occasional heavy rain.

Small fish appeared to abound at this anchorage. I had never before seen the sucking-fish (*Echeneis*

Remora) so plentiful as at this place; they caused much annoyance to our fishermen by carrying off baits and hooks, and appeared always on the alert, darting out in a body of twenty or more from under the ship's bottom when any offal was thrown overboard. Being quite a nuisance, and useless as food, Jack often treated them as he would a shark, by " spritsail-yarding," or some still less refined mode of torture. One day some of us while walking the poop had our attention directed to a sucking-fish about two and a half feet in length which had been made fast by the tail to a billet of wood by a fathom or so of spun yarn, and turned adrift. An immense striped shark, apparently about fourteen feet in length, which had been cruizing about the ship all the morning, sailed slowly up, and, turning slightly on one side, attempted to seize the apparently helpless fish, but the sucker, with great dexterity, made himself fast in a moment to the shark's back—off darted the monster at full speed,—the sucker holding on fast as a limpet to a rock, and the billet towing astern. He then rolled over and over, tumbling about, when, wearied with his efforts, he laid quiet for a little. Seeing the float, the shark got it into his mouth, and disengaging the sucker by the tug on the line, made a bolt at the fish; but his puny antagonist was again too quick, and fixing himself close behind the dorsal fin, defied the efforts of the shark to disengage him, although he rolled over and over, lashing the water with his tail until it foamed all around. What the final result was, we could not clearly make out.

Many water snakes were seen here, swimming about on the surface; and one of two chasing each other and playing about the ship was shot by Captain Stanley from his cabin window, and brought on board. It appeared to be of the genus *Hypotrophis*, and measured 37½ inches in length; it had a pair of minute poison fangs on each side of the upper jaw; the colour was a dirty greenish with numerous pale narrow bands.

July 16*th.*—The pinnace having returned yesterday and reported a clear passage for the ship to the westward close in-shore, we got under weigh and returned on the same line by which we had come out, anchoring for the night in 19 fathoms water, under Observation Reef II. Next day we rounded Brierly Island from the eastward, passed between it and Joannet Island, and after running a few miles further to the westward, anchored in 30 fathoms— 15 miles W.N.W. from Brierly Island, and two miles from the nearest of the Calvados Group. In passing Brierly Island the place appeared to be deserted. We saw a single canoe hauled up on the beach, but no natives.

On July 18th, after standing to the westward 32 miles, we hauled out south, and anchored in 22 fathoms, about eight miles from the nearest of the Calvados. We remained at this anchorage for the next three days. One day we were visited by a canoe from a neighbouring island, and on the following morning two more canoes came off. The people in one canoe kept at a safe distance, but those in the other came alongside, and after exhausting their stock of yams and other articles of barter, went off to their more cautious companions, and speedily returned to us with a fresh supply. The canoe was an old patched-up affair, and while one of the natives was standing up with a foot on each gunwale, a previous fracture in the bow, united only by pitch, gave way, and a piece of the side, four feet long, came out, allowing the water to rush in. The canoe would speedily have been swamped, had not the author of the mischief held on the piece in his hand, while some of the others bailed away as rapidly as possible, and the remainder paddled off with desperation, shouting loudly to the people in the second canoe for help. But their friends seemed as much frightened as themselves, not knowing the nature of the accident, and probably supposing that we had been roughly treating their companions;—they made sail for the shore, and did not stop until they had got half a mile away from the ship, when they waited until the damaged canoe came up in a sinking state, bailed her out, and after taking some people out of her, both made off, under sail, and we saw no more of them.

But for this accident I would probably have got a few words of their language to compare with those obtained at Brierly Island. Our visitors were profusely decorated with the red, feathery, leafy shoots of an *Amaranthus,* which they wore fastened in bunches about the ankles, waist, elbows, and in the hair. In other respects, I saw nothing among them different from what has already been described at Coral Haven.

From this anchorage we enjoyed an extensive view of the south-eastern portion of the Louisiade Archipelago. On the extreme right is the large South-east Island, with its sharply undulating outline, and Mount Rattlesnake clearly visible, although distant 45 miles. Next, after a gap partially filled up by Pig Island, Joannet Island succeeds, $10\frac{1}{2}$ miles in length, not so high as South-east Island but resembling it in dimness of outline,—its highest point, Mount Asp, is 1104 feet in height. Next come the Calvados, of various aspect and size, some with the undulating outline of the larger islands, others rising more or less abruptly to the height of from four to upwards of nine hundred feet. They constitute a numerous group,—upwards of 40—some of which, however, are mere rocks, are delineated upon the Rattlesnake's chart, and there are others to the northward. Behind them, in two of the intervals, the large and distant island of St. Aignan (so named after one of D'Entrecasteaux's lieutenants) fills up the back ground, falling low at its eastern extreme, but the western half high and mountainous, with an elevation of 3279 feet. Further to the westward the last of the Calvados in this view was seen to form a remarkable peak, 518 feet in height, to which the name of Eddystone was applied; and still further to the left Ile Real, of D'Urville's chart, shoots up to the height of 554 feet, as a solitary rocky island with rugged outline and an abruptly peaked summit.

July 23rd.—Yesterday we were prevented from reaching our intended anchorage at the Duchâteau Isles by a strong easterly tide, the wind at the same time being too light to allow us to stem it. To-day the ship was moved closer in, and moored in a convenient berth in 18 fathoms, half a mile north from the middle island.

We remained here for eleven days, thus affording good opportunities for examining the group. The Duchâteau Isles are three low, wooded, coral islets, the largest of which is only three-fourths of a mile in length. The two eastern islands are connected by a reef, partly dry at low water, and separated by a narrow passage from the smaller reef, surrounding the western island. The southern, or windward margin of these reefs, presents a similarity to the barrier class by rising up suddenly from an unknown depth, with constant and very heavy breakers, but the northern, and at present the leeward portion, extends only a little way, with irregular and not well defined outline, and anchorage near it in from twelve to fifteen fathoms. The three islands agree in presenting the same physical characters. They are margined by a beach of white coral sand, with occasional thin beds and ledges of coral conglomerate, succeeded by a belt of tangled bushes and low trees, after which the trees become higher and the ground tolerably free from underwood, with occasional thickets of woody climbers. The cocoa-palm grows here in small numbers, usually several together, overtopping the other trees among which one of the *Bombaceæ* (silk-cotton trees) and *Pisonia grandis* attain the greatest dimensions, having frequently a girth of twelve or fifteen feet, with a height of sixty or seventy. A large leaved *Calophyllum* is the prevailing tree of the island, and among the others I may mention a *Myristica* and a *Caryophyllum*, neither of which, however, are of the species furnishing the nutmegs and cloves of commerce.

Of mammalia a large *Pteropus*, or fruit-eating bat, was seen once or twice, but no specimen was procured. The little Indian rat occurs abundantly on all the islands, taking to hollow logs and holes under the roots of trees for shelter. Here it is tamer than I have elsewhere seen it,—by sitting down in a shady place, and remaining quiet, I have sometimes had three or four within a few yards of me playing about, chacing each other, or turning over the dead leaves. It even climbs bushes and low trees, and gets out among the branches like a squirrel.

Birds were plentiful, and our sportsmen committed great havoc among the megapodii and pigeons. The former were very numerous, running about the

thickets, and calling to each other like pheasants in
a preserve at home.   Among the other game birds,
first in size and splendour comes the Nicobar pigeon
(*Calœnas Nicobarica*).   As its appearance exhibits
a near approach to the gallinaceous birds, so do its
habits.   It lives chiefly on the ground, runs with
great swiftness, and flies up into a tree when disturbed.   A nest found here was of the rude platform
construction usually found among the pigeon family;
it was built in a tree about ten feet from the ground,
and contained a single white egg.   The most common of the family, however, is one of the nutmeg
pigeons, *Carpophaga Oceanica*.   Many of both sexes
were furnished with a large, round, fleshy caruncle
on the bill at the base of the forehead,—this is said
to be present during the breeding season only.   Its
favourite place of resort during the heat of the day
is among the nutmegs and other spreading shady
trees where we found it difficult of detection, even
when led up to the spot by its cooing.   This last
may be represented by the letters *poor-oo-oo-oo
hoor-r-r-r*, the first syllable loud and startling, the
remainder faint and long drawn out; on the other
hand the cry of the Nicobar pigeon is merely *hoo-
hoo*.   In flavour the Oceanic pigeon far surpasses
the white or Torres Strait species, the merits of
which, as an article of food, we had so often fully
appreciated during our last cruize.   Most of them
were very fat, and some even burst open in
falling to the ground after having been shot.   A

solitary specimen of another large pigeon—with the
throat white, and the plumage with purple and
green metallic reflections—was obtained, also a small
dove of a new species, with pink forehead and broad
cream-coloured pectoral band, which has been named
by Mr. Gould *Ptilonopus strophium*. The only
other bird which I shall mention is a very fine kingfisher (*Halcyon saurophaga*), with white head, neck,
and lower parts, green scapulars, and blue wings
and tail, previously known by a single specimen
from New Guinea in the British Museum. It is
a very shy bird, frequenting the margin of the
island, usually seen perched on some detached or
solitary branch, as if sunning itself, and darting off
into the dense brush upon being approached.

Small lizards were plentiful, but we met with no
large ones or snakes during our rambles on the
Duchâteau Isles. These islands are probably much
resorted to by turtle, as they were daily seen swimming about, and one was caught on shore during our
stay by a party of natives. The variety of fishes
caught at this anchorage was considerable, and furnished many additions to the ichthyological collection, to which the paucity of other objects in zoology
for some time back enabled me to bestow much
attention.* Among the genera most remarkable

---

* Besides many kinds preserved in spirits, which have not yet
been examined, my collection contained stuffed specimens of about
forty species of Louisiade fishes. These, I have been informed
by Sir John Richardson, have nearly all been previously described
from other parts of Oceania, the Indian Ocean, and the China

for singularity of form and brilliancy of colouring I may mention *Holocentrum,* five kinds of which were procured here, one brilliantly coloured with blue and silver, and the remainder more or less of a bright scarlet.

The land-shells appear here to be limited to a solitary *Helicina,* found on the leaves and trunks of trees; and the trifling amount of rise and fall of tide, not exceeding three feet, prevented any search for marine species upon the reef. By dredging, however, in some of the sandy channels among the coral patches, in two to three fathoms water, some small *Mitræ, Nassæ, Subulæ,* and other interesting shells were procured, but no zoophytes came up in the dredge, and hardly any crustacea. One can scarcely avoid taking notice of the prodigious numbers of small hermit-crabs (*Cœnobita*) tenanting dead univalve shells, and occurring from the margin of the beach as far back as the centre of the islands, where they are found even in the holes of decaying trees at some height above the ground.

During our stay at this anchorage the weather was fine for the first three days, but afterwards was usually hazy, with strong breezes from between east and south-east, with squalls and occasional showers, the thermometer ranging between 72° and 85°—re-

Sea. The family *Sparidæ* is that best represented in the Louisiade Archipelago so far as I could judge,—three species of *Pentapus* numerically more than equal all the rest, and the next commonest fish is *Diacope octo-lineata.*

spectively the maximum and minimum temperature registered on board.

We were frequently visited by canoes from the Calvados Islands. The parties of natives usually landed on one of the adjacent Duchâteau Islands before communicating with the ship, and sometimes passed the night there before returning on the following morning. They brought with them cocoanuts, yams, and various other articles to barter with; among these were some productions of the country which I had not previously seen — Indian corn, ginger, and sugar-cane. The canoes were of the common description, with the exception of one of large size, closed at the bow and stern, with a high peak at each end, a standing mast, large oval sail, and the platform entirely covered over.* Few additional observations upon the natives were made here. On one occasion I procured a few words of their language, all of which, with one doubtful exception, are similar to those formerly obtained at Brierly Island. At another time we saw squatted down in a canoe alongside, with four men in it, two female children about three years of age, quite naked, with their hair twisted into long yarn-like strands falling over the shoulder; one of the two was a plump, laughing, intelligent creature, with fine features, great black eyes, and long silky eye-lashes.

At this place we had the misfortune to lose by death our carpenter, Mr. Raymond. His remains

* This is the canoe figured on p. 206.

were interred on the largest of the islands, in a clearing made by the wood-cutters, and as an additional precaution, for the purpose of concealing the grave from the keen sight of the natives, a large fire was made upon it to efface all marks of the spade.

Aug. 4th.—We left our anchorage this morning for the Duperré Islands, twenty-one miles to the westward, and reached them before noon. On our way we passed in sight of the Montemont and Jomard groups, each consisting of two low, wooded islets, similar to those which we had left. As the ship went along she raised prodigious numbers of flying fish in large scholes, closely watched by frigate-birds, boobies, and terns. The afternoon was ineffectually spent in searching for an anchorage, the pinnace and one of the cutters having been sent in-shore for that purpose. In the evening the anchor was let go after a cast of fifty fathoms, but slipped off the bank, and had to be hove up again. In company with the Bramble we passed the night in standing off and on the islands, directed by bright moonlight, and a fire on the westernmost of the group which the pinnace's people had been sent in to make.

The following day was spent in a similar manner, and with the like result. The Bramble, when ordered by signal to point out the anchorage which Lieut. Yule had found a week before, at once passed through an opening in the northern margin of the reef connected with the Duperré Isles, and brought up in the smooth and moderately deep water inside, but it was not judged safe for us to follow, so the pinnace was hoisted in-board, and the ship kept under weigh all night.

Aug. 6th.—We passed out to sea to the southward by a wide and clear channel between the Duperré and Jomard Islands. The former are five in number, all uninhabited, small, low, and thickly covered with trees. They extend over a space of about six miles on the northern margin of a large atoll or annular reef extending eleven miles in one direction and seven in another, with several openings leading into the interior, which forms a navigable basin afterwards called Bramble Haven. Inside the greatest depth found was twenty fathoms, with numerous small coral patches shewing themselves so clearly as easily to be avoided,—outside, the water suddenly deepens to no bottom with one hundred fathoms of line, at the distance of a mile from its edge.

For several days we continued making traverses off and on the line of barrier reefs extending to the westward, obtaining negative soundings, and occasionally communicating by signal with the Bramble, which was meanwhile doing the in-shore part of the work. The next islet seen was Ile Lejeune of D'Urville, situated in lat. 10° 11′ S. and long. 151° 50′ E., eight miles to the westward of the nearest of the Duperré group, with a wide intervening passage. The sea face of the barrier now becomes continuous for twenty-one miles further, its northern side broken into numerous openings, leading into shoal water. It is, in fact, an elongated, almost linear atoll, with islands scattered along its sheltered margin. After this, the barrier becomes broken up into a series of small reefs, with passages between, still preserving a westerly trend, until it ends in long. 150° 58′ E. Several small, low islets are scattered along its course; of these the Sandy Isles come first, three in number, two of them mere sand-banks, and the third thinly covered with trees, apparently a kind of Pandanus. The neighbouring Ushant Island (supposed to be that named Ile Ouessant by Bougainville) is larger and densely wooded, and still further to the westward we saw the two Stuers Islands, also low, and wooded. All those islets hitherto mentioned as occurring along the line of the barrier reef are of the same character,— low, of coral formation, and generally wooded—and so are two others situated a few miles to the north-ward of the reef, and unconnected with it. These last are Kosmann Island, in lat. 11° 4½′ S. and long. 151° 33′ E., and Imbert Island, situated thirteen miles further to the westward.

Aug. 11*th.*—To-day we came in sight of two groups of high rocky isles, very different from the low coral islets in the line of the barrier reef, which here ceases to shew itself above water. These are the Teste and Lebrun Islands of D'Urville, the latter two in number, and of small size (the westernmost, in lat. 10° 53' S. and long. 150° 59' E.), the former, a group of four, of which the largest measures two and a half miles in length, while the smallest is a remarkable pyramidal projection, to which the name of Bell Rock was given,—this last is situated in lat. 10° 57½' S. and long. 151° 2' E.

Aug. 12th.—We saw in the distance part of the high land of New Guinea in the neighbourhood of where its south-east cape has been conjectured to be, and approached within a few miles of the Dumoulin* Islands, a group of four rocky isles, the westernmost of which is 400 feet high, and less than a mile in length ; there are besides five rocks, some of con- siderable size. The Dumoulin Isles are inhabited, and appear fertile,—they are tolerably well-wooded with small trees and a sprinkling of cocoa-palms. In standing off for the night, the water suddenly shoaled from no bottom with 80 fathoms to casts of 16 and 12 fathoms, of coral, and sand and shells, and then deepened again as we went out. One is inclined to suspect that this may be a submarine extension of the barrier reef.

The Bramble meanwhile had been ordered in to look for anchorage, and found it under the lee of the largest island in 25 fathoms. She remained in that neighbourhood for several days while we were beating about at sea. Several of the Dumoulin

* The hydrographical engineer attached to D'Urville's last expedition, and the constructor of most of the charts published in the Hydrographical Atlas of " Voyage au Pole Sud, &c."

Islands proved to be inhabited, and the natives exhibited no hostile feeling towards the Bramble's people. A specimen of the rock, taken from the shore and given me by Lieutenant Yule, is a very curious siliceous breccia; when viewed from the sea I had observed the cliffs to exhibit horizontal and vertical fissures—apparently lines of cleavage—as I had seen assumed on various occasions during our last cruize by granite and porphyry. This, at least, indicated a great approaching change in the geological structure of the New Guinea Islands, contrasted with those of the Louisiade Group which had come under our observation.

CHAPTER VII.

August 17th.—WE are once more comfortably at
anchor after many dreary days at sea of thick
blowing weather* spent in sailing backwards and
forwards, daily tantalised by the sight of land,
which was approached only that we might stand
off again for the night. Yesterday afternoon the
Bramble was seen coming out from under the
largest of the Brumer Islands, and on her making
the usual signal for good anchorage, we followed

---

* In working to the eastward (in June) Bougainville for four
days had "the wind constantly blowing very fresh, at E.S.E.
and S.E." (just as we found it) "with rain; a fog so thick that,"
says he, "we were obliged to fire guns in order to keep company
with the Etoile; and lastly, a very great sea, which hove us
towards the shore. We could hardly keep our ground by plying,
being obliged to wear, and to carry but little sail."—Bougainville's
Voyage round the World. Translation by Forster, p. 308.

her in and brought up after sunset in 35 fathoms, mud, about a mile from the shore.

The island under which we thus anchored, is the westernmost and largest of a group of five, the next in size being about a mile in length, moderately high and wooded, and the remaining three mere rocks. The large Brumer Island is long and narrow, running E.N.E. and W.S.W., two miles and two-thirds in greatest width; it is situated in lat. 10° 45′ 30″ S. and long. 150° 23′ E. The whole island presents a luxuriant appearance, being covered with cocoa-palms and other trees, and on the high ground several large fenced enclosures of cultivated ground—where among other plants we could distinguish the banana and sugar-cane— attested the fertility of the soil. The western, and at present the leeward side of the island, as viewed from our anchorage exhibits the appearance of a broken ridge on its southern half with several eminences topped by immense detached blocks of rock, partially concealed by the trees,—to this, in the centre, succeeds a break occupied by a very low irregular cliff behind a bay with a sandy beach,— afterwards the land rises suddenly to form a hill, 665 feet in height, with a steep face to the north-west, and a gradual slope backwards,—and beyond this another hill, not so high (386 feet), but somewhat similar in form, shut out our further view in that direction. The mainland of New Guinea filled the back ground with a broken outline of ridges of wooded hills along the coast in front of a more distant and nearly continuous range of high mountains covered with trees up to their very summits.

Next morning we were visited by a party of natives from the neighbouring island, consisting of six men in a canoe, and one on a catamaran or raft. They were perfectly unarmed and came boldly alongside with a quantity of yams and cocoa-nuts for barter; when their stock was exhausted, they returned for more, and, accompanied by others, repeated the visit several times during the day. Although there was no obvious difference between these natives and those of the southern portion of the Louisiade, yet the catamaran was quite new to us, and the canoe differed considerably from any which we had seen before.

The first catamaran was only nine feet long,—it consisted of three thick planks lashed together, forming a sort of raft, which one man sitting a little behind the middle, with his legs doubled under him, managed very dexterously with his paddle. We afterwards saw others of a larger size, some of them capable of carrying a dozen people with their effects. One of this description is made of three logs—rarely two or four—laid side by ·side, and firmly secured to each other with strips of rattan at each end, and in two or three other places. The upper surface is smoothed down flat, and the central piece projects a little way at each end which usually shews some rude carving touched up with red and

white paint.   As the sea washes over a catamaran
during rough weather, on such an occasion a small
temporary stage is sometimes erected in the centre,
and on this the cargo is secured with strips of cane.

The canoe of this part of New Guinea is usually
about twenty-five feet in length, and carries seven
or eight people.   It is made of the trunk of a tree,
hollowed out like a long trough, roundly pointed at
each end, a foot and a half in extreme width, with
the sides bulging out below and falling in at top,
leaving only eight inches between the gunwales
which are strengthened by a pole running along
from end to end.   The ends—which are alike—are
carved like those of the catamaran in imitation of
the head of a turtle or snake, but more elaborately.
The outrigger consists of a float as long as the

canoe, attached by small sticks or pegs let into the wood to eight or nine supporting poles the inner ends of which rest in notches in both gunwales, and are secured there. A portion, or the whole of this framework, is carefully covered over with planks or long sticks, and occasionally a small stage is formed on the opposite side, over the centre of the canoe, projecting a little outwardly, with room upon it for two people to sit and paddle. The canoes of this description which we saw were not provided with any other sail than a small temporary one, made by interlacing the leaflets of the cocoa-palm, and stuck up on poles when going with the wind free. The paddles used here are similar in shape to those seen in the Louisiade Archipelago, with spear-shaped blades and slender handles, but are larger — measuring six feet in length—and of neater construction, the end of the handle being carved into some fanciful device.

About sunset, and when about to leave us, one of the Brumer Islanders, standing on a large catamaran alongside, put himself into a grotesque attitude, and commenced beating with his hand upon a large tin can which some one had given him, at the same time going through some of the motions of a dance. He seemed to be a most amusing vagabond, for, upon our drummer being set to work in the chains, after joining with the other natives in the first exclamations of surprise, he listened attentively for a little, and then struck up on his own extempore drum, keeping very good time and causing roars of laughter by his strange grimaces and antics. The effect of this pantomime was heightened by the style of painting adopted by the actor whose face had been blackened with charcoal, variegated by a white streak along the eyebrows turned down at the ends, and another along the cheeks passing round the chin.

Aug. 18*th.*—The boisterous state of the weather did not prevent the natives from repeatedly coming off to us with various articles of barter; and we were even visited by a party of seven men from Tissot Island, who paddled up on a catamaran five or six miles to windward against a strong breeze and current. After some little persuasion, several of them were induced to come on board and were shewn round the ship, presented with various articles, and dressed out with scraps of clothing of every description. At first they shewed symptoms of uneasiness, and made frequent protestations of friendship, as if the circumstance of our repeating them gave increased confidence. Their mode of salutation or expression of friendship consists in first touching the nose with the forefinger and thumb of one hand, and then pinching the skin on each side of the navel with the other, calling out at the same time, *magăsúga !* This habit resembles on one hand that of rubbing noses, so general in Polynesia,—and on the other, the custom of pinching the navel and repeating the name for that part, practised by the islanders of Torres Strait. At length our visitors withdrew, well pleased with their reception, during which their common exclamation indicative of surprise and delight, an *aö* long drawn out, was in constant requisition.

Aug. 19th.—A quantity of cooked yams in baskets and large earthen pots was brought off to-day by a party of natives, as if in acknowledgment of our civility to those whom we had invited on board yesterday. Nothing was asked for in return—a very unusual circumstance,—and that it was intended as a present was further shewn by their leaving a proportionate share on board the Bramble, and immediately pushing off for the Rattlesnake with the remainder, explaining that it was intended for us and could not be sold.

The weather being now favourable for communication with the shore, the two cutters were manned and armed for this purpose, and sent away in charge of Lieut. Simpson, and, as usual, I was one of the volunteers who joined the party. Two of the natives gladly went in one of the boats—the same two who had previously invited us on shore, as if to return our hospitality and point out the fresh water about which we had made repeated inquiries, our stock of that all-essential article being now much reduced, and the ship's company on an allowance of six pints each per diem. We landed at a little bay near the centre of the western side of the nearest and largest of the Brumer group. Although perfectly sheltered from the wind, a heavy swell broke upon the margin of a fringing coral reef running out fifty or sixty yards from the sandy beach and stretching across the bay. The boats were backed in from their anchors, and, after seven of us had got on shore by watching an opportunity to jump out up to the middle in water, and cross the reef, hauled out again to await our return.

Some women on the beach retired as we were about to land, but a number of boys and a few men received us, and after a preliminary halt to see that our guns were put to rights after the ducking, we all started together by a narrow path winding up a rugged wall of basaltic rock, fifty feet in height. From the summit a steep declivity of a couple of hundred yards brought us to the village of Tassai, shaded by cocoa-nut trees, and beautifully situated on a level space close to the beach on the windward side of the island, here not more than a quarter of a mile in width. No canoes were seen here, and a heavy surf broke on the outer margin of a fringing reef. On the outskirts of the village we met the women and remainder of the people, and were received without any signs of apprehension. One of our friends immediately got hold of a drum*—a hollow cylinder of palm-wood two feet and a half in length, and four inches in diameter, one end covered over with the skin of a large lizard,— and commenced beating upon it very vigorously with the palm of the hand, singing and dancing at the

* Represented in the uppermost figure on next page.

same time, as if in honour of our arrival. Each of us joined in the merriment as he came up, and in a short time the whole of Tassai was in an uproar. Among the natives every one seemed pleased, bustling about, watching our motions, examining our dress, and laughing and shouting immoderately as each new object was presented to his view. Meanwhile I wandered about the village, accompanied by some women and children, picking up at the same time materials for my vocabulary. One old dame brought me a cocoa-nut shell full of water which I returned after drinking some, but she pressed me in a very motherly way to put it into my bag, having doubtless imagined from our inquiries after water, that even a little constituted a valuable present. We had seen neither stream nor well upon the island, and besides, it is probable that the great abundance of cocoa-nuts enables them to subsist with very little water. We distributed among them some iron-hoop, knives, fish-hooks, and calico, to which I added a quantity of useful seeds,* which last were eagerly sought after when their use had been explained and understood.

The women shewed an unsual amount of curiosity, and were much pleased at the notice taken of them, for, on examining the curious tatooing of one, others immediately pressed forwards to shew me theirs, directing particular attention to the difference of patterns. This practice of tatooing the body—or marking it with colouring matter introduced into the skin by means of punctures or incisions—is rarely exhibited by the men, and in them is usually confined to a few blue lines or stars upon the right breast; in some instances, however, the markings consisted of a double series of large stars and dots stretching from the shoulder toward the pit of the stomach. Among the women the tatooing extends over the face, fore part of the arms, and whole front of body continued backwards a little way over the shoulders, usually, but not always, leaving the back untouched. The pattern for the body consists of series of vertical stripes less than an inch apart, connected by zigzag and

* Part of a large supply procured at Hobart Town by Capt. Stanley from the Government garden there. They were placed under my charge, and were sown wherever circumstances appeared favourable for their growth, chiefly on uninhabited islands, there seldom having been an opportunity of distributing them among the natives of the shores we visited.

other markings,—that over the face is more complicated, and on the fore arm and wrist it is
frequently so elaborate as to assume the appearance
of beautiful lace-work.

Unlike the men—whose only article of dress consists of a small breech-cloth of pandanus leaf passing
between the legs, and secured before and behind to
a string or other girdle round the waist—the females
wear petticoats *(noge)* of the same leaf, divided into
long grass-like shreds, reaching to the knee. That
worn by the girls consists merely of single lengths
made fast to a string which ties round the waist;
but the women wear a larger and thicker kind of
petticoat, composed of three layers of different degrees of fineness and lengths, forming as many
" flounces," the upper one of more finely divided
stuff, neatly plaited above, over a girdle of the same
tough bark *(barrai)* used in making their larger
kinds of rope. Two or three of these petticoats are
usually worn one over the other, and in cold or wet
weather the outer one is untied and fastened round
the neck, covering the upper part of the body like a
cape or short cloak. The hair of the women is also
usually but not invariably twisted up into " thrums"
like those of a mop, a style of dressing it here peculiar to the female sex.

Many pigs were running about the village—small
in size, lean and long legged, usually black, with
coarse bristles—also two or three dogs, similar to
those seen at Brierly Island. One young woman

was seen carrying about in her arms and fondling a very young pig—an incident which afforded us as much amusement as a lady's lap-dog, with one end of a ribbon round its neck and the other attached to a wasp-waisted damsel, would have caused among these utilitarian savages.

The village covers a space of about half an acre ; it consisted of twenty-seven huts built at right angles to each other, but without any other attempt at arrangement. These huts are of various sizes—the largest thirty-five feet long, twelve wide, and twenty-five high. All are constructed on a similar plan, being raised from the ground about four feet on posts, four, five, or six in number, passing through the same circular wooden discs seen at the Louisiade Archipelago, intended, I believe, to keep out rats or other vermin. The sides and roof are continuous, and slope sharply upwards, giving to an end view the appearance of an acute triangle, while a side view exhibits a long ridge rising suddenly at each end to a point and descending by a straight line of gable. The roof is neatly and smoothly thatched with grass, and the sides are covered in with sheets of a bark-like substance, probably the base of the leaf of the cocoa-nut tree flattened out by pressure. The entrance is at one end, overhung by the gable like a curtain, with a small stage to ascend by. I did not examine the interior of the houses, being desirous to avoid any cause of offence by exhibiting too much prying curiosity. From the accounts of

Hullmandel & Walton. lith.

others of the party it appears that there is a second
partial floor above the principal one ; they saw large
bundles of spears stowed along the sides of the hut
which they looked into, and some human skulls suspended near the entrance.*

After a very short stay of a quarter of an hour
only we returned by the path formerly taken, accompanied by about fifty men, women, and children,
and went on board the boats. During our visit we
had met with the most friendly reception ; no weapon
of any kind was seen in the hands of the natives
who at the same time probably thought us perfectly
unarmed, as they at first supposed our guns to be
instruments for carrying water in, and we had no
opportunity of shewing the effects of fire-arms without involving the risk of causing a tumult. The
anchor of one of the boats having caught the coral,
some delay was caused, during which an old man
from the beach swam off to her, as if he perfectly
understood what had happened, and, after diving
several times, cleared the anchor, for which he was
rewarded with an axe. His skill in diving was remarkable,—he went down feet foremost, apparently
without an effort, and after remaining below about
half a minute, came up shewing no signs of exhaus-

---

* These huts resemble in form some found on the Duke of
York and Bowditch Islands, in the western part of the Pacific,
300 miles to the northward of the Samoan group.—See Narrative
of the United States' Exploring Expedition, vol. v. p. 7 ; also
plate opposite p. 3.

tion. But all these natives appeared to feel as much
confidence afloat as on shore; and we had frequent
opportunities of observing their fearlessness of the
water, and dexterity in swimming and diving when
alongside the ship.

Aug. 20th.—It being considered probable that
the natives might be induced to part with some of
their pigs, a party was sent on shore, to endeavour
to procure some by barter. On landing, which was
effected with much less difficulty than yesterday
(for it was now high water, enabling the boats to
go over the reef although heavy rollers were coming
in), we found that most of the men were absent, and
the few remaining, although made to understand
what we wanted, did not appear to like our paying
a visit to their village, as if suspicious of our intentions towards the women, a circumstance which
Europeans must always be on their guard against
in dealing with savage tribes. Our stay therefore
was very short—not exceeding five minutes,—and
on the way back, besides picking up a few scraps
for my vocabulary from a number of women and
children in company, I procured a very fine white
Helix from the branch of a bread-fruit tree, and had
a brief opportunity of examining the rock of the
island. This is of volcanic origin, and consists of
a stratified earthy tufa and volcanic conglomerate,
hollowed out below by the sea, succeeded by a
harder vesicular rock above which one of the forms
of lava has been poured out.

On our return to the beach we found that scarcely any bartering had gone on, and that the exhibition of a number of axes and knives, had been attended with the bad effect of exciting the cupidity of the natives. Soon afterwards a canoe with people from the mainland arrived, and as anything but good feeling appeared to subsist, and we had failed in our object of getting the pigs, we left for the ship—and this was our last communication with the shore during our stay at this anchorage.

Aug. 22nd.—The most interesting occurrence of the day was the arrival from the main of a very large canoe, with twenty-six people on board.* When close to she shortened sail and attempted to paddle up, but being too unwieldy to stem the current, the end of a rope from the ship was carried out to her and she hauled up under our stern and made fast there. Besides the ordinary paddles we observed at each end two others of large size—probably used for steering with, pulled as oars, with cane gromets on the gunwale. We had not before seen so fine a sample of Papuans; several were elderly men of fine figure and commanding appearance. One man among them who sat alone upon a small raised stage over the platform appeared to exercise a considerable degree of authority over the rest; the only instance yet seen by us, either here or at the Louisiade, of any one assuming the functions

* Represented in the frontispiece.

of a chief.   He called a small canoe alongside, and
getting under the mizen chains attempted to climb
up at once, and appeared surprised that the privilege
of coming on board denied to the other natives was
not immediately extended to him.   He was, however, accidentally allowed to come up the side and
remain on deck for a short time.   He was a tall
slender man, of about forty years of age, with sharp
Jewish features,—his face and chest were painted
black, and he wore a crest of cassowary feathers
across his head.

This large canoe measured about forty feet in
length, and was constructed of a hollowed out tree
raised upon with large planks forming a long coffin-
like box, closed with high end boards elegantly
carved and painted.   Two rows of carved fishes ran
along the sides, and both ends were peaked, the bow
rising higher than the stern, and, like it, but more
profusely, decorated with carving painted red and
white, streamers of palm-leaf, egg-cowries, and
plumes of cassowary feathers.   The outrigger frame
work was completely covered over, forming a large
platform above the centre of which a small stage
rested on a strong projecting beam the outer end
of which was carved into the figure of a bird, while
the inner reached to the centre of the body of the
canoe, and served to support the mast.   The planks
forming the sides were strongly supported by knees
where each of the ten or twelve outrigger poles
passes through one side and rests against the other,

and some loose bottom boards form a partial shifting deck. The mast is supported above by two stays fore and aft, and below steps into a massive bent timber crossing the centre of the canoe, resting on the bottom, and is secured above to the inner end of the long cross beam by strong lashings, and some large wedges between it and one side. The sail is of great size, being as long as the platform, but both in construction and mode of management is precisely similar to that formerly described with reference to a canoe seen at Coral Haven, supposed to have come from Piron's Island.

A few days ago we saw another canoe closely resembling the above mentioned, but much smaller and carrying only eleven people. It exhibited, however, one peculiarity in the great breadth of beam amidships—amounting to four feet—which gave it much room for stowage and additional buoyancy.

Of late the number of natives daily coming off to the ship has rapidly increased, so as now to amount to upwards of 100 in about 15 canoes and catamarans. Those from Tissot Island and the mainland usually arrive in the forenoon, and, after an hour's stay, leave us for the northern village on the nearest Brumer Island, where they spend the the night and return the next morning with a fair wind. The noise and scrambling alongside when bartering is going on baffles all description,—besides the usual talking and shouting, they have a singular habit of directing attention to their wares by a loud, sharp *ss, ss,* a kind of hissing sound, equivalent to "look at this." In their bargaining the natives have generally been very honest, far more so than our own people whom I have frequently seen cheating them by passing off scraps of thin worthless iron, and even tin and copper, for pieces of hoop, the imposition not being found out until the property has changed hands. As at the Louisiade iron hoop is the article most prized by the natives, and is valued according to its width and thickness as a substitute for the stone-heads of their axes. They also shewed great eagerness to obtain our hatchets and fish-hooks, but attached little value to calico, although a gaudy pattern, or bright colour, especially red, was sure to arrest attention; but in such matters they are very capricious. Even glass bottles were prized, probably as a substitute for obsidian or volcanic glass, portions of which I saw among them, used in shaving, as was explained to me, and probably also for carving in wood.

Aug. 25th.—Yesterday and to-day, in addition to upwards of a hundred natives alongside bartering, we were honoured with visits from several parties of the Tassai ladies, in whose favour the prohibition to come on board was repealed for the time. The young women were got up with greater attention to dress and finery than when seen on shore, and some had their face blackened as if to heighten their attractions. The outer petticoat, worn on gala days such as this, differs from the common sort in being much finer in texture and workmanship, besides being dyed red and green, with intermediate bands of straw colour and broad white stripes of palm-leaf. It is made of long bunches of very light and soft shreds, like fine, twisted grass, apparently the prepared leaf of a calamus or rattan. None of the women that I saw possessed even a moderate share of beauty (according to our notions) although a few had a pleasing expression and others a very graceful figure, but, on the other hand, many of the boys and young men were strikingly handsome. We had no means of forming a judgment regarding the condition of the women in a social state, but they appeared to be treated by the men as equals and to exercise considerable influence over them. On all occasions they were the loudest talkers, and seemed to act from a perfect right to have every thing their own way. It is worthy of mention, that, even in their own village, and on all other occasions where we had an opportunity of observing them, they acted with perfect propriety, and although some indecent allusions were now and then made by the men, this was never done in the presence of the women. Of their marriages we could find out nothing,—one man appeared to have two wives, but even this was doubtful. The circumstance of children being daily brought off by their fathers to look at the ship, and the strange things there, indicated a considerable degree of parental affection.

Returning to our visitors :—the fiddle, fife, and drum were put in requisition, and a dance got up to amuse them. The women could not be persuaded to join, but two of the men treated us to one of their own dances, each having been previously furnished with a native drum or *baiătŭ*. They advanced and retreated together by sudden jerks, beating to quick or slow time as required, and chaunting an accompanying song, the cadence rising and falling according to the action. The attitude was a singular one— the back straight, chin protruded, knees bent in a crouching position, and the arms advanced ; on another occasion, one of the same men exhibited himself before us in a war dance. In one hand he held a large wooden shield, nearly three feet in length and rather more than one in width, and in the other a formidable looking weapon two feet in length—a portion of the snout of a saw-fish with long sharp teeth projecting on each side. Placing himself in a crouching attitude, with one hand covered by the shield, and holding his weapon in a position to strike, he advanced rapidly in a succession of short bounds, striking the inner side of the shield with his left knee at each jerk, causing the large cowries hung round his waist and ankles to rattle violently. At the same time with fierce gestures he loudly chaunted a song of defiance. The remainder of the panto-mime was expressive of attack and defence, and exultation after victory. But a still more curious dance was one performed a few nights ago by a party of natives which had left the ship after sunset and landed abreast of the anchorage. On seeing a number of lights along the beach, we at first thought they proceeded from a fishing party, but on looking through a night-glass, the group was seen to consist of above a dozen people, each carrying a blazing torch, and going through the movements of a dance. At one time they extended rapidly into line, at another closed, dividing into two parties, advancing and retreating, crossing and re-crossing, and mixing up with each other. This continued for half an hour, and having apparently been got up for our amusement, a rocket was sent up for their's, and a blue-light burned, but the dancing had ceased, and the lights disappeared.

In the evening when the natives were leaving for the shore, one of them volunteered to remain on board on the understanding that some of us should accompany him to Tassai, where, he explained, there would be plenty of dancing and eating, enumerating pigs, dogs, yams, and cocoa-nuts, as the component parts of the feast. He was taken down to the wardroom, and shortly underwent a complete metamorphosis, effected by means of a regatta shirt of gaudy pattern, red neckcloth, flannel trousers, a faded drab "Taglioni" of fashionable cut buttoned up to the throat, and an old black hat stuck on one side of his woolly head. Every now and then he renewed his invitation to go on shore, but was satisfied when given to understand that our visit must be deferred till the morrow.　He was a merry, active, good-humoured fellow, and gave us a number of songs, one of which I wrote down.　Although unfortunately I cannot give an accompanying translation, yet this song exhibits the remarkable softness of the language from the great number of vowels.

> Ama watúya boyama
> Manyúre gerri gege údaeno
> Dagi ginoa dagi gino ama
> 　　Watu yebbo.
>
> Manyure gerri gege údaeno
> Dagi egino da' gino ama
> 　　Watu yebbo—watu yebbo.

Most of them—perhaps all—were extempore, as on turning his attention to the moon, he struck up a song in which the name of that body was frequently mentioned.　He was treated to an exhibition of the magic lantern in the cabin by Capt. Stanley, and a rocket was sent up to his great astonishment and admiration, which he found words to express in "*kaiwa*" (fire) "*kaiwa, oh! dim dim!*"

Aug. 26th.— Our guest became very uneasy when he saw no canoes from the island coming off, and no symptoms of lowering a boat to land him.　His invitation to the shore and pantomime of killing a pig were repeated time after time, and he became very despondent.　Two canoes from the mainland came alongside, and he got into one which shoved off, but quickly returned and put him on board, as they were not going to the island.　The poor fellow at last appeared so miserable, being actually in tears, that a boat was sent to put him on shore abreast of the ship, and, when he landed, two young women and a child came running up to meet him. A number of natives on the sandy beach were anxiously watching the boat, as if the long detention of the man on board the ship had made them suspicious of our treatment of him.

Without entering into details of uninteresting daily occurrences, I may here give a general account of such circumstances regarding the natives as have not previously been alluded to or insufficiently described. It would be difficult to state the peculiarities of this portion of the Papuan* Race (including also the inhabitants of the Louisiade) for even the features exhibit nearly as many differences as exist among a miscellaneous collection of individuals of any European nation. They appear to me to be resolvable into several indistinct types, with intermediate gradations; thus occasionally we met with strongly marked Negro characteristics, but still more frequently with the Jewish cast of features, while every now and then a face presented itself which struck me as being perfectly Malayan. In general the head is narrow in front, and wide and

---

* As the term Papuan when applied to a Race of Mankind is not strictly correct, I may here mention that whenever used in this work, it includes merely the woolly or frizzled haired inhabitants of the Louisiade, S.E. coast of New Guinea, and the islands of Torres Strait.

very high behind, the face broad from the great projection and height of the cheek bones and depression at the temples; the chin narrow in front, slightly receding, with prominent angles to the jaw; the nose more or less flattened and widened at the wings, with dilated nostrils, a broad, slightly arched and gradually rounded bridge, pulled down at the tip by the use of the nose-stick; and the mouth rather wide, with thickened lips, and incisors flattened on top as if ground down.

Although the hair of the head is almost invariably woolly, and, if not cropped close, or shaved, frizzled out into a mop, instances were met with in which it had no woolly tendency, but was either in short curls, or long and soft without conveying any harsh feeling to the touch.   In colour too it varied, although usually black, and when long, pale or reddish at the tips;* yet some people of both sexes were observed having it naturally of a bright red colour, but still woolly.   The beard and moustache, when present, which is seldom the case, are always scanty, and there is very little scattered hair upon the body.

The colour of the skin varies from a light to a dark copper colour, the former being the prevailing hue; individuals of a light yellowish brown hue are often met with, but this colour of the skin is not accompanied by distinctive features.

* Probably artificially produced, as is known to be effected by means of lime water, by the inhabitants of the north-west coast of New Guinea.

The average stature of these Papuans is less than our own, being only about five feet four inches; this did not appear to be the case when seen alongside, but on board the ship, and especially when clothed, the difference became very apparent. Although well made, and far surpassing us in agility, they were our inferiors in muscular power. Their strength was tested by means of a deep-sea lead weighing twenty-two pounds which none of the natives could hold out at arm's length, although most of us who tried it experienced no difficulty in sustaining the weight for a few seconds.

Among the people who came alongside the ship one day we noticed two cases of that kind of *elephantiasis* called "Barbadoes Leg," in one combined with enormous distention of the scrotum, which was larger than a man's head, and studded with warts. One of these unfortunate objects had both legs much swollen, especially about the ankle, where the skin was almost obliterated by large scab-like warts, the other, besides the diseased leg, had a huge tumour on the inner side of the right thigh.

The weapons procured at this place consist of spears, clubs, a wooden sword, and a shield. Of the first there are several kinds, all larger and heavier than those obtained at the Louisiade, but, like them, made of hard, heavy, well polished cocoa-nut wood. The spears vary in length from nine to eleven feet, with a diameter, where thickest, of rather more than an inch. From their great weight it would scarcely be possible to throw them with effect to a greater distance than from fifteen to twenty yards, and, judging from the signs and gestures of the natives on various occasions when explaining their mode of warfare, they are also used for charging and thrusting with, the neighbourhood of the armpit being the part aimed at as most vulnerable.

The spear in most common use tapers to a point at each end, more suddenly in front and very gradually behind where it usually terminates in a small knob with two or three ornamental rings. Sometimes a gromet, or ring of cordage, is worked upon the spear near one end, to prevent the hand slipping when making a thrust. There are many other kinds of spears variously barbed on one or both sides near the head. The fishing spear is usually headed by a bundle of about four or six slender, sharp pointed pieces of wood, two feet in length, sometimes barbed at the point.

We obtained three clubs here—the only ones seen—one, closely resembling the stone-headed club of Darnley Island, consists of a wooden shaft, four feet long, sharp pointed at one end and at the other passing through a hole in the centre of a sharp-edged circular disk of quartz, shaped like a quoit, four inches in diameter; the second is twenty-seven inches in length, cut out of a heavy piece of wood, leaving a slender handle and cylindrical head, three and a half inches long, studded with knobs; the

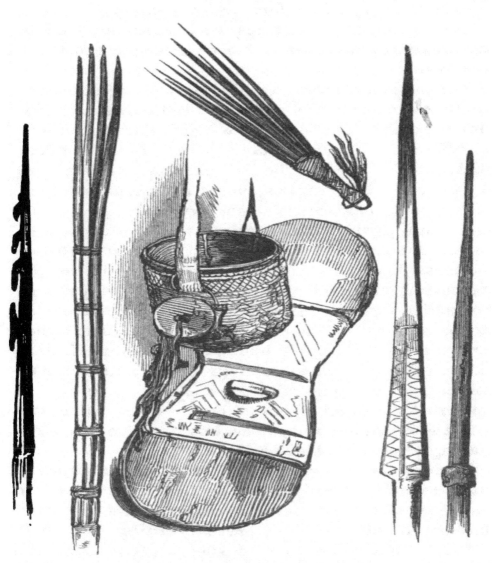

Spears, Shield, Basket, and Comb.
New Guinea.

remaining one, a less formidable weapon than the others, is flat on both sides, with a serrated edge, and measures twenty-two inches in length and three in width.

The ornaments worn on this part of the coast are in general so precisely similar to those of the Louisiade, already described, that a brief allusion to them is sufficient. In both places we saw the same nose-sticks, combs stuck in the hair, flat circular earrings, woven and shell armlets, round ornaments made of melon shell, necklaces of dog's teeth and black seeds, and white cowries strung round the legs, arms, and neck. I observed here none of the human jawbones worn as bracelets so frequently met with in the Louisiade, nor did painting the body appear to be carried to the same extent, although the mode of doing so was the same. Here too we sometimes saw the hair collected and twisted behind into a single or double queue, and procured a neatly constructed bushy wig of frizzled hair. A girdle of split rattan wound about a dozen times round the waist is in common use here, but I do not recollect having seen it in the Louisiade.

Among other articles of native manufacture I may mention large baked earthen pots * used in cooking, also very neatly made round flat-bottomed baskets in sets of four, partially fitting into each other, with a woven belt to suspend them from the

* Similar to that figured on p. 261.

shoulders by,—in these various small articles are carried, among them the spatula and calabash, with lime to be used in betel chewing—and a netted bag, a foot and a half in width and one in depth. Their rope is beautifully made of the long tough stringy bark of a tree, strongly twisted and laid up in three strands, and for finer lines and twine a kind of flax, resembling the New Zealand, but still more the Manila sort, is used here. The finest sample of the prepared material which I saw measured eleven feet in length, and consisted of a bundle of rather fine white fibres. Although very much coarser than our hemp, it is of nearly uniform size, and possesses considerable strength, but breaks easily when knotted. We saw it in considerable quantity, but had no means of ascertaining the plant from which it is derived, probably, however, a banana of some kind. We occasionally saw pieces of a white soft papery cloth, apparently similar to the tapa of Polynesia, and like it made of the inner bark of some small tree, but it did not appear to be applied to much use.

In the Louisiade we had not observed the betel pepper, but here it was found in common use—both the leaf and green fruit, especially the latter, being added to the lime and areca-nut. Still betel chewing, although a very general habit, is by no means universally practised, for many elderly people retained the original whiteness of the teeth. By the males it appears to be adopted only after attaining the state of manhood, and among the females is almost entirely confined to the old women.

The fondness of these people for flowers and strong-scented plants is remarkable,—they wear them in their hair, thrust under the armlets and girdle, or as garlands round the neck. Among the chief favourites may be mentioned an amaranth with purple leaves, giving out a very rich colour upon pressure being applied, and a species of mint-like herb which they dry in bunches, and carry about with them.

In addition to the drum formerly mentioned, and large shells—*Cassis* or *Triton*—with a hole at one end, used as trumpets, we saw a small Pandean pipe made of portions of reed of different lengths, and a tube of bamboo, two feet long, which gives out a sound like a horn when blown into.

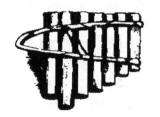

The staple article of food is the yam, which is produced here in great abundance, of large size, and excellent quality. Several other tubers, or roots, are eaten. Among them is that of a species of *Calladium*, which requires much cooking to destroy its acridity. The cocoa-nut tree grows everywhere. In the canoes we saw abundance of sugar-cane in pieces two feet in length and an inch in thickness, and the natives brought off to us bananas, bread-fruit, mangos, and prepared arrow-root. To a certain extent also the natives feed upon fish, judging from the nets and fishing-spears seen among them. The former, although frequently thirty or forty feet in length, did not exceed eighteen inches in depth,— they have small meshes, thin triangular wooden floats, and shells at the bottom as sinkers. Although we saw many pigs on shore in the village, only one was obtained by barter, in this one a spear wound behind the shoulder was made alongside the ship before handing it on board, but for what purpose we could not understand, as it did not kill the animal. Dogs also I have reason to believe are occasionally eaten, but whether cannibalism is ever practised by these people is a question which we have not the means of settling, as no evidence bearing upon the point could be obtained.

August 29th.—During our stay of thirteen days at this anchorage the wind has usually been strong from East to E. S. E., with dull, gloomy, squally weather, and occasionally showers of drizzling rain. To-day, however, the rain was so heavy that we caught seven tons in the awning. To this haziness, which by obscuring distant objects was unfavourable for surveying purposes, we owed our long detention here. As our intercourse with the shore was limited to the two brief visits formerly mentioned, I made no addition to the collection, with the exception of a solitary Helix, nor was anything of zoological interest brought off by the natives, except a string of heads of a species of hornbill (*Buceros plicatus*), and feathers of a cassowary, a scarlet lory, and a few other birds.   No fish were caught at the anchorage, probably on account of the nature of the bottom—a tenacious, greenish, muddy clay—and the strength of the current which prevented our lines from resting on the bottom.   Observations made with the lead alongside at the time of high and low water indicated by the shore shewed in thirteen days' observations a rise and fall of only from two to six feet.   Neither during the ebb nor the flood tide was there any appreciable difference in the direction of the current at our anchorage which set constantly to the westward between West and W. S. W., at the rate of from one to one-and-a-half knots an hour.   This current may reasonably be conjectured to come from the northward and sweep round the S. E. cape of New Guinea (distant from this anchorage about fifty miles), thus making it appear probable that a clear passage exists between the S. E. extreme of New Guinea and the western termination of the Louisiade Archipelago : indeed so far as Lieut. Yule's observations were carried in this direction no reefs were seen to impede his progress to the north-east.

Sept. 4th.—Five days ago we sailed from the Brumer Islands, and continued running lines of soundings off and on the coast, the in-shore details being left as usual to the Bramble.   On one occasion, while within a few miles of the shore, the water suddenly shoaled to twelve, ten, and six fathoms, rock or coral, although half an hour before no

bottom could be got with a hundred fathoms of line,
—apparently an indication of a submarine barrier,
more or less continuous, running at a variable
distance from the shore, and following the general
trend of the coast.   The appearance of the land seen
lately is very fine : the coast being backed by ranges
of high mountains presenting a very diversified outline ; one of them, named upon the chart Cloudy
Mount, attains an elevation of 4477 feet.   Yesterday and to-day great numbers of a storm petrel
(*Thalassidroma leucogastra*) have been following
in our wake.   This afternoon, while off the eastern
end of the bay called by Bougainville the "Cul de
sac de l'Orangerie," the Bramble was signalled to
lead in towards the land off which we anchored at
9 p.m. in 30 fathoms.

From our anchorage we next morning saw on
Dufaure Island, from which we were distant about
three miles, a village in a grove of cocoa-nut trees
behind a sandy beach, and the natives came off in
considerable numbers bringing large quantities of
cocoa-nuts and bread-fruit ;* they did not appear
however to have any yams.   Two or three small
pigs, of the same description as that hitherto seen
(*Sus Papuensis*), were procured ; and we obtained
two fine live opossums, of a rare and singular kind
(*Cuscus maculatus*), for an axe a-piece.   They ap-

* This was of smaller size than it attains in the South Sea
Islands ; we cooked it in various ways but failed to make
it palatable.

peared to be quiet gentle animals, until much irritated, when they bite hard. We fed them at first on ripe cocoa-nuts, of which they were very fond; but latterly they became accustomed to pea-soup. They spent most of the day in sleep in a corner of the hen-coop where they were kept, each on its haunches with the tail coiled up in front, the body arched, and the head covered by the fore paws and doubled down between the thighs; at night, however, they were more active and restless, their large reddish yellow eyes being then obscured by the dilated pupil, which during the day appears as a narrow vertical line. One was frequently taken on deck towards evening and allowed to climb about the rigging, moving very slowly, and endeavouring to get up as high as possible.

The natives resemble those seen at Brumer islands (from which we were distant about thirty-six miles) so closely that I saw no points regarding them deserving of separate notice, and their language is the same, judging from a small vocabulary of about seventy words. The only manufactured article new

to us was a small wooden pillow* about a foot long and six inches high, with a slight concavity above to receive the neck of the person using it. Both women and children came off with the men to traffic with us and look at the ship, but none could be tempted to come on board, although they paddled up alongside without the slightest hesitation. We were frequently solicited to accompany them on shore, but no one was allowed to leave the ship.

The northern shores of the Cul de Sac are low and wooded, forming an extensive tract of level land stretching backwards towards the mountains, with a large opening at its eastern end, which is probably the mouth of a great river. The Bramble was sent to examine this bay, but the shoalness of the water, and the unfavourable nature of the weather prevented the completion of this work. During her absence a large canoe was seen in the bay, differing from all those hitherto observed in having a triangular or latteen sail set with the apex downwards, thus resembling those in use on the north coast of New Guinea, among some of the Malay Islands, and those of the Viti Archipelago.

The weather, since leaving Brumer Islands, has usually been gloomy, with frequent rain, occasionally very heavy, and a close muggy feeling in the atmosphere as if one were living in a vapour bath; the

* Wooden pillows are also in use in some of the islands of Polynesia and in New Caledonia.

temperature on board ship ranged between 72° and 83°. During our five days' stay off Dufaure Island we were daily employed in catching rain water for ship's use, being on reduced allowance of that necessary article. The wind throughout has been steady at S.E., occasionally varying a point or two towards east.

Sept. 18*th.*—For the last three days the coast has appeared as a strip of low land, backed by mountain ranges of moderate elevation.* We observed several openings, apparently creeks or mouths of rivers, and saw much smoke and some canoes, but our distance from the shore was too great to allow of communication. In the evening we stood off to seaward, and during the night, while trying to avoid it, probably passed over the assigned position of a reef laid down on one of the charts as having been seen in 1804, but without being able to confirm or disprove its existence.†

* From the haze involving distant objects—less frequent (as we afterwards had reason to believe) during the westerly monsoon—the much higher Owen Stanley Range was not then visible; it had also, probably from the same cause, quite escaped the notice of D'Urville who passed this portion of the coast at the distance of about eight or nine miles.

† Although this reef does not exist in the position assigned to it, I may state that its presence upon the charts rests upon the authority of Coutance; Freycinet, rejecting Coutance's longitude of Cape Deliverance and adopting that of D'Entrecasteaux, has laid down the reef in question as bearing W.S.W. from Point Hood, at a distance of twelve leagues. Another but smaller reef is stated on the same authority to exist five leagues S.E. ¼ E. from Cape Rodney.

Sept. 19th.—Passed Mount Astrolabe, a series of long flat-topped ridges parallel with the coast, but were unable clearly to identify the Cape Passy of D'Urville where his running survey terminated, and where the Astrolabe and Zelée bore away to the westward for Torres Strait.

Sept. 20th.—During the forenoon the Bramble was observed to windward, and in the afternoon she was sent in-shore to look for anchorage. Following her we stood in towards a remarkable headland (365 feet high) which afterwards received the name of Redscar Head, from the reddish colour of its cliffs. At the distance of six and a half miles from the shore we struck soundings in twenty-seven fathoms, and soon afterwards crossed a narrow ridge of coral, with only five fathoms over it; after this the bottom consisted of tenacious mud, and we carried in from twenty-two to eighteen fathoms, in the last of which we anchored two miles and two-thirds off the point.

When Lieut. Yule came on board we heard that since we left the Bramble near Dufaure Island to do the in-shore work, he had on one occasion an affray with the natives in the neighbourhood of the Toulon Islands. When the Bramble was nearly becalmed close in-shore, several canoes with about thirty people, including several women and children, came off to barter. A small pig* was handed up

* As has often happened the bone of contention did not rest with the belligerents, for the pig was eventually handed over to me

into the chains, but, owing to an unavoidable occurrence, no return was made for it, upon which the owner snatched the cap from off the head of a marine attending at the gangway. The canoe which had brought the pig then shoved off, and, on being directed by gestures to return the cap, one man stood up and poised his spear, and the others got their arms ready. Several musket shots were fired into the canoe from a distance of six or seven yards, but, regarding the effect, conflicting statements have been made. No resistance was attempted, as, after the first shot, some of the natives jumped into the water and all made off in confusion, which was further increased when a round shot was fired in the direction of a distant canoe coming out from the shore.

Sept. 21st.—Took a passage in a boat sent with Lieut. Simpson to get a round of angles on one of three neighbouring islands (afterwards called Pariwara, the native name), situated two miles and a half N.W. from Redscar Point, with which they appear formerly to have been continuous, and, like it, are remarkable for their red and white cliffs. The largest, that on which we landed, is only three-fourths of a mile in length. In shape it is somewhat triangular : one side is formed by a rounded ridge, the highest point of which is 234 feet in height, with irregular cliffs along the sea margin; the opposite

and prepared as a specimen, now in the British Museum, the only *Sus Papuensis* in England at the present time.

angle is occupied by a rounded hill projecting as a
headland with rocky cliffs; and these two opposite
portions are connected by low land forming a sandy
beach on two of the sides. The island is covered
with long coarse grass growing in tufts; there are
also some pandanus trees of two kinds (*P. spiralis*
and *P. pedunculata*), and some low brush of stunted
bushy trees, their tops matted together, and indicating by the direction in which their branches are
bent that the prevailing wind is from the south-east.

Strictly speaking, there is no soil upon the island:
what may, however, be considered as such consists
of the disintegrated calcareous rock, on the low part
mixed up with sand. This rock, acted upon by the
weather, has a tendency to fall down in large
masses, leaving cliffs, steep and rugged in some
places and smooth in others; in colour it varies
from white to red, and is usually of a light pink.
Behind one of the beaches, a few feet distant from
high water mark, I observed a bank twelve feet high
of slightly agglutinated coral sand in parallel beds,
mixed up with large depositions of weather-worn
shells: *Tridacna, Hippopus, Strombus, &c.*, all of
species now living on the reef. At one end this
deposit appears to have been tilted up, forming a
slight ridge stretching across the low part of the
island. The shores in some places are fringed with
coral conglomerate composed of shells and sand,
fragments of coral, and rolled pieces of rock from
above. The reef surrounding the islands does not

dry at low water, and in crossing it in the boat very little live coral was observed, except on the outer margin, outside of which the bottom is a tenacious mud, effervescing on the application of hydrochloric acid.

I collected a few plants, among which are a yellow flowered *Cleome,* a purple *Pongamia, Convolvulus multivalvis, Evolvulus villosus, Guettarda speciosa, &c.* The only birds seen were a white-headed eagle and an osprey, neither of which were molested although the latter frequently came within shot, and followed me as if from motives of curiosity. Almost the only insects seen were small grass-hoppers, rising in numbers at every step, and green ants which have nests in the bushes, and appear identical with those of the Louisiade and Australia.

No fresh water was found here. Some recent traces of natives were met with—including two fire places where turtle and fish had been cooked on a framework of sticks over a fire,—precisely similar to one of large size, formerly seen on the Duchâteau Islands. I saw many places where turtle eggs had been dug out of the sand behind the beach, where besides were numerous burrows of a maritime crab (*Ocypode cursor*), which also appeared to feed upon the eggs—judging from the quantity of empty shells about the holes of those creatures.

Of the two remaining islands of the group, one, less than a quarter of a mile long, is covered with trees, probably a *Bombax* or *Erythrina*,—at this time destitute of leaves,—on the other is a high bare rock with three other small detached, needle-shaped ones lying off it. The observations with the theodolite having been completed we obtained some soundings and returned to the ship.

The view we had to-day from the Pariwara Islands was not so interesting as I had expected. The shores of the bay stretching to the northward of Redscar Head for many miles are low and covered with tall trees behind a strip of sandy beach. At the back of the point in the corner of the bay, we saw an opening two hundred yards wide, with tall mangroves on the northern bank, apparently one of the mouths of a river traversing the great extent of low wooded country behind. A very large fire two or three miles behind the beach, sending up great volumes of smoke, might have been intended for a signal, but neither canoes nor natives were seen during our absence from the ship.

Sept. 24th.—A canoe with twelve young men and lads came off from the shore, and approached within two hundred yards of the ship, but although tempted by the exhibition of a large piece of red cloth, they would come no closer. Their visit was apparently prompted by mere curiosity as they had nothing to barter with. These natives closely resembled the other Papuans seen to the eastward, but were smaller in stature, and wore the hair frizzled up into a mop projecting backwards, nor had

I before seen in one canoe so many handsome faces. As a breech-cloth they wore a narrow strip of white cloth passing between the legs and secured to a string round the waist, but this was too narrow to serve as a fig-leaf.   Among their ornaments we saw necklaces of small white cowries, and round flat pieces of shell two inches in diameter worn on the breast, also black, tightly fitting, woven armlets, in which they had stuck bunches of apparently the same purple odoriferous amaranth seen elsewhere, while other tufts of this plant were attached to the ankles and elbows.   The canoe was nearly of the same description as those commonly seen at the Brumer and Dufaure Islands, but the outrigger float was rather shorter, having only five poles to support it instead of seven or eight, and the bow and stern,

especially the former, much sharper and more raking. On the side opposite to the outrigger there was a small slightly projecting stage of two planks only. The paddles were six and a half feet in length, much clumsier than those seen in other parts of New Guinea, and without the carving on the handle, the blade also differed slightly in shape, being more elliptical. After paddling inshore a short distance they made sail and landed near the point. The sail resembled the common one of the Louisiade, being long, narrow, square at the ends, and stretched between two yards or masts, and in setting was merely stuck upon end and supported by guys fore and aft.

During our stay at this anchorage we had fine weather, with light variable winds of short duration, generally from the westward, but sometimes from the northward, and the thermometer ranged between 77° and 84°.

Sept. 25th.—Weighed in the afternoon with a very light air from S.W., and stood to the N.W., but by sunset, when we anchored in 27 fathoms mud, we had made only about eight miles. The weather was very sultry all day with the thermometer from 82° to 84° in the shade. In the evening we got a land breeze from about east, which lasted most of the night.

Sept. 26th.—Soon after daylight we were visited by a party of natives who came from an opening in the low land at the north-east corner of the bay—

apparantly the mouth of a large river. They were in three canoes carrying respectively seven, four, and three people, and paddled up alongside without hesitation, appearing anxious to be admitted on board, holding on by the chains and peeping into the ports in a most inquisitive manner. With the exception of two or three cocoa-nuts nothing was brought to barter with, but they readily parted with bows and arrows, of which they had a very large supply. These bows appear to be made of the hard heavy wood of the cocoa-nut tree, pointed at each end, and varying in length from five to six feet, with a greatest width of an inch and a quarter and thickness of five-eighths. The string is a strip of rattan three-eighths of an inch wide. The arrows are precisely similar to those used by the Torres Strait Islanders, consisting of a head of cocoa-nut wood, nine to eighteen inches in length, shipped into a light reed $2\frac{1}{2}$ to $3\frac{1}{2}$ feet in length, and secured by a neat cane plaiting. They are variously barbed on the edges in one or more series, or furnished with constrictions at short intervals which would cause a piece readily to break off in a wound and remain there. Some were headed with a piece of bamboo shaped like a gouge or scoop, and several other varieties were observed. This is the first occasion of our meeting with these weapons, which appear almost completely to have superseded the spear of which only a few small ones were seen in the canoes. In exchange for their bows and arrows the natives attached most value to articles of clothing of every description. Glass bottles were also eagerly sought after—but iron was not prized—indeed its use appeared to be unknown, nor had they any name for it. While leaning out of one of the wardroom ports, and getting words from a very intelligent native whose attention I secured by giving him various little presents from time to time, I had occasion to point to a bamboo scoop* lying in the canoe in order to get its name. The man, to my surprise, immediately bit off a narrow strip from one side, as if to sharpen the edge, and taking up a piece of stick, shewed me that this scoop was used as a knife. Not to be outdone I took one of our common knives and cut away vigorously at a piece of wood to shew the superiority of our knives over his one; he appeared suddenly to become terrified, talked vehemently to the others, drew their attention to me, and repeated my motions of cutting the wood, after which his canoe pushed off from the ship's side. My friend refused to accept of the knife—as I afterwards found the natives had also done to other people when iron implements were offered them—nor would he pay any further attention to my attempts to effect a reconciliation.

The greatest peculiarity among these people is their mode of dressing the hair; it is usually shaved off the temples and occasionally a little way up the

* Resembling that figured in Jukes' Voyage of the Fly, vol. i. p. 277,—but smaller.

forehead, then combed out at length, and tied midway with a string, leaving one part straight, and
the remainder frizzled out into a mop projecting
horizontally backwards. Some also had a long
pigtail hanging down behind, in one case decorated
with a bunch of dog's teeth at the end. Across the
forehead they wore fillets of small shells strung
together over a broad white band of some leafy substance. The septum of the nose was perforated,
and some wore a long straight nose-stick of bone
with black bands. All our visitors had their teeth
darkened with the practice of betel chewing,—we saw
them use the leaf of the betel pepper, the green areca
nut, and lime, the last carried in a small calabash
with a spatula.

We had been becalmed all the morning, but before
noon the sea-breeze set in from the S. S. E., and we

got under weigh, ran past S. W. Cape, and anchored in 22 fathoms mud, off a large island afterwards named in honour of Lieut. Yule.

Sept. 27th.—This has proved a very uneasy anchorage under the combined influence of a strong breeze from the south-east and a heavy sea. At one, p.m., we got under weigh in company with the Bramble, and left the coast of New Guinea, running to the westward for Cape York, in order to meet the vessel with our supplies from Sydney.

Next evening Bramble Cay was seen on our weather beam; being so low and so small an object, we had nearly missed it. We hauled upon a wind immediately but could not fetch its lee, so anchored two and-a-half miles N. W. by W. from it. Great numbers of boobies and noddies came about us, but our distance from the shore was too great and our stay too short to send on shore for bird's eggs.

Sept. 29th.—With a strong south-easterly breeze we passed to the westward of Campbell and Stephens' Islands, the Bramble leading, and anchored in the evening near Marsden Island. On Campbell Island, numbers of the natives came down to the edge of the reef, waving to us as we passed by, and inviting us to land. There were many cocoa-nut trees, and we saw a village on the north-west side of the island, beautifully situated on the shady skirts of the wood. The huts resemble those of Darnley Island, being shaped like a haycock or bee-hive, with a projecting central pole ornamented with a

large shell or two attached to it.   Most of the huts
were situated in small enclosures, and there were
other portions of ground fenced in with tall bamboo
paling.

On the following day the Bramble* left us for
Booby Island, to call at the "post-office" there,
and rejoin company at Cape York, and we reached
as far as the neighbourhood of Cocoa-nut Island at
noon, passing close to Arden Island, then covered
with prodigious numbers of blue and white herons,
small terns, curlews, and other waders.

Oct. 1st.—We had a fine breeze and pleasant
weather, and in the afternoon reached our former
anchorage in Evans' Bay, Cape York, and moored
ship in seven fathoms.   A party was immediately
sent to examine the water-holes, which promised,
after a little clearing out, as abundant a supply as
they afforded us last year.   We met some of the
natives who came down to the rocks as the boat
landed, and among them I saw many old acquaint-
ances who joyfully greeted us.

* On his return, Lieut. Yule reported that the boats of an
American whaler, lost on the Alert Reef (outside the Barrier),
had reached Booby Island, and the crews had been saved from
starvation by the depot of provisions there.   That this supply
will be renewed from time to time is most likely, as the Legislative
Council of New South Wales, last year, voted the sum of £50
for provisions to be left on Booby Island for the use of ship-
wrecked people.

CHAPTER VIII.

ON the day after our arrival at Cape York the vessel from Sydney with our supplies anchored beside us, and besides provisions and stores, we had the additional pleasure of receiving five months' news from home.

On Oct. 16th, a startling incident occurred to break the monotony of our stay. In the afternoon some of our people on shore were surprised to see a young white woman come up to claim their protection from a party of natives from whom she had recently made her escape, and who, she thought, would otherwise bring her back. Of course she received every attention, and was taken on board the ship by the first boat, when she told her story, which is briefly as follows. Her name is Barbara Thomson: she was born at Aberdeen in Scotland, and along with her parents, emigrated to New South

Wales.   About four years and a half ago she left Moreton Bay with her husband in a small cutter (called the America), of which he was owner, for the purpose of picking up some of the oil from the wreck of a whaler, lost on the Bampton Shoal, to which place one of her late crew undertook to guide them; their ultimate intention was to go on to Port Essington.   The man who acted as pilot was unable to find the wreck, and after much quarrelling on board in consequence, and the loss of two men by drowning, and of another who was left upon a small uninhabited island, they made their way up to Torres Strait, where, during a gale of wind, their vessel struck upon a reef on the Eastern Prince of Wales Island.   The two remaining men were lost in attempting to swim on shore through the surf, but the woman was afterwards rescued by a party of natives on a turtling excursion, who, when the gale subsided, swam on board, and supported her on shore between two of their number.   One of these blacks, Boroto by name, took possession of the woman as his share of the plunder; she was compelled to live with him, but was well treated by all the men, although many of the women, jealous of the attention shewn her, for a long time evinced anything but kindness.   A curious circumstance secured for her the protection of one of the principal men of the tribe a party from which had been the fortunate means of rescuing her, and which she afterwards found to be the Kowrárĕga, chiefly inhabiting

Múralug, or the Western Prince of Wales Island. This person, named Piaquai, acting upon the belief (universal throughout Australia and the Islands of Torres Strait so far as hitherto known) that white people are the ghosts of the aborigines, fancied that in the stranger he recognised a long-lost daughter of the name of Gi(a)ōm, and at once admitted her to the relationship which he thought had formerly subsisted between them; she was immediately acknowledged by the whole tribe as one of themselves, thus ensuring an extensive connection in relatives of all denominations. From the head-quarters of the tribe with which Gi'om thus became associated being upon an island which all vessels passing through Torres Strait from the eastward must approach within two or three miles, she had the mortification of seeing from twenty to thirty or more ships go through every summer without anchoring in the neighbourhood, so as to afford the slightest opportunity of making her escape. Last year she heard of our two vessels (described as two war canoes, a big and a little one) being at Cape York—only twenty miles distant—from some of the tribe who had communicated with us and been well treated, but they would not take her over, and even watched her more narrowly than before. On our second and present visit, however, which the Cape York people immediately announced by smoke signals to their friends in Múralug, she was successful in persuading some of her more immediate friends to bring her across to the main land within a short distance of where the vessels lay. The blacks were credulous enough to believe that "as she had been so long with them, and had been so well treated, she did not intend to leave them,—only she felt a strong desire to see the white people once more and shake hands with them;" adding, that she would be certain to procure some axes, knives, tobacco, and other much prized articles. This appeal to their cupidity decided the question at once. After landing at the sandy bay on the western side of Cape York, she hurried across to Evans' Bay, as quickly as her lameness would allow, fearful that the blacks might change their mind; and well it was that she did so, as a small party of men followed to detain her, but arrived too late. Three of these people were brought on board at her own request, and as they had been instrumental in saving her from the wreck, they were presented with an axe a-piece, and other presents.

Upon being asked by Captain Stanley whether she really preferred remaining with us to accompanying the natives back to their island, as she would be allowed her free choice in the matter, she was so much agitated as to find difficulty in expressing her thankfulness, making use of scraps of English alternately with the Kowrárĕga language, and then, suddenly awaking to the recollection that she was not understood, the poor creature blushed all over, and with downcast eyes, beat her forehead with her hand, as if to assist in collecting her scattered thoughts. At length, after a pause, she found words to say,—" Sir, I am a Christian, and would rather go back to my own friends." At the same time, it was remarked by every one that she had not lost the feelings of womanly modesty—even after having lived so long among naked blacks; she seemed acutely to feel the singularity of her position—dressed only in a couple of shirts, in the midst of a crowd of her own countrymen.

When first seen on shore our new shipmate presented so dirty and wretched an appearance that some people who were out shooting at first mistook her for a *gin*, and were passing by without taking further notice, when she called out to them in English, " I am a white woman, why do you leave me ?" With the exception of a narrow fringe of leaves in front, she wore no clothing, and her skin was tanned and blistered with the sun, and shewed the marks of several large burns which had been received from sleeping too near the fire on cold nights; besides, she was suffering from ophthalmia, which had previously deprived her of the sight of one eye. But good living, and every comfort (for Captain Stanley kindly provided her with a cabin and a seat at his table), combined with medical attention, very soon restored her health, and she was eventually handed over to her parents in Sydney in excellent condition.

Although perfectly illiterate, Mrs. Thomson had made good use of her powers of observation, and evinced much shrewdness in her remarks upon various subjects connected with her residence among the blacks, joined to great willingness to communicate any information which she possessed. Much of this will be found in another part of this volume, incorporated with the result of my own observations. Several hundred words of the Kowrárĕga language, and a portion of its grammar, were also obtained from time to time, and most of these were subsequently verified. And, although she did not understand the language spoken at Cape York, yet, as some of the Gúdang people there knew the Kowrárĕga, through its medium I was usually able to make myself tolerably well understood, and thus obtain an explanation of some matters which had formerly puzzled me, and correct various errors into which I had fallen. It was well, too, that I took an early opportunity of procuring these words, for my informant afterwards forgot much of her lately acquired language, and her value as an authority on that subject gradually diminished.

Gi'om was evidently a great favourite with the blacks, and hardly a day passed on which she was not obliged to hold a levee in her cabin for the reception of friends from the shore, while other visitors, less favoured, were content to talk to her through the port. They occasionally brought presents of fish and turtle, but always expected an equivalent of some kind. Her friend Boroto, the nature of the intimacy with whom was not at first understood, after in vain attempting by smooth words and fair promises to induce her to go back to live with him, left the ship in a rage, and we were not sorry to get rid of so impudent and troublesome a visitor as he had become. Previous to leaving, he had threatened that, should he or any of his friends ever catch his faithless spouse on shore, they would take off her head to carry back with them to Múralug; and so likely to be fulfilled did she consider this threat, being in perfect accordance with their customs, that she never afterwards ventured on shore at Cape York.

During the period of our stay at Cape York, the Bramble, Asp, and Rattlesnake's pinnace were sent away to the western entrance of Torres Strait to finish the survey, and returned after a month's absence. The boats had held no intercourse with any of the natives, except a small party of Kowrárĕgas, the inhabitants of Mulgrave and Banks Islands having carefully avoided them. Hopes had been entertained prior to starting of seeing something of a white man of the name of Wini, who had lived with the Badús for many years. Gi'om had seen and conversed with him during a visit to Múralug which he had made in hopes of inducing her to share his fortunes. She supposed him to be a foreigner, from his not appearing to understand the English she used when asked by him to speak in her native tongue. He had reached Mulgrave Island in a boat after having, by his own account, killed

x 2

his companions, some three or four in number.   In
course of time he became the most important
person in the tribe, having gained an ascendancy
by procuring the death of his principal enemies and
intimidating others, which led to the establishment
of his fame as a warrior, and he became in consequence the possessor of several wives, a canoe, and
some property in land, the cultivation of which last
he pays great attention to.   Wini's character appears from the accounts I have heard—for others
corroborated part of Gi'om's statement—to be a compound of villany and cunning, in addition to the
ferocity and headstrong passions of a thorough
savage,—it strikes me that he must have been a
runaway convict, probably from Norfolk Island.
It is fortunate that his sphere of mischief is so
limited, for a more dangerous ruffian could not easily
be found.   As matters stand at present, it is probable
that not only during his life, but for years afterwards, every European who falls into the hands of
the Badú people will meet with certain death.*

* In further illustration of this assertion I give the following
note with which I have lately been furnished by Mr. J. Sweatman,
R.N., who served in the Bramble at the time of the occurrence
of the murder to which it alludes.   In June 1846 the supercargo
and a boat's crew of a small vessel from Sydney procuring
trepang and tortoise-shell in Torres Strait, landed upon Mulgrave
Island (the vessel being about seven miles off) in order to barter
for tortoise-shell.   The natives appeared at first to be friendly
enough, but, towards evening some circumstances occurred which
induced the boat's crew to re-embark, and they then went to a

The inhabitants of the neighbouring Banks Island are described by Gi'om as evincing the same hostility towards Europeans. Only a few years ago the Italegas, one of the two tribes inhabiting that island, murdered two white men and a boy, who had reached their inhospitable shores in a small boat, probably from a wreck. Such savage outrages committed by the inhabitants of the north-western islands would probably be completely prevented were they oftener visited by Europeans; such was the case with the people of Darnley Island, once dangerous savages, now safely to be dealt with by taking the usual precautions, and where, as at the Murray Islands, I believe strangers in distress, without valuable property, would now be kindly treated.

We remained nine weeks at our anchorage in

small sand-bank about a mile off to pass the night there. The supercargo and three men landed, leaving two men in the boat at anchor; about midnight the latter were alarmed at hearing shouts and yells on shore, and, landing in haste, found that the natives had attacked their comrades, whose muskets, being damp, were quite useless. The supercargo and two men were killed—a shot from the boat however dispersed the natives sufficiently for the two men to drag their surviving comrade into the boat, but he had an arrow through the body, and his hands were partially severed, and he soon died. The bodies of the three people on the sand-bank could not be recovered, the natives returning to the attack with showers of arrows, nor could the small force on board the schooner attempt to punish the perpetrators of this unprovoked murder.

Evans Bay. The natives, of whom there were usually a number encamped in the neighbourhood, attracted by the presence of the ship, as vultures by a carcass, continued on perfectly friendly terms, assisted the wooding and watering parties, brought off fish and portions of turtle to the ship, and accompanied us on our walks on shore. The usual remuneration for their services was biscuit, and, next to that, tobacco, besides which axes and knives were highly prized and occasionally given them. Immediately on landing for the purpose of an excursion, each of us looked out for his *kotaiga*** from among a crowd of applicants surrounding the boat, the haversack was thrown across his shoulders, and away we started for the bush. It was often difficult for the possessor of a good stock of biscuit to shake off other useless volunteers; these hangers-on, with few exceptions, were more remarkable for their capacity for food than for their powers of endurance, shewing a deeply rooted antipathy to any exertion not actually necessary, and for every trifling additional service asking for *bisiker múro, choka múro, neipa,* or some such thing. Still a few of these same blacks make a very agreeable addition to a shooting party, as besides their services as guides, and in pointing out game, they formed amusing companions and enlivened many a noonday bivouac

---

* Derived from the Kowrarega word Kutaig (younger brother); here in the jargon used between us it signified friend, associate, companion, &c.

or dull thirsty march in the hot sun with their songs, jokes, and mimicry.

One evening I was asked to join a party made up for the purpose of witnessing a native dance. Many strange blacks were then encamped on the margin of the beach, and altogether about 150 people belonging to four or five tribes had collected. Not being apprised of our coming they shewed much surprise and suspicion at our landing after dark, but, with some trouble, a number were induced by the promise of a quantity of biscuit to get up a dance round a large fire on the sand to the music of a drum which we had taken with us to announce our approach. The dance after all was a very poor affair,— none of the performers were painted and decorated, there was little scenic effect, and they seemed glad when it was over. The bag containing the promised biscuit was most injudiciously handed over to an old woman named Baki, or "*queena woman Baki*," as some one had taught her to call herself, for distribution among the party. She doled out a few handfuls to some women and children who had not been at all concerned in the matter, and would have marched off with the remainder had she not been prevented. The appointment of a woman to this office gave great offence to the men who had been dancing,—while not one among them would have scrupled forcibly to deprive her of the whole on the very first opportunity, yet every man there scorned the idea of having to *ask* a woman for anything,—

the consequence was that the performers were not
rewarded, and naturally imagined that we had
broken faith with them. The discontent increased,
some of the men left in a state of great excitement,
and went for their spears and throwing sticks. One
or two rockets were sent up soon after to amuse
them, on which the few remaining women and
children hurried to their sheds of bark and hid their
faces in terror. When a blue light was burned, and
lit up the gloomy shadows of the neighbouring
bush, it disclosed the spectral figures of many
armed men among the trees, singly and in groups,
intently watching our motions. Paida, who with
other native allies of ours still remained with us,
was very urgent for us to be off, telling me that
spears would be thrown immediately (*kaibú kalaka
múro*); being a *kotaig* of mine, he considered himself bound to attend to my safety, so conducted me
to the boat which he assisted in shoving off, nor did
he retire from the beach until we had got into deep
water.

I have alluded to this occurrence, trivial as it
may appear, not without an object. It serves as
an illustration of the policy of respecting the known
customs of the Australian race, even in apparently
trifling matters, at least during the early period of
intercourse with a tribe, and shews how a little
want of judgment in the director of our party caused
the most friendly intentions to be misconstrued, and
might have led to fatal results. I must confess

that I should have considered any injury sustained on our side to have been most richly merited; moreover, I am convinced that some at least of the collisions which have taken place in Australia, between the first European visitors and the natives of any given district, have originated in causes of offence brought on by the indiscretion of one or more of the party, and revenged on others who were innocent. As a memorable instance I may give that which happened during Leichhardt's overland journey to Port Essington, when his camp was attacked one evening, and Mr. Gilbert lost his life. Long afterwards the undoubted cause of this apparently unaccountable attack transpired in the acknowledgment, while intoxicated, by one of the persons concerned, that a gross outrage had been committed upon an aboriginal woman a day or two previously, by the two blacks belonging to the expedition.

One day I witnessed a native fight, which may be described here, as such occurrences, although frequent enough in Australia, have by Europeans been witnessed only in the settled districts. It was one of those smaller fights, or usual modes of settling a quarrel when more than two people are concerned, and assumed quite the character of a duel upon a large scale. At day-break, I landed in company with six or seven people who were going out on different shooting parties. The natives came down to the boat as usual, but all carried throwing-sticks

—contrary to their usual practice of late; and at the place where they had slept, numbers of spears were stuck up on end in the sand. These preparations surprised me, but Paida would not explain the cause and seemed anxious to get me away. The shooters marched off—each with his black—but I loitered behind, walking slowly along the beach.

About 200 yards from the first camping-place, two groups of strange natives, chiefly men, were assembled with throwing-sticks in their hands and bundles of spears. While passing them they moved along in twos and threes towards the Evans Bay party, the men of which advanced to meet them. The women and children began to make off, but a few remained as spectators on the sands, it being then low water. A great deal of violent gesticulation and shouting took place, the parties became more and more excited, and took up their position in two scattered lines facing each other, extending from the margin of the beach to a little way in the bush, and about twenty-five yards apart. Paida, too, partook of the excitement and could refrain no longer from joining in the fight; he dropped my haversack and bounded away at full speed to his camping-place, where he received his spears from little Purom his son, and quickly made his appearance upon the scene of action.

The two parties were pretty equally matched— about fifteen men in each. The noise now became deafening; shouts of defiance, insulting expressions, and every kind of abusive epithet were bandied about, and the women and children in the bush kept up a wailing cry all the while rising and falling in cadence. The pantomimic movements were of various descriptions; besides the singular quivering motion given to the thighs placed wide apart (common to all the Australian dances), they frequently invited each other to throw at them, turning the body half round and exposing the breech, or dropping on one knee or hand as if to offer a fair mark. At length a spear was thrown and returned, followed by many others, and the fighting became general, with an occasional pause. The precision with which the spears were thrown was not less remarkable than the dexterity with which they were avoided. In nearly every case the person thrown at would, apparently, have been struck had he stood still, but, his keenness of sight enabled him to escape by springing aside as required, variously inclining the body, or sometimes merely lifting up a leg to allow the spear to pass by, and had two been thrown at one person at the same moment he could scarcely have escaped, but this I observed was never attempted, as it would have been in war,—here each individual appeared to have a particular opponent. I had a capital view of the whole of the proceedings, being seated about fifty yards behind and slightly on the flank of one of the two contending parties. One spear thrown higher than usual passed within five yards of me, but this I was satisfied was the result of accident, as I had seen it come from Paida's party. Soon afterwards I observed a man at the right extreme of the line next me, who had been dodging round a large scævola bush for some time back, make a sudden dart at one of the opposite party and chop him down the shoulder with an iron tomahawk. The wounded man fell, and instantly a yell of triumph denoted that the whole matter was at an end.

Paida rejoined me five minutes afterwards, apparently much refreshed by this little excitement, and accompanied me on my walk, still he would not explain the cause of the fight. The wounded man had his arm tied up by one of our people who landed soon afterwards, and, although the cut was both large and deep, he soon recovered.

The frequent excursions of our shooting parties being more extended than during our last visit became the means of adding considerably to our knowledge of the surrounding country. One of the immediate consequences was the discovery of several small streams of fresh water. The principal of these, which we named Mew River (after its first finder, the sergeant of marines on board), has its mouth in a small mangrove creek three-quarters of a mile to the eastward of Evans Bay. About five miles further up its source was found to be a spring among rocks in a dense calamus scrub. It waters a fine valley running nearly east and west behind the range of hills to the southward of Evans Bay, and its line is marked by a belt of tangled brush exceeding in luxuriance anything of the same description which I had seen elsewhere. The variety of trees in this dense brush is very great, and many were quite new to me. The Seaforthia palm attained the height of 60 to 80 feet, and the rattan was very abundant, and from the recurved prickles catching and tearing the clothes, it was often no easy matter to penetrate the thickets. Among the plants along the river the most interesting is an indigenous species of banana or plantain, probably the same as that found at Endeavour River during Cook's first voyage. The fruit is of small size with numerous hard seeds and a small quantity of delicious pulp; cultivation would, doubtless, wonderfully improve it. Another remarkable plant found on the grassy borders of the jungle and characteristic of rich damp soil is a beautiful species of *Roscœa* (?), (one of the Scitamineæ or ginger family), about a foot high, with a solitary leaf and large bracteæ, the lower green and the upper ones pink, partially concealing handsome yellow flowers. From its succulent nature I failed in preparing specimens for the herbarium, but some roots were preserved and given to the Botanical Garden at Sydney.

The lower part of the valley is open forest land, or nearly level and thinly wooded country covered with tall coarse grass. Further up it becomes more beautiful. From the belt of wood, concealing the windings of the river, grassy sloping meadows extend

upwards on each side to the flanking ridges which are
covered with dense scrub occasionally extending in
straggling patches down to the water, and forming
a kind of imperfect natural fence.   The soil of these
meadows is rich sandy loam, affording great apparent facilities for cultivation from their proximity
to what is probably a never failing supply of fresh
water.   Here, at the end of the dry season, and
before the periodical rains had fairly set in, we found
the stream at half way up to be about six feet in
average breadth, slowly running over a shallow,
gravelly, or earthy bed, with occasional pools from
two to four feet in depth.

I have alluded to this subject at greater length
than under ordinary circumstances I would have
done, in the belief that, should a settlement ever be
established at Cape York, the strip of good land
that runs along the upper part of Mew River may
hereafter be turned to good account.   Several other
valleys watered by small and apparently permanent
streams were discovered by our shooting parties,
chiefly by Wilcox and the sergeant of marines; these
were afterwards visited by me, and my opinion of
the productiveness of the country about Cape York
almost daily became more and more favourable the
further I extended my excursions.

I need scarcely repeat the arguments which have
been adduced in favour of the expediency, I may
almost say necessity, of establishing a military post,
or small settlement of some kind, in the vicinity of

Cape York, simply because, while perfectly agreeing with Mr. Jukes* and several other persons who have drawn the public attention to the subject, I have little in addition to offer. Still a few words on the question may not be out of place. The beneficial results to be looked for were such a settlement to be formed would be —

1st. A port of refuge would be afforded to the crews of vessels wrecked in Torres Strait, and its approaches, who otherwise must make for Booby Island, and there await the uncertainty of being picked up by some passing vessel, or even attempt in the boats to reach Coupang in Timor, a distance of 1100 miles further. And now that the settlement at Port Essington has been abandoned the necessity for such a place of refuge is still greater.

2nd. Passing vessels might be supplied with water and other refreshments, also stores, such as anchors, &c., which last are frequently lost during the passage of the Strait.

3rd. The knowledge of the existence of such a post would speedily exercise a beneficial influence over our intercourse with the natives of Torres Strait, and induce them to refrain from a repetition of the outrages which they have frequently committed upon Europeans; the little trade in tortoiseshell which might be pushed in the Strait (as has frequently been done before by small vessels from Sydney and even from Hong Kong) would no longer

* Voyage of the Fly, vol. i. p. 302.

be a dangerous one—and protection would be afforded to the coaling depôt for steamers at Port Albany.*

4th. In a military point of view the importance of such a post has been urged upon the ground, that in the event of war, a single enemy's ship stationed in the neighbourhood, if previously unoccupied, could completely command the whole of our commerce passing through the Strait.

5th. From what more central point could operations be conducted with the view of extending our knowledge of the interior of New Guinea by ascending some of the large rivers of that country, disemboguing on the shores of the Great Bight?

6th and lastly. But on this point I would advance my opinion with much diffidence—I believe that were a settlement to be established at Cape York, missionary enterprize, *judiciously conducted*, might find a useful field for its labours in Torres Strait, beginning with the Murray and Darnley Islanders, people of a much higher intellectual standard than the Australians, and consequently more likely to appreciate any humanizing influence which might be exercised for their benefit.

Several kangaroos or wallabies, the largest of

* I adduce this last advantage on the presumption, which now assumes a greater degree of probability than before—that the steam communication before alluded to (p. 132), will be established, and that the Torres Strait route, the one which is almost generally advocated, will be the one adopted.

which weighed forty pounds, were killed during our stay at Cape York. A kangaroo dog belonging to Captain Stanley made several fine runs, all of them unsuccessful however, as the chase was seldom upon open ground, and there was little chance of overtaking the kangaroo before it got into some neighbouring thicket where the dog could not follow it. This wallaby proved to be the *Halmaturus agilis,* first found at Port Essington, and afterwards by Leichhardt in Carpentaria. A singular bat of a reddish brown colour was shot one day while asleep suspended from a branch of a tree; it belonged to the genus *Harpyia,* and was therefore a contribution to the Australian fauna.

Among many additions to the ornithological collections of the voyage were eight or nine new species of birds, and about seven others previously known only as inhabitants of New Guinea and the neighbouring islands.* The first of these which came under my notice was an enormous black parrot (*Microglossus aterrimus*) with crimson cheeks; at Cape York it feeds upon the cabbage of various palms, stripping down the sheath at the base of the leaves with its powerful, acutely-hooked upper mandible. The next in order of occurrence was a third species of the genus *Tanysiptera* (*T. Sylvia*), a gorgeous kingfisher with two long, white, central tail-feathers, inhabiting

---

* Many of these have since been figured and described, with accompanying notes on their habits, &c , in the recently published Supplement to Mr. Gould's Birds of Australia.

the brushes, where the glancing of its bright colours
as it darts past in rapid flight arrests the attention
for a moment ere it is lost among the dense foliage.

I may next allude to *Aplonis metallica*—a bird
somewhat resembling a starling, of a dark glossy
green and purple hue, with metallic reflections—in
connection with its singular nest. One day I was
taken by a native to the centre of a brush, where a
gigantic cotton tree standing alone was hung with
about fifty of the large pensile nests of this species.
After I had made several unsuccessful attempts to
shoot down one of the nests by firing with ball at
the supporting branch, the black volunteered to
climb the tree, provided I would give him a knife.
I was puzzled to know how he proposed to act,
the trunk being upwards of four feet in diameter
at the base, and the nearest branch being about
sixty feet from the ground. He procured a tough
and pliant shoot of a kind of vine (*Cissus*), of
sufficient length to pass nearly round the tree, and
holding one end of this in each hand and pressing his
legs and feet against the tree, he ascended by a series
of jerks, resting occasionally, holding on for half a
minute at a time with one end of the vine in his
mouth. At length he reached the branches and
threw me down as many nests as I required. He
afterwards filled the bag which he carried round
his neck with the unfledged young birds, which
on our return to the native camp on the beach were
thrown alive upon the fire, in spite of my remon-

strances, and when warmed through were devoured
with great apparent relish by himself and his
friends.

Two days before we left Cape York I was told
that some bower-birds had been seen in a thicket,
or patch of low scrub, half a mile from the beach,
and after a long search I found a recently constructed bower, four feet long and eighteen inches
high, with some fresh berries lying upon it. .The

bower was situated near the border of the thicket,
the bushes composing which were seldom more than
ten feet high, growing in smooth sandy soil without
grass.

Next morning I was landed before daylight, and
proceeded to the place in company with Paida,
taking with us a large board on which to carry off
the bower as a specimen. I had great difficulty in

inducing my friend to accompany me, as he was afraid of a war party of Gomokudins, which tribe had lately given notice that they were coming to fight the Evans Bay people. However I promised to protect him, and loaded one barrel with ball, which gave him increased confidence, still he insisted upon carrying a large bundle of spears and a throwing-stick. Of late Paida's tribe have taken steps to prevent being surprised by their enemies. At night they remove in their canoes to the neighbouring island Robumo, and sleep there, returning in the morning to the shore, and take care not to go away to a distance singly or unarmed.

While watching in the scrub I caught several glimpses of the *tewinya* (the native name) as it darted through the bushes in the neighbourhood of the bower, announcing its presence by an occasional loud *churr-r-r*, and imitating the notes of various other birds, especially the leather-head. I never before met with a more wary bird, and for a long time it enticed me to follow it to a short distance, then flying off and alighting on the bower, it would deposit a berry or two, run through, and be off again (as the black told me) before I could reach the spot. All this time it was impossible to get a shot. At length, just as my patience was becoming exhausted, I saw the bird enter the bower and disappear, when I fired at random through the twigs, fortunately with effect. So closely had we concealed ourselves latterly, and so silent had we

been, that a kangaroo while feeding actually hop-
ped up within fifteen yards, unconscious of our
presence until fired at. My bower-bird proved to
be a new species, since described by Mr. Gould as
Chlamydera cerviniventris, and the bower is ex-
bited in the British Museum.

Among the game birds of Cape York, the emu
is entitled to the first rank. Only two or three,
however, were seen, and we were not fortunate
enough to procure one. One day an emu allowed
me to approach within fifty yards by stalking it
cautiously, holding up a large green bough before
me, when, becoming alarmed, it darted in its fright
into a thicket and was lost to view. Many brush
turkeys (*Talegalla Lathami*) were shot by our sportsmen, and scarcely a day passed on which the
natives did not procure for us some of their eggs.
The mode in which these and other eggs are cooked
by the blacks is to roll them up in two or three
large leaves, and roast them in the ashes; the eggs
burst, of course, but the leaves prevent the contents
from escaping. Both bird and eggs are excellent
eating; the latter, averaging three and a half inches
in length, of a pure white colour, are deposited in
low mounds of earth and leaves in the dense brushes
in a similar manner to those of the megapodius, and
are easily dug out with the hand. I have seen
three or four taken out of one mound where they
were arranged in a large circle, a foot and a half
from the surface. The laying bird carefully effaces

any mark she may have made in scooping out a place for the eggs, but the keen eye of a native quickly detects the slightest sign of recent disturbance of the mound, and he seldom fails to hit upon the eggs.

As at Port Essington, the year at Cape York is divided into two seasons,* the dry and the rainy. From personal observation and other sources of information, it would appear that the limits and duration of these admit of so much variation that it is impossible to determine with certainty, even within a month, when one ceases and the other begins. It would appear however that the dry season, characterized by the prevalence of the south-east trade, usually terminates in November, the change having for some time previous been indicated by calms, light winds, sometimes from the westward, a gloomy unsettled appearance in the weather, and occasional showers—violent squalls of wind and rain are frequent about this time until the westerly breezes set in, when the weather becomes moderate with frequent rain, occasionally very heavy, and intervals, often of many days duration, of dry weather. In the month of March the south-east trade usually resumes its former influence, the change being often attended with the same thick squally weather, and

---

* The natives of the neighbouring Prince of Wales Island distinguish the dry season (*aibú* or the fine weather), the wet (*kúki* or the N.W. wind which then prevails), and the period of change (*malgúi*), equivalent to our Spring and Autumn.

perhaps a gale from the north-west, which ushered in the westerly monsoon.

Our own experience of the winds during our last stay at Cape York, at the period when the change of the monsoon was to be expected, may be summed up as follows. During the month of October the trade wind prevailed, keeping pretty steady at E. S. E., and generally blowing rather strongly, with hazy weather and an occasional shower. For three days in the middle of the month we experienced light north-westerly winds dying away again in the evening, and on the 25th a violent squall from the same quarter accompanied by very heavy rain rendered it expedient that the ship should next day be moved a cable's length further off shore. During the four last days in the month we had calms and light winds from the northward of east, as if the trade were about to cease, but it commenced afresh and continued until the 26th of November, generally very moderate, with fine weather. During the last six days of our stay we had light airs from about N. W., succeeded in the evening by a slight puff of south-easterly wind followed by a calm lasting all night. Last year, during the month of October, we experienced no northerly or westerly winds, but a moderate trade prevailed throughout, pretty steady at E. S. E., but varying much in strength.

In a place situated like Cape York, only about 640 miles distant from the equator, the atmospheric temperature may be expected to be very high; still the heat, although occasionally very oppressive for a time, caused very different sensations from those experienced during the almost stifling calms of Port Essington. At Cape York, however, calms seldom lasted above a few hours, as from its peninsular position the land receives the full influence of nearly every breeze. An abstract of the thermometrical observations made on board the Rattlesnake shews the following results :—

Oct. 1848.	aver.	81°	aver. max.	85°	aver. min.	77° 5
„ 1849.	„	81°	„	83° 8	„	78° 7
Nov. 1849.	„	81°9	„	84° 8	„	79°

During the above period, the highest and lowest temperatures recorded by the self-registering maximum and minimum thermometer are, for October 1848, 88° and 73°; for October 1849, 83°. 8 and 77°; and for November 1849, 88° and 76°.

APPENDIX.

No. I.

Observations on the temperature of the Sea, made during the Voyage of H.M.S. Rattlesnake, Dec. 1846—July, 1847.

BY

JOSEPH DAYMAN, R.N.

Lieut. and Assistant Surveyor.

Date	Position of Ship		Temp. of Air	Temperature of Sea		
	Lat.	Long.		Surface	Depth in fath.	Depth in fath.
1846						
Dec. 17	34°52′ N	16°24′W	59°	61°	61° 132	
,, 28	28 34	18 38	66	67	63 130	
,, 30	23 22	20 58	68	69	66 66	61• 190
,, 31	21 13	22 1	66	71	61 193	
1847						
Jan. 1	18 40	23 18	68	73	70 78	57 178
,, 2	15 28	23 22	72	73	53 180	
,, 3	8 55	22 38	78	82	59 191	
,, 5	6 28	22 39	82	84	51 185	
,, 6	5 54	22 34	79	82	50 361	
,, 7	5 8	22 19	82	83	49 340	
,, 12	1 5	22 32	77	83	52 335	
,, 14	2 37 S	26 15	79	80	53 268	
,, 15	5 9	27 51	78	80	54 153	60 293
,, 16	7 55	29 11	79	80	53 183	47 273
,, 17	12 49	32 23	79	81	80 59	
,, 19	15 5	34 44	79	80	59 226	62 317
,, 20	17 48	36 20	80	81	67 132	
,, 21	20 10	37 58	78	80	59 146	50 306
Feb. 4	26 7	40 30	66	77	60 231	51 351
,, 5	27 21	38 1	73	76	65 182	51 342
,, 8	30 52	36 48	71	73	61 200	51 360
,, 9	33 22	36 54	68	70	60 184	50 324
,, 10	35 21	35 31	68	68	62 168	49 309
,, 12	37 20	30 58	69	66	57 205	45 355
,, 13	36 50	27 50	66	66	62 215	45 370
,, 15	36 31	24 7	63	64	58 194	45 339
,, 16	36 7	21 4	59	66	55 196	47 336
,, 17	35 30	19 34	64	69	58 215	51 366
,, 18	36 47	18 47	64	68	57 128	50 257
,, 19	38 7	16 43	65	63	48 370	

Date	Position of Ship		Temp. of Air	Temperature of Sea		
	Lat.	Long.		Surface	Depth in fath.	Depth in fath.
1847	° ′	° ′	°	°	°	°
Feb. 21	37 54 S	10 28 W	59	62	53 205	43 345
,, 23	36 4	4 53	62	67	61 205	48 345
,, 24	34 42	4 15	69	70	51 364	44 650
,, 25	35 28	3 6	68	69	54 195	46 335
,, 26	36 57	1 31	65	67	53 195	49 335
,, 27	38 22	0 28	64	62	55 192	45 338
Mar. 1	38 25	4 1 E	56	55	48 195	44 335
,, 3	36 47	10 24	63	66	54 208	46 348
,, 4	36 41	12 1	66	64	55 188	46 328
,, 5	36 22	13 40	66	68	52 217	46 367
,, 6	36 24	14 42	71	70	65 147	56 284
Apr. 13	36 17	26 43	61	68	62 215	60 360
,, 14	36 53	27 49	66	69	65 215	56 360
,, 15	38 10	29 39	67	69	67 205	58 350
,, 16	38 8	32 54	69	69	64 128	60 278
,, 19	37 49	39 50	64	59	51 266	53 316
,, 21	38 13	45 36	66	60	55 158	52 293
,, 24	34 24	54 14	60	64	60 157	58 287
,, 26	30 13	56 50	65	71	61 162	60 283
,, 27	28 16	57 18	70	73	60 210	57 360
,, 28	26 56	57 31	70	74	60 200	57 350
May 1	25 48	61 6	74	—	62 165	59 320
,, 3	20 42	58 47	76	77	74 140	57 300
,, 18	21 53	56 45	77	77	63 182	
,, 19	24 16	56 58	76	75	71 182	
,, 20	26 9	58 45	74	71	63 140	73 360
,, 21	27 36	61 9	69	73	54 333	
,, 22	28 6	63 30	68	69	53 300	
,, 24	28 1	67 28	67	69	54 286	
,, 25	29 49	67 14	66	66	54 360	
,, 26	32 4	68 6	65	65	55 340	
,, 27	33 48	70 11	63	63	54 350	
,, 28	35 33	72 6	61	60	55 350	
,, 29	36 6	74 15	60	59	52 350	
June 1	35 0	80 56	61	59	55 346	
,, 6	36 42	97 54	55	56	51 320	
,, 12	39 57	118 0	48	54	45 320	
,, 14	40 46	123 26	49	53	50 380	
July 9	15 miles E. of Cape Pillar, VanDiemen's Land.		53	55	48 375	

No. II.

THE following pages contain abstracts of the meridian distances measured in H.M. Surveying Ship "Rattlesnake" and her tender the "Bramble," in the survey of the Inner Route through Torres Strait, the Louisiade Archipelago, and the S. E. Coast of New Guinea, during the years 1847-8-9 and 50, under the command of the late Captain Owen Stanley, R.N., F.R.S.

The 1st three columns require no explanation.

The 4th (interval of days) is the elapsed time between the last day at the first station and first day at the second.

The 7th (meridian distance in arc) is the result of the particular measurement specified between the two places named.

The 8th (mean meridian distance from Sydney) is that deduced by a mean value of two or more distances by the same T. K.'s, and in some instances of *one only*, in some of the principal stations connected with the survey.

The times throughout these abstracts have been determined by equal altitudes of the sun, excepting in those instances where the contrary is specified by A.A. The interpolations in the "Rattlesnake's" distances have been calculated by Owen's method : those of the "Bramble" by a method of Lieut. Yule's.

In the "Rattlesnake's" distances interpolation has been employed throughout ; in the "Bramble's" only where an intermediate distance is measured between two rates.

The asterisks point out the place to which the mean meridian from Sydney refers.

Abstract of Meridian Distances measured in H. M. Surveying

Year.	PLACES MEASURED BETWEEN.	No. of T. K.'s used.	Interval in days.	Ex. difference of results in seconds of time.	Range of Temperature.	Meridian distance in Arc.	Mean Mer. distance from Fort Macquarie, Sydney.
				sec.		° ′ ″	° ′ ″
1846	Greenwich and Madeira	14	10	7·7	..	16 53 22W	.. ..
1847	Madeira & Rat. I. Rio de Janeiro	12	31	31·6	..	26 14 38W	.. ..
,,	Rat. I. Rio Janeiro and Simon's Bay	12	36	50	..	61 32 52E	.. ..
,,	Simon's Bay and Mauritius I.	13	28	20	..	39 1 6E	.. ..
,,	Mauritius I. and Hobarton, V. D. L.	14	40	40	..	89 45 43E	.. ..
,,	Hobarton and Sydney	11	11	5	..	3 52 39E	.. ..
,,	Sydney and *Parramatta	10	1	0·6	..	0 13 13W	*0 13 13W
,,	Sydney and *Twofold Bay	9	3·5	3	..	1 17 53W	*1 17 53W
,,	Twofold Bay and *Gabo I.	8	5	2·1	..	0 00 37W	*1 18 35W
,,	Gabo I. and Fort Macquarie	8	4	9·5	..	1 18 40E	.. ..
,,	Twofold Bay and Fort Macquarie	9	9	12·6	..	1 17 54E	.. ..
,,	Fort Macquarie and *Moreton I.	16	8	8	60 to 81	2 9 59E	.. ..
1841	Moreton I. and Fort Macquarie	15	10	10	..	2 8 25W	} *2 9 30E
1849	Sydney and Moreton I.	17	7·5	15	62 to 75	2 10 7E	
1847	Moreton I. and *Port Curtis	16	12	14	71 81	1 59 59W	*0 8 37E
,,	Port Curtis and Port Molle	15	11	8·3	64 84	2 30 48W	.. ..
,,	Port Molle and Cape Upstart	16	2·4	1·5	..	1 5 42W	.. ..
,,	Cape Upstart and *Port Molle	16	4	1·5	..	1 5 42E	*2 21 53W
,,	Port Molle and Moreton I.	15	22·5	28	..	4 31 59E	.. ..
1848	Sydney and *Port Phillip	15	11	6·4	..	6 18 14W	*6 19 48W
,,	Point Gellibrand and Shortlands Bluff	16	3	2·6	..	0 14 18W	.. ..
,,	Point Gellibrand and Port Dalrymple	16	9	12·5	..	1 55 30E	.. ..
,,	Port Dalrymple and Sydney	16	14	14·2	..	4 25 53E	.. ..
,,	Sydney and *Rockingham Bay	16	31	28·9	64 to 84	5 3 27W	*5 3 27W
,,	Sydney and *Cape Upstart	16	22	25·8	64 79	3 27 00W	*3 27 37W
,,	Rockingham Bay and Cape Upstart	16	9	8·2	73 84	1 36 32E	.. ..
,,	Mound Islet and No. 3 Barnard Group	16	4	3·8	71 84	0 2 18E	.. ..
,,	No. 3 Barnard Gp. & No. 4 Frankland Gp.	16	5	5·5	72 78	0 6 4W	.. ..
,,	No. 4 Frankland and Fitzroy I.	16	7	6	72 79	0 5 34W	.. ..
,,	Mound Islet and *Fitzroy I.	15	16	7·9	84 72	0 9 28W	*5 12 55W
,,	Fitzroy I. and Islet Trinity Bay	16	6	4·4	73 79	0 18 25W	.. ..
,,	Islet Trinity Bay and Low Isles	16	4	2·4	73 77	0 7 23W	.. ..
,,	Low Isles and East Hope I.	16	10	5·4	72 79	0 6 2W	.. ..
,,	Fitzroy I. and *East Hope I.	16	20	9·1	73 79	0 31 57W	*5 44 52W
,,	East Hope I. and *Lizard I.	15	9	3·7	73 79	0 00 7E	*5 44 45W
,,	Lizard I. and No. 1 Howick Group	16	3	1·4	73 79	0 29 49W	.. ..
,,	No. 1 Howick, and No. 6 Howick Group	16	3·5	1·3	76 79	0 8 56W	.. ..
,,	No. 6 Howick and Pipon I.	16	3·5	2·5	76 82	0 17 45W	.. ..
,,	Lizard I. and *Pipon I.	16	10	2·7	73 82	0 56 14W	*6 40 59W
,,	Pipon I. and Pelican I.	16	2	1·4	76 83	0 41 00W	.. ..
,,	Pelican I. and Night I.	16	12	6·9	78 83	0 16 14W	.. ..
,,	Night I. and C. Reef	16	9	9·4	78 83	0 4 32W	.. ..
,,	Pipon I. and *C. Reef	16	23	9·7	76 84	1 1 25W	*7 42 24W
,,	C. Reef and Piper's I.	16	4	5·6	80 84	0 17 19W	.. ..
,,	Piper's I. and Sunday I.	16	4	4·8	80 84	0 1 4W	.. ..
,,	Sunday I. and Cairncross I.	16	3	1·6	81 84	0 17 37W	.. ..
,,	Cairncross I. and Z. Reef	16	2	2·5	81 84	0 12 7W	.. ..
,,	Z. Reef and Cape York	16	4	3·7	81 85	0 10 22W	.. ..
,,	C. Reef and *Cape York	16	17	13·5	78 86	0 58 33W	*8 42 8W
,,	Cape York and *Port Essington	16	10	8·5	81 90	10 23 50W	*19 5 58W
1848	Port Essington and Sydney	15	71	60	62 90	19 00 16W	.. ..

Ship, " Rattlesnake," by Capt. Owen Stanley, R.N., F.R.S.

SPOT OF OBSERVATION.	Latitude of Spot of Observation.	REMARKS.	
Mr. Veitch's Garden, Funchal	32 37 42 N	16 53 22 W ⎫ of Greenwich.	
Rat I. Rio de Janeiro	22 53 30 S	43 8 0 ⎬	
N.W. end of Dockyard, Simon's Bay	34 11 28 S		
West side of Tonnelier's I.			
Ross bank Observatory	42 52 10 S		A A
Fort Macquarie	33 51 33 S		A A
Parramatta Observatory	33 48 50 S	*By the Bramble's T. K.'s	
Jetty at Eden, Twofold Bay	37 4 20 S	*By the Bramble's T. K.'s mean of	A A
Landing place on West side	37 34 0 S	* do. [2 measurements	A A
Fort Macquarie	33 51 33 S	do.	A A
Ditto	33 51 33 S	do.	A A
Watering place near the N.W. end	27 5 44 S		A A
Fort Macquarie, Sydney	33 51 33 S	*Mean of 3 measurements	
Watering place near the N.W. end	27 5 44 S		
West side of Facing I , Port Curtis	23 51 45 S	*Mean of 2 measurements	
1-10th mile N. of Sandy Bay, E. side of har.	20 19 48 S		
Sandy Bay, near the Cape	19 42 3 S		A A
1-10th mile N. of Sandy Bay, E. side of har.	20 19 48 S	*Mean of 2 measurements	A A
Watering place near the N.W end	27 5 44 S		AA
Lighthouse, Point Gellibrand	37 52 31 S	* do. do.	
Lighthouse, Shortland's Bluff	38 16 0 S		
North point of Lagoon Bay	41 5 0 S	Latitude from Chart	
Fort Macquarie	33 51 33 S		
Summit of Mound Islet	17 55 25 S	*One measurement	A A
Sandy Bay, near the Cape	19 42 3 S	*Mean of 2 measurements	A A
Ditto ditto	19 42 3 S		
Sandy beach, West extreme	17 40 20 S		A A
Sandy beach, West side	17 12 22 S		
Ditto ditto	16 55 57 S		
Ditto ditto	16 55 57 S		
Centre of North side of Islet	16 43 26 S	*One measurement	A A
N.E. point of Western Isle	16 22 56 S		A A
Beach on West side of I.	15 43 45 S		
Ditto ditto	15 43 45 S	*One measurement	
South end of Sandy Bay on West side	14 39 56 S	*One measurement	
N.W. extreme of I.	14 29 46 S		
Middle of West side of I.	14 26 0 S		
S.W. side of West I.	14 7 9 S		
Ditto ditto	14 7 9 S	*One measurement	
S.W. side of Island	13 54 21 S		
Coral patch, N.W. end of Island	13 9 58 S		A A
Dry sand, N.W. end of reef	12 34 50 S		A A
Ditto ditto	12 34 50 S	*One measurement	
N.E. extreme of West I. on large reef	12 14 30 S		
S.W. side on sandy beach	11 55 54 S		
N.W. extreme on sandy beach	11 14 34 S		
Dry sand on N.W. end	10 48 50 S		
Sextant Rock, Evans' Bay	10 41 31 S		
Ditto ditto	10 41 31 S	*The mean of 3 measurements	
Government House, Victoria	11 22 2 S	*One measurement	
Fort Macquarie	33 51 33 S	*Useless (interval being too long)	

Year.	PLACES MEASURED BETWEEN.	No. of T.K.'s used.	Interval in days.	Er. difference of results in seconds of time.	Range of Temperature.	Meridian distance in Arc.	Mean Mer. distance from Fort Macquarie, Sydney.
				sec.		° ′ ″	° ′ ″
1849	Sydney and Moreton I.	17	7·5	15·0	62 to 75	2 10 7E	.. ..
,,	Moreton I. & No. 1 Obs. Reef C. Haven	17	21·5	24·8	66 85	0 4 46W	.. ..
,,	No. 1 Obs. Reef & No. 2. Obs. Reef C. Ha.	17	12	11·5	81 85	0 12 7W	.. ..
,,	No. 2 Obs. Reef and *Duchâteau Isles	17	14	10·9	81 87	0 43 30W	*1 9 7E
,,	Duchâteau Isles and *Brumer I.	17	14	9·3	79 87	2 1 56W	*0 53 9W
,,	Brumer I. and *Dufaure I.	17	16	20·7	79 85	0 37 7W	*1 29 58W
,,	Brumer I. and Redscar Bay	17	30	14·3	79 86	3 32 8W	.. ..
,,	Redscar Bay and Cape York	17	12	12·3	82 86	4 20 4W	.. ..
,,	Brumer I. and Cape York	17	42	22·7		7 51 23W	.. ..
,,	Cape York and *Mount Ernest	17	3	6·9	83 88	0 4 12W	*8 45 2W
,,	Mid. Duchâteau and Cape York	17	61	45·1	..	9 51 56W	.. ..
,,	Cape York and *Bramble Cay	15	16	17·4	82 88	1 19 55E	*7 20 55W
,,	Cape York and *Redscar Bay	15	21	16·7	82 88	4 19 51E	*4 21 51W
1850	Redscar Bay and Midd. Duchâteau	17	9·5	6·6	83 88	5 29 55E	.. ..
,,	Middle Duchâteau and Sydney	16	29·5	43·4	..	1 5 59W	.. ..
,,	Redscar Bay and Sydney	16	39	52·4	73 88	4 22 47E	.. ..
,,	Sydney and Bay of Is. New Zealand	15	18·5	16·6	63 77	22 54 20E	.. ..
,,	Bay of Is. and Port Stanley, E. Falkland	15	56·5	90·5	44 67	128 3 9E	.. ..
1847	Fort Macquarie and Port Stephens	9	3	2	9	0 47 15E	
,,	Port Stephens and *Moreton I.	9	12	6·2	5	1 22 24E	
1848	Moreton Bay and Sydney	9	10	8·5	13·5	2 9 9W	*2 9 25E
1849	Moreton Bay and Sydney	10	18	15·8	3·5	2 9 41W	
,,	Fort Macquarie and Moreton Bay	10	10·5	16·2	8	2 9 10E	
1847	Moreton Bay and Port Curtis	10	8	2·6	6·5	2 0 7W	
1848	Sydney and *Port Curtis	9	19	24	11	0 7 19E	*0 8 35E
1847	Port Curtis and Moreton Bay	10	17	18	10	2 0 16E	
1848	Sydney and *Kent's Group, Lt. H.	10	9·5	5·0	9	3 55 11W	*3 55 11W
,,	Sydney and *Hobson Bay, Port Phillip	10	16·5	4·8	9	6 18 56W	*6 19 00W
,,	Hobson's Bay and Sydney	10	17	7	10·5	6 19 4E	
,,	Sail Rocks, Pt. Curtis, & Rockingham B.	10	4	3·8	7	5 20 3W	.. ..
,,	Goold I. (Rockingh. Bay) & *Fitzroy I.	10	15	5·6	4	0 9 50W	*5 14 19W
,,	Fitzroy I. and a rocky Islet, C. Melville	10	36	23·5	4	1 38 00W	.. ..
,,	A rocky Islet, C. Melville, and Pelican I.	10	7	8·3	3·5	0 31 38W	.. ..
,,	Pelican I. and *Cape York	10	15	10·8	2·5	1 17 3W	*8 40 52W
,,	Cape York and Booby I.	10	2	0·7	1·5	0 38 18W	.. ..
1849	Booby I. and Cape York	10	2·5	3·4	2·5	0 38 19W	.. ..
1848	Cape York and Moreton I.	10	38	23·4	6	10 49 10E	.. ..
1849	Moreton I. and North Solitary I.	10	7	4·2	..	0 1 7E	.. ..
,,	Moreton I. & No. 1 Obs. Reef Cor. Haven	10	21	41	20	0 4 29W	.. ..
,,	No. 1 Obs. Reef and No 2 Obs. Reef	10	13	8·2	3·5	0 12 14W	.. ..
,,	No. 2 Obs. Reef and Green I.	10	6	5·2	3	0 26 48W	.. ..
,,	No. 2 Obs. Reef and Green I.	10	6	3·2	3	0 26 48W	.. ..
,,	Green I. and Duchâteau Isles	10	3	4·6	3	0 15 53W	.. ..
,,	Green I. and *Middle Duchâteau	10	1	1·1	3	0 16 43W	*1 8 34E
,,	Middle Duchâteau & Duperre sandbank	10	3	1·9	3·5	0 19 54W	.. ..
,,	Middle Duchâteau and Lejeune Isle	10	5	3·4	4	0 33 26W	.. ..
,,	Lejeune I. and Kosmann I.	10	2	2	3	0 16 52W	.. ..
,,	Lejeune I. and East Sable I.	10	2·9	2·8	3	0 25 47W	.. ..
,,	Lejeune I. and West Barrier I.	10	3	2·7	3	0 40 28W	.. ..
,,	Lejeune I. and West Dumoulin I.	10	5	4·5	3	1 4 18W	.. ..
,,	Middle Duchâteau and *Brumer I.	10	14	15·6	4	2 1 13W	*0 52 40W
,,	Brumer I. and *Dufaure I.	10	17	5·0	2·5	0 35 20W	*1 27 43W
,,	Brumer I. and Cape York	10	43	17·9	4	7 48 19W	.. ..
,,	Cape York and Darnley I.	10	12·5	7	2	1 13 39E	.. ..
,,	Cape York and Bramble Cay	10	16	10·3	1·5	1 20 34E	.. ..
1850	Redscar Bay and Bramble, off Round I.	10	8	7	3	0 37 45E	.. ..
,,	Redscar Bay & Bramble, off C. Rodney	10	16	8·4	3	1 35 25E	.. ..
,,	Redscar Bay and Bramble, off Dufaure	10	21	14·2	3	2 48 41E	.. ..
,,	Redscar Bay & Bramble, off Brumer I.	10	23	17·9	3	3 27 34E	.. ..
,,	Redscar Bay and Middle Duchâteau	10	31·5	24·7	3	5 29 46E	.. ..
,,	Middle Duchâteau I. and Sydney	8	28	41·3	..	1 7 30W	.. ..
,,	Sydney and Bay of Is. New Zealand	7	18·5	7·1	..	22 55 24E	.. ..
,,	Bay of Is. and Falkland I.	7	57	95	..	128 3 9E	.. ..

SPOT OF OBSERVATION.	Latitude of Spot of Observation.	REMARKS.	
	° ′ ″		
Watering place near the N.W. end	27 5 44 S		
Dry sand, W. extreme of reef	11 18 39 S	N.B.—The distances in the	
Dry sand, E. extreme of reef	11 21 30 S	Louisiade and New Guinea are	
Centre of Middle I., North side	11 16 51 S	calculated with the mer. dist. of	
At the ship's anchorage	10 45 30 S	the Sextant Rock, Cape York,	A A
At the ship's anchorage	10 30 36 S	assumed to be 8° 40′ 50″ W.	A A
At the ship's anchorage	9 16 14 S	of Sydney, to adapt them to	A A
Sextant Rock, Evans' Bay	10 41 31 S	the original △ of the N.E.	A A
Ditto ditto	10 41 31 S	Coast of Australia.	A A
N.W. end of Island	10 14 58 S	*One measurement	
Sextant Rock, Evans' Bay	10 41 31 S		
Centre of Bramble Cay	9 8 38 S	*One measurement	
Sandy point, N. extremity Pariwara I.	9 14 21 S		
Centre of Middle I., North side	11 16 51 S		
Fort Macquarie	33 51 33 S		
Ditto	33 51 33 S		
Kairaro I., Kororareka Bay	35 16 0 S		
In front of Chaplain's house	51 41 19 S		
In the Garden, Tahlee House	32 40 18 S		
Watering place on N.W. end of Island	27 5 44 S		
Fort Macquarie	33 51 33 S	The mean of 4 measurements	
Ditto	33 51 33 S		
Watering place near N.W. end of Island	27 5 44 S	[to Observ. spot by Charts	
At the Observ. spot W. side of Facing I.	23 51 45 S	Measured to Sail Rocks, & reduced	
Ditto ditto	23 51 45 S	Mean of 3 measurements	
Watering place near N.W. end of I.	27 5 44 S	One measurement	
At the Lighthouse	39 29 58 S		
Near the Lighthouse, Point Gellibrand	37 52 31 S	Mean of 2 measurements	
Fort Macquarie	33 51 33 S		
Rocky point, ½ mile S. of N.W. ex. Goold I.	18 9 33 S	One measurement	
The same as "Rattlesnake's"	16 55 57 S	*By Capt. King's Sextant	
On its summit	*14 15 13 S		
S.W. side of Island	13 54 21 S	Mean of 4 measurements	
Sextant Rock, Evans' Bay	10 41 31 S		
N.W. end of I.	none observ.	Two measurements	
Sextant Rock, Evans' Bay	10 41 31 S		
Watering place, near N.W. end of I.	27 5 44 S	*Capt. King's Sext. Sea horizon	
Summit of Island	*29 56 8 S		
Dry sand, W. extremity of reef	11 18 39 S		
Dry sand, E. extremity of reef	11 21 30 S		
On Coral Islet, near Green I. (S. side)	11 8 36 S		
Ditto ditto	11 8 36 S	Repeated	
On the N.E. ex. of Eastern Duchâteau	11 16 45 S		
Rattlesnake's Observation spot	*11 16 51 S	*By triangulation	A A
On sandbank E. of Duperre Isles	11 10 48 S	N.B.—The distances in the	A A
On N.W. extreme of the I.	11 10 38 S	Louisiade and New Guinea are	A A
On middle of North side of Island	11 4 20 S	calculated with the mer. dist. of	A A
Centre of Island	11 10 6 S	the Sextant Rock, Cape York,	A A
East end of Island	11 5 36 S	assumed to be 8° 40′ 50″ W.	A A
N.W. end, on a detached rock	10 54 20 S	of Sydney, to adapt them to	A A
Rattlesnake's anchorage	10 45 30 S	the original △ of the N.E.	A A
Rattlesnake's anchorage	10 30 36 S	Coast of Australia.	A A
Sextant Rock, Evans' Bay	10 41 31 S	*From Chart	A A
East end of Treacherous Bay	*9 35 0 S		
On the centre of the Cay	9 8 38 S		
On board the "Bramble," at anchor	9 58 53 S		
Ditto ditto	10 16 20 S		
Ditto ditto			
Ditto ditto			
On centre of N. side of Island	11 16 51 S		
Fort Macquarie	33 51 33 S		
Kairaro I. Kororareka Bay	35 16 0 S		
Near Chaplain's house, Stanley, E. Falkl.	51 41 19 S		

THE following is a summary of the results obtained from the Chronometric measurements of H. M. S. "Rattlesnake" and "Bramble," giving a proportionate value to each, according to the number of T. K.'s employed.

SPOT OF OBSERVATION.	Mean Mer. distance from Port Macquarie, Sydney.	East or West	Longitude E. of Greenwich, assuming the longitude of Port Macquarie to be 151° 14' 47" E.	Observed Latitude.	Instrument used to observe Latitude.	Initials of Observers of Latitude.
Parramatta Observatory .	0 13 13	W	151 1 34 E	33 48 50 S	From	Naut. Alm.
Eden Jetty, Twofold Bay .	1 17 53	W	149 56 54 E	37 4 20 S	Circle.	O. S.
Gabo Island . . .	1 18 35	W	149 56 12 E	None observed.		
Lighthouse, Pt. Gellibrand, Pt. Philip	6 19 29	W	144 55 18 E	37 52 31 S	As. & Alt.	O. S.
Lighthouse, Kent's Group .	3 55 11	W	147 19 36 E	39 28 58 S	Sext.	C. B. Y.
Rossbank Observatory, Hobarton	3 52 39	W	147 22 8 E	42 52 10 S	Circle and As. Alt.	O. S.
Tahlee H., Port Stephens .	0 47 15	E	152 2 2 E	32 40 18 S		Capt. King
N. pt. of Lagoon Bay, Port Dalrymple	4 24 56	W	146 49 51 E	None observed.		
North Solitary Island . .	2 10 35	E	153 25 22 E	29 56 8 S	Sext.	C. B. Y.
Moreton I. watering place, N.W. end	2 9 28	E	153 24 15 E	27 5 44 S	Sea hor. Cir. & As. Alt.	O. S.
Obs. spot, W. side Facing I. Port Curtis	0 8 36	E	151 23 23 E	23 51 45 S	As. & Alt. and Sext.	O.S., C.B.Y. and J. D.
Port Molle, near Sandy Bay, E. side of harbour	2 21 53	W	148 52 54 E	20 19 48 S	As. Alt.	O. S.
Cape Upstart, Sandy Bay near Cape	3 27 37	W	147 47 10 E	19 42 3 S	As. Alt.	O. S.
Mound Islet, Rockingham B.	5 3 27	W	146 11 20 E	17 55 25 S	Circle.	O. S.
Fitzroy I. sandy beach, W. side	5 13 27	W	146 1 20 E	16 55 57 S	Circle.	O. S.
East Hope I., beach on W. side	5 44 52	W	145 29 55 E	15 43 45 S	Circle.	O. S.
Lizard I. sandy beach, W. side	5 44 45	W	145 30 2 E	14 39 56 S	Circle.	O. S.
West Pipon I., S.W. side	6 40 59	W	144 33 48 E	14 7 9 S	Circle.	O. S.
C. reef dry sand, off Restoration I.	7 42 24	W	143 32 23 E	12 34 50 S	As. Alt.	W. H. O.
Sextant Rock, Evans' Bay, C. York	8 41 33	W	142 33 14 E	10 41 31 S	As. Alt.	W. H. O.
Port Essington, Government House	19 5 23	W	132 9 24 E	11 22 2 S	As. Alt.	W. H. O.
Booby Island . . .	9 19 51	W	141 54 56 E	10 35 56 S	△ n.	
Bramble Cay . . .	7 21 23	W	143 53 24 E	9 8 38 S	As. Alt.	W. H. O.
Pariwara I. (N. side) Redscar Bay	5 9 25	W	146 5 22 E	9 14 25 S	As. Alt.	W. H. O.
Middle Duchâteau Island .	1 7 50	E	152 22 37 E	11 16 51 S	Circle.	O. S.
No. 1 Obs. reef, Coral haven, Louisiade	2 4 48	E	153 19 35 E	11 18 39 S	Circle.	O. S.
Kairaro I., Bay of Islands, New Zealand	22 54 40	E	174 9 27 E	35 16 0 S	Sext.	W. H. O.
Chaplain's House, Stanley, E. Falkland	150 57 49	E	57 47 24 W	51 41 19 S	As. Alt.	W. H. O.

Initials: O. S.—Captain Owen Stanley.   C. B. Y.—Lieut. C. B. Yule.
J. D.—Lieut. J. Dayman.   W. H. O.—Mr. Obree.

No. III.

Observations of the mean magnetic inclination made on shore in the Voyage of H.M.S. Rattlesnake, by Lieut. Joseph Dayman, R.N. Instruments employed : Robinson's 6-inch Inclinometer ; Fox's Dipping Apparatus.

The following tables contain the absolute determinations of the magnetic inclination and declination made in the Voyage of H.M.S. Rattlesnake on shore. A very large series made almost daily at sea with Fox's instrument and the Azimuth Compass require several corrections before they are fit for publication.

Madeira.

In Mr. Veitch's verandah, Funchal, by Robinson's Needle, A.	59° 41′ 7 N	
Ditto ditto, by Fox's Needle, A	60 40 2 N	
On the summit of the Pico dos Bodes, ditto .	64 10 5 N	
Ther. 64. Ditto angle of deflection, 2 grains ditto .	33 13 6	
Ther. 59. Funchal ditto, 2 grains	38 8 8	

Rat Island, Rio de Janeiro.

By Robinson's Needle, A. 1 . . .	12 15 1 S
Ditto A. 2 . . .	12 19 1 S
Mean	12 17 1 S

Simon's Bay, Cape of Good Hope.

In the dockyard near the Observation spot of Erebus and Terror, by Fox's Needle A, with index error applied	53 40 0 S

Tonnelier's Island, Port Louis, Mauritius.

By Robinson's Needle, A 1 . . .	53 48 9 S
Ditto A 2 . . .	53 48 8 S
Mean	53 48 8 S

Hobarton, Van Diemen's Land.

At the Magnetic Observatory, Ross bank, by Robinson's Needle, A 1	.	.	.	70° 36′. 0 S
Ditto A 2	.	.	.	70 41 5 S
			Mean	70 38 7 S

Port Jackson.

On Garden Island, by Robinson's Needle, A 1	.	62 45 3 S
Ditto ditto A 2	.	62 47 7 S
	Mean	62 46 5 S

Port Curtis, N.E. Coast of Australia.

On Facing Island, by Robinson's Needle, A 1	.	51 28 9 S
Ditto A 2	.	51 30 9 S
	Mean	51 29 9 S

No. 1. Percy Island.

In a sandy Bay, on North side of Island, by Robinson's Needle, A 1	.	.	.	49 3 5 S
Ditto A 2	.	.	.	49 0 2 S
			Mean	49 1 8 S

Keppel Island.

In a small Bay, on North side, by Robinson's Needle, A 1	.	.	.	50 46 6 S
Ditto ditto	.	.	.	50 49 5 S
			Mean	50 48 0 S

Moreton Bay.

Near the N.W. end of Moreton Island, by Robinson's Needle, A 1	.	.	.	55 20 1 S
Ditto A 2	.	.	.	55 13 5 S
			Mean	55 16 8 S

Port Phillip.

Near Capt. Bunbury's House, Williamstown, by
Robinson's Needle, A 1 . . . 67° 12'. 7 S
    Ditto   A 2 . . . 67 16 7 S

                               Mean 67 14 7 S

Port Dalrymple, V. D. Land.

In Lagoon Bay, by Robinson's Needle, A 1 . 69 29 0 S
    Ditto   A 2 . 69 19 5 S

                               Mean 69 24 2 S

Swan Island, Banks' Strait.

Near the Lighthouse, by Fox's Needle B, with
index error applied . . . 68 56 1 S

Port Jackson.

On Garden Island, by Robinson's Needle A 1 . 62 48 9 S
    Ditto   ditto   A 2 . 62 39 1 S

       April 1848   Mean 62 44 0 S

Rockingham Bay, N.E. Coast of Australia.

On Mound Islet, by Robinson's Needle A 1 . 44 15 5 S
    Ditto   ditto   A 2 . 44 10 6 S

                               Mean 44 13 0 S

No. 2. Barnard Island.

On the West Point of the Island, with Fox's Needle
C (index error applied) . . . 44 8 8 S

Low Isles, Trinity Bay.

On the North Point of North Low Islet, Fox's
Needle C (index error applied) . . 42 22 4 S

Lizard Island.

On the West side of the Island, by Robinson's
Needle A 1 . . . . 39 32 9 S
Ditto   A 2 . . . . 39 31 8 S

                               Mean 39 32 3 S

No. 5. *Claremont Isle.*

On the North side of the Island, by Robinson's
Needle A 1   .   .   .   .   38° 11′ 9. S

Cape York.

In Evans Bay, by Robinson's Needle A 1   .   33 10 2 S
  Ditto by Fox's Needle C, corrected for
index error .   .   .   .   .   33 8 4 S

                  33 9 3 S

Port Essington.

In Proa Bay, 1 mile west of Settlement, by Fox's
Needle C (with error applied)   .   .   35 14 6 S
On board the ship, at anchor at Port Essington,
same needle corrected for local attraction and
index error   .   .   .   .   33 48 0 S

Note.—The observations on board the ship at this station are
the nearest to the truth, there being much iron-stone strewed
over the country about the observation spot on shore.

Port Jackson.

Garden Island, by Robinson's Needle A 1, March
1849   .   .   .   .   62 44 2 S

Moreton Bay.

On the N.W. side of Moreton Island, by Robinson's
Needle A 1   .   .   .   .   55 21 3 S

Coral Haven, Louisiade Archipelago.

On a patch of Coral near Pig Island, by Robinson's
Needle A 1   .   .   .   .   32 35 2 S
    Ditto   by Fox's Needle,
index error applied   .   .   32 33 0 S

           Mean   32 34 1 S

Duchâteau Islands, Louisiade Archipelago.

On the Middle Island, by Robinson's Needle A 1   32 48 6 S
  Ditto   Fox's Needle B (with
index error applied)   .   .   32 56 4 S

           Mean   32 52 5 S

Cape York.
In Evans Bay, by Robinson's Needle A 1 . 33° 22'. 4 S

Bramble Cay, South Coast of New Guinea.
By Fox's Needle B, with index errror applied . 31 49 2 S

Garden Island, Port Jackson.
By Fox's Needle A, corrected for index error, &c. 62 44 9 S
Ditto   B   ditto . 62 44 9 S
Ditto   C   ditto . 62 44 9 S

Bay of Islands, New Zealand.
Near Kororareka Bay, by Fox's Needle A, corrected
for index error . . . . 59 37 6 S
     Ditto   B . 59 44 2 S
     Ditto   C . 59 28 1 S

Mean   59 36 6 S

East Falkland Island.
Near the Chaplain's house at Stanley, by Fox's
Needle A, corrected for index error . . 52 19 6 S
     B   Ditto . . 51 43 3 S
     C   Ditto . . 50 58 8 S

Mean   51 40 6 S

At the Observation spot of the Erebus and Terror
near the old settlement, Berkeley Sound, by
Fox's Needle B, corrected for index error . 51 25 6 S

Fayal, Azores.
In the Consul's garden, Horta, by Fox's Needle B,
corrected for index error . . . 66 58 4 N
     Ditto   ditto   A 67 26 9 N

Mean   67 12 6 N

The following absolute determinations of the magnetic declination were made with a declinometer, and A.M. and P.M. azimuths of the sun :

William Town, Port Phillip	9° 10′ 52″ E
Lagoon Bay, Port Dalrymple, V. D. Land	10 29 16 E
Garden Island, Port Jackson, March and April, 1848	9 6 43 E
Mound Islet, Rockingham Bay, N.E. Coast of Australia	6 19 18 E
Lizard Island ditto	5 46 7 E
Evans Bay, Cape York, North Coast of Australia	4 42 31 E
Garden Island, Port Jackson, March and April, 1849	10 9 10 E
Moreton Island, East Coast of Australia	9 21 14 E
Coral Haven, Louisiade Archipelago	7 44 17 E
Duchâteau Isles ditto	7 14 5 E
Bramble Cay, S.E. Coast of New Guinea	4 22 37 E
Kororareka Bay, Bay of Islands, New Zealand	13 27 20 E
Stanley, East Falkland Island, July 1850	16 54 46 E

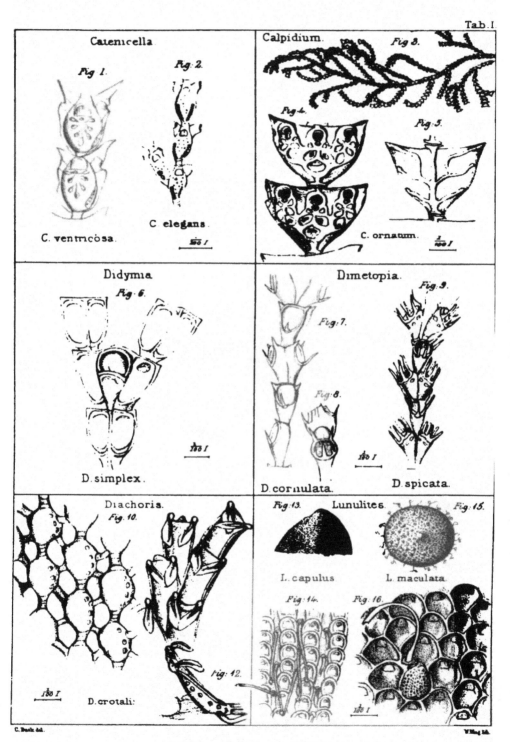

Tab. I.

Catenicella.

Fig. 1.

Fig. 2.

C. ventricosa.

C. elegans.

Calpidium.

Fig. 3.

Fig. 4.

Fig. 5.

C. ornatum.

Didymia.

Fig. 6.

D. simplex.

Dimetopia.

Fig. 9.

Fig. 7.

Fig. 8.

D. cornulata.

D. spicata.

Diachoris.

Fig. 10.

Fig. 12.

D. crotali:

Fig. 13.

Lunulites.

Fig. 15.

L. capulus.

L. maculata.

Fig. 14.

Fig. 16.

C. Beek del.

W.West lith.

T. & W. Boone, Publishers, London, 1851.

No. IV.

AN ACCOUNT OF THE POLYZOA, AND SERTULARIAN ZOO-
PHYTES, *collected in the Voyage of the Rattlesnake, on
the Coasts of Australia and the Louisiade Archipelago,
&c. By* GEORGE BUSK, F.R.S.

THIS collection includes about eighty-five species, distributed in twenty-nine genera, and may perhaps be
regarded as the largest and most interesting of the kind
ever brought to this country.

When it is stated that seventy-eight of the species are
new or undescribed, the number will appear extraordinarily
great, but when the comparatively neglected state of
exotic Zoophytology is considered the wonder will be much
diminished, and still further, as it may safely be assumed,
that many of the species here given as new have been
previously noticed, though so insufficiently described, as
in the absence of figures not to admit of correct identification.

Making, however, a considerable deduction on this
account, the remainder will still stamp the present collection with extreme value. As an instance, may be cited
the genus *Catenicella*, of which this collection affords about
fifteen species, and of which certainly not more than three
have been previously noticed in any way, and of these no
sufficient descriptions or figures are extant by which even
that small number could be identified. The explanation
of this is perhaps to be sought in the circumstance that
the species of *Catenicella* are deep sea forms, and only to
be obtained by dredging in deep water—very few being
apparently found on the shores.

Though the number of new or supposed new species is so great, the number of new genera is comparatively small, not amounting to more than four. It has, however, been found necessary considerably to modify the characters of several other established genera, so as to include new species.

With respect to the geographical distribution of the species, my means of comparison have been pretty extensive. They have been derived from the examination of Mr. Darwin's and Dr. Hooker's collections, placed at my disposal by the kind liberality of Mr. Darwin,—a considerable collection of South African species mainly procured from Mr. Bowerbank—and from the Collection of British and exotic Zoophytes in the British Museum, for the freest opportunities of examining which I have to thank Mr. Gray. From these various sources, and others of less account, I have been able to examine species from a very considerable extent of the earth's surface—more especially in the Southern hemisphere, and to arrive perhaps at as fair a view of the geographical distribution of species as the present imperfect state of Zoophytology will allow.

POLYZOA.

The number of species of Polyzoa is about fifty-four—belonging to twenty-four genera. Of these genera it is believed that four will be found to be new, or hitherto undescribed, and it has been deemed requisite to modify the characters of several others upon the more extended survey of species afforded mainly by the present collection. The new genera here instituted are :

Calpidium	*Didymia*
Diachoris	*Dimetopia*

And the genera whose characters it has been found requisite to modify are :

Catenicella	*Canda*
Salicornaria	*Emma*
Cellularia	*Acamarchis*
Scrupocellaria	*Cuberea.*
Bicellaria	

Of the twenty-four genera, three, or perhaps four, appear to be peculiar to the Australian seas. These are :

Calpidium	*Didymia*
Canda ?	*Dimetopia.*

All the rest, excepting two, Emma and Diachoris, appear to be distributed over the globe in both hemispheres. The above two are perhaps limited to the southern.

Of the fifty-three species, about thirty-three seem to be new, or to have been so imperfectly described as not to admit of precise identification, and five others have synonyms more or less doubtful applied to them.

Six species only are common to the seas of Europe, viz. :

Tubulipora phalangea?	*Anguinaria spatulata*
Crisia denticulata	*Acamarchis neritina*
Eucratea chelata	*Retepora cellulosa.*

Sixteen others are met with in other parts of the Southern hemisphere, viz. :

Catenicella elegans?	*Catenicella cribraria*
——————— *ventricosa*	——————- *cornuta*
Eschara lichenoides, occurring in Algoa Bay ;	*Cellularia monotrypa*
Caberea Zelanica	*Bicellaria tuba*, in New Zealand ; and
Acamarchis tridentata, in Algoa Bay and New Zealand;	*Emma crystallina*
Caberea lata	——————- *tricellata*, in New Zealand and Campbell's Island.
Catenicella hastata	

Thus of the fifty-four species, about thirty-four would

seem to be peculiar to the Australian seas. Ten of these belong to the genus Catenicella, and one to the closely-allied Calpidium, three to Didymia and Dimetopia, and one to Diachoris, of which genus two other species are found in the Straits of Magellan.

The method according to which the Polyzoa are arranged, is, in the primary divisions at least, pretty nearly identical with that indicated in the Synopsis of the Families and Genera of Polyzoa Infundibulata, given in Dr. Johnston's "British Zoophytes."*

A few words, however, will be necessary to explain more particularly the subsequent subdivisions here adopted.

The order, *Polyzoa infundibulata,* is divided into three suborders, coinciding very nearly with the Tubuliporina, Celleporina, and Vesicularina of the work above referred to, but as the characters of these suborders are derived from the conformation of the opening of the cell, I have thought it more convenient to name them accordingly. The first suborder, having a round, simple opening to the cell, is here termed the CYCLOSTOMATA; the second, with the opening of the cell filled up by a usually thin, membranous or calcareous velum, and with a crescentic mouth provided with a moveable lip, the CHEILOSTOMATA; and the third suborder, which might perhaps include the Halcyonellea of Ehrenberg, as well as the Vesiculariadæ, distinguished by the existence of a more or less well-marked fringe of setæ (sometimes only rudimentary) around the opening of the cell when the animal is protruded, the CTENOSTOMATA.

The following synoptical arrangement—which it must be remarked, includes only the genera occurring in the Rattlesnake collection—will serve to indicate the subsequent divisions.

* Vol. 1, p. 263, 2nd Edit.

Synoptical Arrangement of the Polyzoa included in the Rattlesnake Collection.

Suborder I. CYCLOSTOMATA (Tubuliporina).

Fam. 1. TUBULIPORIDÆ.
Gen. 1. Tubulipora.
Sp. 1. *T. phalangea?*
2. Pustulipora.
2. *P. australis,* n. sp.
3. Idmonea.
3. *I. radians.*
Fam. 2. CRISIADÆ.
4. Crisia.
4. *C. denticulata.*
5. *C. acropora,* n. sp.

Suborder II. CHEILOSTOMATA (Celleporina).

§. 1. UNISERIALARIA.

Fam. 1. CATENICELLIDÆ.
5. Catenicella.
a. fenestratæ.
6. *C. hastata,* n. sp.?
7. *C. amphora,* n. sp.
8. *C. margaritacea,* n. sp.
9. *C. ventricosa,* n. sp.
10. *C. plagiostoma,* n. sp.
11. *C. lorica,* n. sp.
12. *C. cribaria,* n. sp.
b. vittatæ.
13. *C. formosa,* n. sp.
14. *C. gibbosa,* n. sp.
15. *C. elegans,* n. sp.
16. *C. cornuta,* n. sp.
17. *C. umbonata,* n. sp.

Suborder 1. CYCLOSTOMATA.
Fam. 1. TUBULIPORIDÆ.
1. TUBULIPORA, *Lamarck.*

1. *T. phalangea*, Couch.
Hab.—Bass Strait, 45 fathoms.
A small, imperfect specimen, which may be referred to the variety noticed in "British Zoophytes," and figured Pl. 46, fig. 3, 4.

2. PUSTULIPORA, *Blainville.*

1. *P. australis*, n. sp.
  P. deflexa? Couch.
Branched dichotomously; branches short, incrassated, truncate. Cells wholly immersed, or about half free, numerous; surface minutely papillose, summits of papillæ of a dark brown or black colour.
Hab.—Bass Strait, 45 fathoms; and elsewhere in the Australian seas.
About half an inch high. The stem becomes thicker as it ascends, and divides into two equal short branches, each of which again subdivides into two short truncate branches, in a plane at right angles to the primary division. The cells in the upper part of the stem appear free for nearly half their length, and are gently curved outwards. The surface is covered with pretty regularly and quincuncially arranged minute papillæ, the apex of each of which is flattened or rounded, and of a dark brown or black colour. The mode of subdivision of the polyzoary, and the truncated ends of the branches, and the more numerous cells, suffice to distinguish this species from *P. proboscidea.* The cells in the figure of *P. deflexa* appear to be much more slender in proportion, and the branches in that species are not truncated, but attenuated at the extremity.

3. IDMONEA, *Lamouroux.*

1. *I. radians,* M. Edwards.   Ann. de Sc. N. tom. 9, p. 25, Pl. 12, fig. 4.

Retepora radians, Lamarck.

Hab.—Bass Strait, 45 fathoms.

One minute specimen, but very perfect, has been examined; but it is undoubtedly the one described and figured by M. Edwards, and noticed by Lamarck as inhabiting the seas of New Holland. M. Edwards' doubt therefore as to this locality is now removed.

Fam. 2. CRISIADÆ.

4. CRISIA, *Lamouroux.*

1. *C. denticulata,* Fleming.

Hab.—Bass Strait, 45 fathoms.

Parasitic upon a species of Salicornaria. The only difference, if there be any, between this form and the British, consists in the rather greater projection or freedom of the extremities of the cells, which are curved towards the front.

2. *C. acropora,* n. sp.

Cells 9 to 13 in each internode; lateral branches given off between the 1st and 2nd, or between the 2nd and 3rd cells above a joint. A small conical tooth, sometimes bifid, above and behind the mouth.

Hab.—Bass Strait, 45 fathoms.

A small parasitic species, distinguished from *C. denticulata,* which it much resembles, by the less average number of cells in each internode, and the less number intervening between the origin of a branch and the joint below it, and by the small conical tooth or tubercle above and behind, or to the outer side of the mouth.

Suborder II.   CHEILOSTOMATA.

§ 1.   *Uniserialaria.*   Cells disposed in a simple series.

Fam. 1. CATENICELLIDÆ. Cells connected by flexible joints.

5.   CATENICELLA, M. Edwards, (Lamarck, An. s. Vert. t. ii, p. 181.)

Cells arising one from the upper and back part of another by a short corneous tube, and disposed in a linear series, all facing the same way, and forming dichotomously divided branches of a phytoid polyzoary; cells geminate at the bifurcation of the branches; each cell furnished with two lateral processes usually supporting an avicularium. Ovicells either subglobose and terminal, or galeriform and placed below the mouth of a cell in front.

This interesting and important genus may be regarded as characteristic, not only of the present collection, but perhaps also of the Australian seas, as far as the Polyzoa are concerned.   Thirteen species are here described, and as it has been found extremely difficult in most cases to identify any of them with the very few hitherto noticed forms, the synonyms given must be regarded as at least extremely doubtful.

Each cell arises from the upper and back part of another, with the intervention of a short corneous tube which is prolonged from the interior of one cell to that of the one above.   The cell is furnished on each side at the top with an usually well-developed avicularium, in some species of huge size, and in some very minute, or entirely aborted.   This avicularian process in most cases supports above a hollow process, which is sometimes closed and more or less elongated, constituting a conical or acerose spine, sometimes open above and assuming the form of a shallow cup or receptacle.   In some species both modifications of this portion of the lateral process are met with in the same specimen.   This form of spine or cup—as the case may be, is always distinctly separated by a septum from the cavity of the avicularium itself. Below the avicularium there is also in many cases a third distinct cavity which is usually widely open, the opening being covered in very frequently by a convex transparent membrane, and its bottom apparently perforated by several minute foramina—from this part of the lateral process there is in many species a prominent ala or keel prolonged to the bottom of the cell—which ala not unfrequently divides into two branches, which, again coalescing at the bottom of the cell, circumscribe a more or less oval space, the bottom of which is also perforated by minute foramina or apparent foramina, and which is often covered over by a transparent convex membrane. This membrane, however, as well as that which covers in the subavicularian space, is more usually broken off and wanting.

The inferior oval space above described is here termed the lateral area, and it is employed in the specific characters. It would thus be correct to say—that each cell is furnished with two lateral processes, each of which in the fully developed state consists of three distinct compartments,—one superior, a cup or spine : a middle one, which is the avicularium : and an inferior ; and it would appear that one or more of these elementary compartments of the lateral process may be more developed than the next, or sometimes entirely aborted. The mouth of the cell is situated at the upper part in front, and is of the same conformation as in the rest of the Cheilostomatous sub-order. An important generic character consists in the gemination of the cell at each bifurcation.*

These characters are common to all the species included in the genus, which furthermore admits of being subdivided into two extremely natural sections or subgenera, (or perhaps into three). These subdivisions are named respectively the " fenestratæ," and the " vittatæ."

* Tab. I. fig. 1, 2.

In the fenestrate division, in the whole of which the cells are of larger size and stronger than in the other, the wall of the cell appears to be constituted of at least two distinct laminæ. The external lamina, on the front of the cell, is perforated by a certain number of holes, is wanting rather in a certain number of spaces, for which spaces the term " fenestræ" is employed. These apparent openings do not, therefore, penetrate into the cavity of the cell. But besides the fenestræ, there is, in some cases, a small central opening which does penetrate through the wall. In most cases the fenestræ are arranged in a crescentic, or rather horse-shoe shaped line, indicative, as it were, of the limits of a regular oval space, in the front wall of the cell, the upper part of which oval would be formed by the mouth, and the remainder filled up by the deposition of calcareous matter, as happens for instance in the older cells towards the bottom of the polyzoary in certain Cellulariæ, &c.

A further characteristic of the fenestrate Catenicellæ is the terminal position of the ovicells. These organs are clearly transformed cells, or cells dilated to considerably more than their natural bulk, and assuming a subglobose form. And what is worthy of remark, these terminal ovicells always have a sessile avicularium on the summit.

In the " Vittatæ" the cell is smaller, and usually more delicate and transparent. They probably want the outer lamina, or have it very thin, and consequently present no fenestrate spaces, and the front of the cell is beset (sometimes very sparingly) with more or less prominent, minute, acuminate " papillæ." On each side, sometimes on the anterior aspect, sometimes quite laterally, is a narrow elongated band or " vitta," as it is here designated, from which the distinctive sectional appellation is derived. This band or stripe varies in width and proportionate length and position in different species ; it is slightly elevated, and marked with larger, or small circular discoid, or acuminated eminences. This subdivision is further distinguished by the situation of the ovicells, which are not terminal, but occur at irregular intervals on cells in the course of the series. They are of the same galeate form as in many others of the Escharinæ, but are not as in them placed above the mouth of the cell, but below it in front : and in all cases the shape of the ovicell-bearing cell is much altered from the rest, and in all the vittate species the cell upon which the ovicell is produced arises from its predecessor, not with the intervention of a short tube, but is immediately sessile upon it, by a broad base.

a. Fenestratæ.

Cells large, fenestrate in front ; ovicells terminal.

1. *C. hastata,* n. sp. ?

C. bicuspis? Gray. Dieffenbach's New Zealand, Vol. ii. p. 293.

Fenestræ, 7—9, disposed in a crescent, and with elongated fissures radiating towards them from the median line. Avicularia supporting a large pyramidal pointed hollow process, compressed, and perforated before and behind by five or six small circular pores.

Hab.—Bass Strait, 45 fathoms, dead shells.

Of a yellowish white colour, sometimes reddish. Forms fine bushy tufts, with long wavy branches, arising from a short common stem, and it attains a height of five or six inches. It appears sometimes to be parasitic upon other polyzoa, and is then much smaller. Its peculiar characteristics are the perforated and striated scutiform area on the front of the cell and the perforated, or apparently perforated pyramidal lateral processes above each avicularium ; these processes are much developed, and give the cell the form of a broad inverted shear-head. It seems to be an abundant species in Bass' Strait, and it occurs also in New Zealand. (Dr. Hooker's Collection.)

2. *C. amphora,* n. sp.

Cellaria catenulata ? var. B. Lamarck. Anim. sans Vert. Vol. ii. p. 180, (2nd ed.).

Cells oval, sides rendered straight upwards by the broad avicularia which are prolonged upwards into an acute spinous angle, and support a shallow cup. Front of cell with nine pyriform fenestræ, with fissures proceeding from their pointed ends towards an oval central perforation. An elevated band, extending from the sides of the mouth to the upper angular processes of the avicularia. An elevated flattened band along the middle of the back, which at the top sends off a narrower lateral band to each avicularian spine.

Hab.—Bass Strait, 45 fathoms.

A fine species of a bright reddish brown, and in the younger cells very transparent. Forms small, irregularly branched bushes, four to six inches high and wide. It is peculiar by its extremely regular vase-like form of cell, which is given by the continuation upwards of the broad avicularia in nearly a straight line, and their prolongation into a sharp angular spine, on the inner side of which is a shallow cube-like cavity, whose sides are usually more horny than calcareous. The number of fenestræ appears to be very constant.

The length of the branches before their dividing, and their straightness, together with the colour of this species, render it not improbable that it is the form intended by Lamarck, (l. c.).

3. *C. margaritacea,* n. sp.

Cellaria vesiculosa ? Lamarck.

Cells oval or sub-globular, much compressed; avicularia short and broad, supporting a deep cup-like cavity. Fenestræ 5, large. Lower margin of mouth notched in the middle; back of cell minutely sulcated; sulci short, interrupted, and irregular. A small lateral " area."

Hab.—Swan Island, Banks Strait.

A very beautiful species, the branches resembling strings of minute pearls. The pearly lustre (in the dry state) owing without doubt to the minute sulci on the backs of the cells. These sulci are not, however, consequent upon the drying, because they are equally apparent and constant when the specimen has been immersed in fluid. The species may almost at once be distinguished by the notch in the lower margin of the mouth, which notch represents the central suboval opening present in some other species.

4. *C. ventricosa*, n. sp. Tab. i. fig. 1.

Cells oval, compressed, rather wide below; avicularia wide, supporting sometimes a cup-like cavity, sometimes a closed broad conical spine. The prehensile part of the avicularium itself small, seated in a deep notch below the acuminate summit; lateral area large and well defined. Fenestræ 7, with fissures radiating to a rounded central opening. Anterior surface of cell studded with minute acuminate papillæ; posterior surface smooth, sometimes spotted.

Hab.—Bass Strait, 45 fathoms.

Colour dirty white or brown. Habit stiff, stem strong, straight, branches short and crowded—probably attains a height of four or five inches. The only other species with which it can be confounded is *C. amphora*, from which it differs in the greater size and more irregular form of the lateral processes, in the presence of the minute papillæ on the surface, and in the absence of the narrow longitudinal band on the back; instead of which the older cells in *C. ventricosa* exhibit a sort of broad scutum, almost covering the back of the cell and sending off two lateral bands on the sides of the cell, one passing below the avicularium and above the lateral area, and the other towards the acuminated apex of the avicularium. It also wants the raised bands which in *C., amphora* pass from the sides of the mouth to the apex of the avicularium in front. One large specimen presents a variety worthy of note—in this the backs of all the cells, except one here and there, exhibit (internally?) numerous irregular-sized leopard-like spots.

5. *C. plagiostoma*, n. sp.

Cells short-ovoid; avicularia very large and long, ascending from near the bottom of the cell into an acute spinous point, and supporting a deep cupped cavity; mouth placed obliquely; front of cell divided into fine large subtriangular fenestræ by four broad bands. Back of cell with a broad central band and two narrower bands branching from it on each side; surface of spaces left uncovered by the bands on the back beset with scattered, long setose spines.

Hab.—Bass Strait, 45 fathoms.

Colour brownish white; habit stiff, branches short. This species is at once recognisable by the peculiar oblique position of the mouth—the enormously developed avicularium usually only on one side of the cell, and by the sculpture of the cell—which appears as if it were swathed with broad tapes or bands. The wide spaces left between the bands in front clearly represent the true nature of the fenestræ of other species. It is the only species furnished with elongated setose spines.

6. *C. lorica*, n. sp.

Cellaria catenulata? Lamarck.

Cells elongated rhomboidal, truncated at each end. Fenestræ three, large, the lowest the largest, arranged in a triangle. Mouth very large; avicularia wide and strong; two lateral areæ on each side, well developed; surface in front with a few indistinct circular spots around the fenestræ, and behind marked with faint longitudinal striæ.

Hab.—Bass Strait, 45 fathoms.

Colour white, transparent. A fine widely branching species, in which the catenulate aspect is more evident to the eye than in almost any other. It is at once recognisable by the rhomboidal scutate form of the cell viewed anteriorly, and, when the back is also viewed, the resemblance of the two aspects to the back, and breast-plates of a coat of mail, is very striking. The structure of the lateral processes is more distinctly to be made out in this species than in any other. Each lateral process consists, 1st, of a deep cuplike cavity above; 2nd, a middle compartment, the *avicularium*; and 3rd, a third loculament below the avicularium, the wide opening of which is covered in by a convex transparent membrane. The bottom of this loculament appears to be perforated, and it is to be noticed also that there is a small central perforation in the septum separating it from the cavity of the avicularium. Towards the bottom of the cell, on each side, is a well developed lateral area of exactly the same conformation as the sub-avicularian loculament, and like it covered in by a convex transparent membrane. It might be supposed that these cavities were for the purpose of containing air, in order to render the otherwise heavy branches of the polyzoary buoyant. They, at all events, appear to be perfectly empty.

7. *C. cribraria*, n. sp.

Cells sub-globular, compressed, more or less alate. Avicularia large, without any superior appendage, and prolonged downwards into elevated lateral alæ. Anterior surface with numerous small round fenestræ, placed at equal distances apart, and evenly distributed over the surface, the circumferential fenestræ being larger than the rest. A minute central perforation of a crescentic form, the lower lip projecting, and the upper lip, lingulate in the middle, falling behind the lower.

Hab.—Bass Strait? This species also occurs in New Zealand.

Colour brown, loosely branched and several inches high. Distinguished readily by the cribriform aspect of the front of the cell, and by the curiously formed central orifice, and by the absence of any superior appendage to the avicularium.

b. Vittatæ. Cells furnished with a narrow elongated band or vitta on each side, without fenestræ. Ovicells not terminal, galeriform.

8. *C. formosa*, n. sp.

Cells oval; avicularia large, flat, or cupped above. Vittæ elliptical, rather anterior.

Hab.—Swan Island, Banks Strait.

Colour light plumbeous. Parasitic upon *C. margaritacea.* The cells are the largest of any in the Vittate division, and very regular and uniform in size and outline. The more distinctive characters are taken from the comparatively broad vittæ, and the flat or cupped upper surface of the avicularia, which are usually continued downwards into a prominent ridge or ala.

9. *C. gibbosa*, n. sp.

Cells pyriform, ventricose posteriorly, much attenuated at bottom. Avicularia small, placed in front close to the sides of the mouth, at the base of strong conical pointed processes which project in front, and are connected across the top of the cell by a prominent toothed ridge. Vittæ long linear, entirely lateral.

Hab.—Prince of Wales Channel, Torres Strait, 9 fathoms, mud.

Of a dark lead colour, when dry. Forms an elegantly branched bush about two inches high. The gibbous form of the cells, and the peculiar anterior position of the avicularia, at the base of the projecting lateral processes, at once distinguish it from all the other vittate species. The toothed (sometimes entire) ridge extending between the two lateral processes across the top of the cell and overlapping the mouth like a pent-house is also a very peculiar feature.

10. *C. elegans,* n. sp.   Tab. i. fig. 2.

Cells elongated ovoid; avicularia large and projecting, without any superior appendage; vittæ narrow, rather anterior.

Hab.——Bass Strait, 48 fathoms.   Port Dalrymple, on stones at low water.

A delicate and beautiful parasitic species; the branches slender and spreading; colour white and very transparent. Cells regular and uniform in size and shape. A very similar if not identical species occurs in Algoa Bay, South Africa, the only difference between them being that the latter is rather larger and has the vittæ much longer; in the Australian forms these bands do not reach above the middle of the cell, whilst in the South African they extend as high as the mouth.

11. *C. cornuta.* n. sp.

Cells oval; avicularia in many cells wholly transformed into long pointed retrocedent spines, on one or both sides, in others into shorter spines or unaltered. Vittæ linear, extremely narrow, entirely lateral, and extending the whole length of the cell from the base of the avicularium.

Hab.——Bass Strait, 45 fathoms.

Colour yellowish white, growth small; parasitic upon *C. amphora.* As some difficulty might be experienced in the discrimination of this species from *C. elegans,* and another South African species (not the variety of *C. elegans* above noticed), it is requisite to remark that the long retrocedent spines when present are not placed upon or superadded to the avicularia, but that they seem to represent an aborted or transformed state of those organs. They vary much in length and size in different cells, and even in those of the same branch; as it frequently happens that there is a spine, usually of diminutive size, on one side and a very large avicularium on the other, and sometimes (but rarely) an avicularium of more moderate size on both sides. But the character of the species by which it is more particularly distinguished consists in the presence on a great many cells, in one part or other of the polyzoary, of the two large and strong spines projecting *backwards*. This retrocession of the spines is alone a sufficient character to distinguish the present species from the South African form above alluded to (*C. taurina*, B.) And the length and lateral position of the vittæ would distinguish the unarmed cells from those of *C. elegans*.

12. *C. umbonata*, n. sp.

Cells more or less pyriform, alate, narrow below, bulging or ventricose upwards. Avicularia large and strong. Vittæ strap-shaped, anterior, extending from the level of the mouth to the bottom of the cell, with elevated acuminate papillæ or short spines. A broad compressed projecting process on the middle of the back.

Hab.—Bass Strait, 45 fathoms.

The cells in this species are small, inflated or ventricose, and as it were sub-globular above, becoming much attenuated below—but the cavity of the cell does not appear to extend into this contracted portion, in which is contained the connecting tube strengthened by calcareous matter—the inferior continuation of the lateral alæ, which descend from the base of the avicularium. Owing to the large size of the avicularia, the upper part of the cell is much widened, and the whole acquires somewhat of a triangular form, and has a peculiar rugose aspect, derived, in part also, from the large size and elevation of the acuminated papillæ, not only of the vittæ but on the surface of the cell itself. The central umbo or crest posteriorly is a marked feature.

c. Without vittæ or fenestræ.

13. C. *carinata*, n. sp.

Cells oval, narrowed at both ends; lateral processes, (without avicularia?) projecting horizontally outwards from the sides of the mouth about the middle of the cell. Mouth nearly central, with a small tooth on each side, and below it a triangular space with three strong conical eminences. The cell which bears the ovicell geminate.

Hab.—Bass Strait, 45 fathoms.

This remarkable form differs so widely in many respects from any of its congeners, as almost to deserve to be considered as the type of a distinct sub-genus. The lateral processes, which may be taken to represent the perfect avicularia of the other species, are, as far as can be ascertained from specimens that have been dried, without a moveable mandible, and are probably really so, because there is no corresponding beak. These processes are channelled in front, nearly from the base to the extremity; they arise by a broad base on each side of the mouth, and on the front of the cell, and from the conjoined bases is continued upwards and downwards, or to the top and bottom of the cell, a prominent flattened band. The expanded bases circumscribe an oval space, nearly in the centre of the front of the cell, the upper two-thirds of which space are occupied by the circular mouth, on each side of which is a small calcareous tooth, to which apparently are articulated the horns of the semilunar lateral cartilage. The lower third is filled up by a yellow, horny(?) membrane, upon which are placed three conical eminences, disposed in a triangular manner. The back of the cell is very convex, and has running along the middle of it an elevated crest or keel, which is acuminate in the middle. The ovicell is situated in front of the cell below the mouth, and below it are three considerable-sized areolated spots, disposed, like the three conical spines, in a triangle. The

cells upon which the ovicells are placed are always geminate, that is to say, have a smaller cell growing out from
one side.

6. CALPIDIUM, n. gen.   Tab. i. fig. 3—5.

Char.—Cells with an avicularium on each side; with
two or three distinct mouths, arising one from the upper
part of another, in a linear series, all facing the same way,
and forming dichotomously-divided branches; cells at the
bifurcations single; ovicells—?

This very peculiar genus, remarkable as it is, seems
hitherto to have escaped notice. It is distinguishable
from Catenicella, in the first place, by the anomalous circumstance that each cell is furnished with two or more,
usually three, distinct keyhole-shaped mouths, and is
doubtless inhabited by three distinct individuals. Whether
these are separated from each other by internal partitions
is unknown, but the closest examination of cells rendered
transparent by means of acid fails to discover such. In
cells thus prepared, there are apparent, however, three
distinct masses, reaching from the bottom of the cell to
each orifice, and which are probably the remains either of
the body or of the retractor muscles of the animals. Another point of difference from Catenicella is the non-gemi-
nation of the cell at the dichotomy of a branch. The
avicularia, moreover, do not form lateral projections, but
are sessile, or imbedded, as it were, in the sides of the cell
immediately below the upper angles.

1. *C. ornatum*, n. sp.   Tab. i. fig. 3—5.

Cells triangular-urn shaped, very broad above, with a
straight border, much compressed; mouths, 2—3, keyhole
shaped. Five fenestræ below each mouth; numerous
branching bands on the back of the cell.

Hab.—Bass Strait, 45 fathoms.

This curious species is the only one belonging to the
genus. The cells are very large, regular, and uniform,

resembling very closely an antique sculptured urn. Colour dark brown, and the walls so thick as to be nearly opaque. The polyzoary, which appears to attain a height of four or five inches, is bipinnate (with all the branches on one plane), the branches alternate, and given off with extreme regularity. The ultimate ramules are incurved. The whole forms a very elegant object. The central stem, or series of cells, differs in no respect as regards the size or disposition of the cells composing it, from the branches.

Fam. 2. EUCRATIADÆ.

7. EUCRATEA, *Lamouroux.*

1. *Eucratea chelata,* Lamouroux.
Hab.—Bass Strait, 45 fathoms.
In all respects identical with the British form. It also occurs at Port Adelaide.

8. ANGUINARIA. *Lamarck.*

1. *A. spatulata,* Lamarck.
   Ætea anguina, Lamouroux.
Hab.—Bass Strait, and other localities.
This species (which appears to be pretty generally distributed over the globe) is identical with the European form. It is to be remarked, however, that a second species (*A. dilatata,* Busk. Ann. Nat. Hist. 2nd Ser. vol. 7, p. 81, pl. 9, fig. 14) is found in Torres Strait, but which does not occur in the Rattlesnake collection.

----

§. 2. *Multiserialaria.* Cells disposed alternately in a double or multiple series.

1. *Articulata.* Polyzoary divided into distinct internodes by flexible articulations.

a. Internodes elongated, or composed of numerous cells.

Fam. 1. SALICORNARIADÆ. Cells disposed around an ideal axis.

9. SALICORNARIA, *Cuvier*.

a. Surface divided into more or less regular hexagonal spaces by elevated ridges.

1.   *S. punctata.* n. sp.

Cellaria salicornioides? Audouin. Savigny, Egypt. Pl. 6. fig. 7.

Hexagonal areas with an acute angle above and below; bottom of area pyriform, surface covered with minute transparent granulations.   Mouth of cell in the upper third, with a minute tooth on each side.

Hab.—Bass Strait, 45 fathoms.   Off Cumberland Islands, 27 fathoms, fine grey mud.

Parasitic upon Sertularians and Polyzoa; branches straggling of irregular lengths.

2.   *S. bicornis.* n. sp.

Areas with an obtuse angle above and below, sometimes rounded above; a minute projection on each side near the top.   Bottom of area long-oval, smooth, sometimes with a perforation above the mouth.   Mouth with a minute tooth on each side.

Hab.—Bass Strait, 45 fathoms.

Parasitic. Branches shorter and thicker than in the preceding species.   In the shape of the area they are very much alike, but in *S. bicornis,* in some cells, and occasionally throughout the greater part of the internode, the area differs widely from the more usual form.   It is much expanded, and presents a wide arch above.   In this case there is usually a considerable-sized perforation above the mouth of the cell, as occurs not unfrequently also in *S.*

farciminoides in the younger cells, and which opening is probably normal, until it becomes filled up by the gradual deposition of calcareous matter. What more especially distinguishes the present from the preceding species are the minute projections on either side at the two upper lateral angles of the hexagonal area, and the smoothness of the surface of the cell. They are both perfectly distinct from *S. farciminoides*.

b. Surface not divided into distinct areas by raised ridges.

3. *S. dichotoma.* n. sp.

Mouth of cell elliptical, occupying two-thirds of its length. Two small perforations on each side immediately above the mouth, protected by a convex transparent hood, which has a rounded opening on its under surface.

Hab.—Prince of Wales Channel, Torres Strait, nine fathoms.

Forms small crowded tufts from one to two or three inches high; branches very regularly dichotomous.

4. *S. marginata.* n. sp.

Cell circumscribed by an acute raised border; opening oval, rather more than half the length of the cell. Cell attenuated below the opening.

Hab.—Prince of Wales Channel, Torres Strait, nine fathoms.

A small broken fragment only preserved; parasitic upon *Sertularia mutulata,* so that its habit cannot be satisfactorily determined. It is of a greenish colour, but this may be adventitious, although general and uniform throughout the specimen. This species differs from the above in being much larger, and in wanting the two perforations on each side above the mouth—in the less comparative size of the opening of the cell, and in the remarkable elevation of the sharp margin surrounding the upper half of the cell. In the looser aggregation, and in the form of the cells, it shews the transition from *Salicornaria* to *Cellularia*.

Fam. 2. CELLULARIADÆ. Cells disposed in the same plane.

10. CELLULARIA, *Pallas.*

Char. (B.) Cells bi-triserial, oblong* or rhomboidal, contiguous. Opening of cell occupying at least half of the front. Margin thickened, sometimes spinous above. A short spine or a sessile avicularium on the upper and outer angle.

A. *inarmatæ*—without avicularium.

1. *C. monotrypa.* n. sp.

Cells oblong, narrowed below, with a single perforation, in the upper and outer part behind. Opening oval, margin smooth; a short spinous process at the upper and outer angle; a sharp short spine in the middle of the upper border of the middle cell, at a bifurcation. Ovicell? in form of a very shallow excavation in the upper part of the cell in front.

Hab.—Bass Strait, 45 fathoms.

The only species with which this can be confounded, is *C. Peachii*, (Busk. Annals. Nat. Hist. Vol. 7. 2nd Series, p. 82. Pl. VIII. fig. 1.)

The latter, however, is very much smaller, the cells narrower in proportion to their length, and the margin of the opening minutely verrucose. The cell has more than one posterior perforation; and the central cell at a bifurcation is rounded above and without a spinous process; lastly, the ovicell is much loftier and tesselated on the surface.

* This shape of the cells is given from the back view of them.

11. SCRUPOCELLARIA, *Van Beneden.*

Char. (modified.) Cells rhomboidal, with a sinnous depression on the outer and posterior aspect. Each furnished with a sessile avicularium at the upper and outer angle in front, and with a vibraculum placed in the sinus on the outer and lower part of the cell behind. Opening oval, or subrotund, spinous above. Ovicells galeriform.

This natural genus is characterized more particularly by the presence upon *each* cell of a sessile avicularium seated on, or in fact forming the upper and outer angle, and of a vibraculum placed on the back of the cell. The cells in some species are provided with a pedunculate operculum, by which it is intended to designate a process, which arising by a short tube from the anterior wall of the cell, immediately beyond the inner margin of the opening, projects forwards and bends over the front of the cell, expanding into a variously formed limb, and serving as protection to the mouth of the cell in front. The cavity of the tube by which the process arises, becomes, in the expanded portion, continuous with variously disposed grooves or channels, which terminate at the edges of the operculum. This organ affords excellent specific characters (not in this genus alone). Besides the sessile avicularia above noticed, many species of this genus also possess avicularia of another kind, and which are placed on the front of the cell below the opening and towards the inner side, or in other words, towards the middle line of the branch. In this genus, in all those species in which the second avicularium occurs, each individual cell is provided with one. This additional avicularium appears to be composed of a flexible material, and it is very easily broken off, so that in many instances, perhaps throughout an entire specimen the organ itself may be wanting, although its position is clearly evidenced by the existence of a rounded opening in the usual situation of the organ. It is necessary to distinguish this form of flexible (if such it be) avicularium from the truly articulated and moveable avicularia, in the form of bird's heads, and which form does not occur in the genus Scrupocellaria.

a.—OPERCULATÆ. Cells furnished with a pedunculate operculum.

1. *S. cervicornis*, n. sp.

Veins or channels in the oval operculum, branching so as to resemble the antlers of a stag. The marginal spine next above the pedunculated operculum, bifurcate.

Hab.—Off Cumberland Islands, 25 fathoms, fine grey mud.

A small, delicate, parasitic species, very transparent. The very peculiar markings on the operculum at once distinguish it. The upper margin of the mouth is furnished with five elongated spines, the innermost of which is forked at the extremity.

2. *S. diadema*, n. sp.

Cells elongate, external side nearly straight, vibraculum sublateral, very prominent. Limit of operculum entire, or obscurely bi-trilobed. A flexible avicularium in front. Ovicell usually with a single row of four or five openings immediately above its mouth.

Hab.—Moreton Bay.

b. INOPERCULATÆ. Cells without a pedunculate operculum.

3. *S. cyclostoma*, n. sp.

Opening of cell nearly or quite circular, margin much thickened, with three or four short indistinct spines above. Vibraculum sublateral. A flexible avicularium in front. Ovicells — ?

Hab.—Bass Strait, 45 fathoms.

4. *S. ferox*, n. sp.

Opening of cell broad oval, pointed below; three short

indistinct spines above; vibraculum large, sinus deep. An enormous anterior avicularium, as wide as the cell. Ovicell lofty, with numerous punctures over the surface.

Hab.—Louisiade Archipelago. Bass Strait.

Distinguished from the former species by the enormous anterior avicularium, and the form of the opening. Another peculiarity of this species is the curious serrated appearance of the radical tubes.

12. CANDA, Lamouroux.

Char. (B.) Cells rhomboidal, sinuated on the outer side for the lodgment of a vibraculum. No sessile avicularium on the upper and outer angle in front. An uncertain number of flexible avicularia, arranged along the middle of the branches, and in much less number than the cells.

This genus is at once distinguished from Scrupocellaria, to which it is otherwise closely allied, by the absence of the sessile avicularium on the upper and outer angle in front, and also by the circumstance, that although there are flexible anterior avicularia, they do not correspond in number with the cells, but seem to be disposed in a special tract along the middle of the branch or internode. The connexion of the branches by transverse tubular fibres is not a character of either generic or specific importance, though it is more striking in the only species hitherto known as belonging to this genus, than in any other. These transverse tubular fibres are, like the radical fibres in Scrupocellaria, always inserted, not into the body of a cell, but into a vibraculum. They are evidently of the nature of a byssus.

1. *C. arachnoides*, Lamouroux.

Cells biserial; opening oval, truncated above, and the upper margin recedent, with a spine on each side, the outer the longer surface of cell covered with transparent granulations.

Hab.—Bass Strait, 45 fathoms.

b. Internodes composed of two-four cells.

13. EMMA, Gray.   Dieffenbach's New Zealand, Vol. ii. p. 293.

Char. (B.)   Cells in pairs or triplets.   Opening more or less oblique, subtriangular, partially filled up by a granulated calcareous expansion.   A sessile avicularium (not always present) on the outer side, below the level of the opening.

This genus appears to be a natural one, though very closely allied to Tricellaria (Fleming).   The more important points of distinction consist in the conformation of the opening of the cell, and in the position of the avicularium when the latter organ is present.   The lower half of what would otherwise be the oval opening of the cell is filled up by a thin plate of calcareous matter, granulated on the surface, and by which the actual opening is rendered more or less subtriangular, the mouth being placed just below the apex of the triangle.   The margin of the opening is considerably raised, especially at the oval end, so that the opening appears to be situated in a deep depression.   This character of opening, however, occurs also in a triserial species of Cellularia from Algoa Bay.   The position of the avicularium entirely *below* the level of the opening on the outer side of the cell, is the peculiar characteristic of Emma as distinguished from Tricellaria, in which that organ when present is placed on the upper and outer angle as in Cellularia proper, and Scrupocellaria.   It is worthy of notice that avicularia may be present on every cell in some specimens, and most usually, whilst in others of equal size there will be none at all apparent.   So that the position of these organs in this genus, as well as in Tricellaria, is of more importance systematically than even their existence.

1. *E. crystallina*, Gray, l. c.

Cells in pairs; three spines on the outer edge, the central usually the longest and strongest.

Hab.—Bass Strait, 45 fathoms.

Parasitic upon Polyzoa, &c. circinate branched—branches irregular divaricate. The opening of the cell triangular, very obliquely placed.

2. *Emma tricellata*, n. sp.

Cells in triplets; three or four long spines on the upper and outer part; a small spine on the inner and lower part of the edge of the opening.

Hab.—Bass Strait.

Parasitic upon Catenicella, &c. Habit long straggling, very like the preceding species. The cells are more infundibuliform, and the avicularium, which, as in *E. crystallina* is not always present, is larger, but occupies the same position on the cell.

2. Polyzoary continuous throughout.

Fam. 3. BICELLARIADÆ. Frond wholly divided into narrow ligulate, dichotomous, bi or multiserial branches; no vibracula. Avicularia when present pedunculate.

14. BICELLARIA, Blainville.

Char. (B.) Cells turbinate, distant. Opening directed more or less upwards. Mouth submarginal. Several curved spines, marginal or submarginal.

1. *B. tuba*, n. sp.

Opening round, looking nearly directly upwards; a digitiform hollow process below the outer border supporting 2—4 long incurved spines; 2—3 other long curved submarginal spines behind or above the opening, none below it in front—a solitary spine on the back a short way down the cell. Avicularia very long, trumpet-shaped, arising on the back of the cell.

Hab.—Bass Strait, 45 fathoms.

This species is at once recognisable by the remarkable form and unusual position of the avicularium, and also by the peculiar digitiform spiniferous process on the outer side of the opening.

2. *B. gracilis*, n. sp.

Cells elongated, slender, opening round or suboval, looking obliquely forwards and upwards; three marginal (sometimes slightly submarginal) spines above and behind the opening, and two much longer curved hair-like spines arising from the anterior and lower edge of the opening. Ovicells globose, subpedunculate, attached to the upper and inner part of the margin of the opening. Avicularia small, like bird's heads.

Hab.—Bass Strait.

A delicate slender species, not unlike *B. ciliata* or *avicularis* in habit. The two long spines arising from the anterior edge of the opening suffice to distinguish it from the former of these two species.

3. *B. grandis*, n. sp.

Cells much elongated outwards, horizontal or projecting portion oblong, rounded at the extremity; 2—5 long curved submarginal spines, externally a single dorsal spine about half way down the cell; opening oval, narrower outwards; very oblique mouth at the outer end. Avicularia—?

Hab.—Bass Strait, 45 fathoms.

Quite distinct from *B. ciliata* not only in its size, which is nearly three times as great, but in the form of the cell and the opening. The number of spines varies very much, and two or three of them, not unfrequently, arise from a common projecting process or base.

4. *B. flexilis*, n. sp.

Cells obliquely truncated above with a short spine on the outer angle; opening large, suboval, with an obtuse angle outwardly; margin slightly thickened, wholly unarmed.

Hab.——Off Cumberland Islands, 27 fathoms, fine grey mud.

Of a light grey colour : grows in large loose tufts, composed of long forked ascending branches. It is a very peculiar species, and some difficulty has been found in finding it a place. In the opening of the mouth, and the external short spine, it is a Cellaria; and in the colour and want of distinct articulation, it approaches Acamarchis; whilst in the form of the cell, and their mode of mutual connexion, it is a Bicellaria : it differs from all other species of that genus, however, in the absence of any long spines, and in general habit. Were it not referred to that genus, it would probably constitute the type of a distinct one. A curious little trident-like organ is visible in the narrow part of some cells.

15. ACAMARCHIS, Lamouroux.

Char. (B.)——Cells elliptical,* closely contiguous; opening very large, margin simple, not thickened. Avicularia not always present, like birds' heads.

To which may be added, that the species are frequently coloured, red or bluish.

1. *A. neritina.* Lamouroux.

Hab.——Rio de Janiero. Broken Bay, N. S. Wales.

This species appears to be one of the most generally distributed of the Polyzoa; it occurs in nearly every latitude in both hemispheres.

(?) 2. *A. tridentata.* Krauss. Corall. d. Südsee, p. 3. fig. 2.

Hab.——Bass Strait (?)

* Viewed posteriorly.

This species is placed doubtfully in the Rattlesnake Collection. It occurs, however, in Van Diemen's Land and New Zealand (Dr. Hooker), and is abundant in South Africa.

Fam. 4. CABEREADÆ.

Polyzoarium entirely divided into ligulate dichotomous bi or multiserial branches; back nearly covered by large vibracula; avicularia sessile.

16. CABEREA, Lamouroux.

Selbia, Gray. op. c. Vol. II. p. 292.

Cells bi-multiserial, in the latter case quincuncial. Posterior surface of branches concealed by large vibracula, which are placed obliquely in a double row, diverging in an upward direction from the middle line, where the vibracula of either row decussate with those of the other. Avicularia when present of the flexible kind, sessile on the front of the cell.

The remarkable feature of this genus resides in the vibracula, which here appear to attain their utmost development. Each vibraculum appears to belong not to a single cell as in *Scrupocellaria*, but to be common to, or applied to the backs of several. They are more or less pyriform or long oval in shape, and the two rows decussate with each other along the middle of the branch—giving in the narrower species, especially, much the aspect of an ear of barley, and in the wider of a straw plait. The walls of the vibracula are usually thin, and very transparent, so as to allow the outlines of the cells to be seen imperfectly through them. The upper and outer extremity of the vibraculum is bifid, and to the inner horn is articulated the seta, and from the notch between the two horns there is continued nearly, if not quite, to the inner extremity of the organ, and along its upper border, a shallow groove, in which is lodged the seta when in a state of rest. In most species the seta is serrated with distant teeth on one side.

Where there are more than two rows of cells, the marginal cells differ in conformation from the central.

As in *Scrupocellaria*, the opening of the cell is sometimes protected by a pedunculate operculum. The genus, therefore, may, like that, admit of being divided into sections, distinguished respectively by the presence or absence of a pedunculate operculum.

a. Operculatæ.

1. *C. rudis,* n. sp.

Multiserial; opening of cells oval, margin much thickened, with a strong projecting upturned spine on each side in the central cells, and with three strong and long similar spines on the outer side, and a smaller one on the inner side in the marginal cells. Operculum spatulate, or pointed above, entire. Each cell of the central rows with two small avicularia in front, immediately below the mouth. Each marginal cell with a single large vibraculum in front below the mouth. Vibracula slender, very transparent. Setæ short, not serrated.

Hab.—Bass Strait.

Colour dirty white : forms a broad frondose polyzoarium 1½ to 2 inches, or perhaps more, in height. The branches, all disposed in the same plane, are flat, thick, and about ⅛th of an inch wide, composed of from four to six rows of comparatively small cells, which viewed behind appear lozenge or diamond shaped, and arranged quincunically. It is not always easy to observe with accuracy the outline of the vibracula, owing to the extreme tenuity of their walls, but the groove along the upper border is very distinct and most usually has the seta lying in it. The avicularia on the marginal cells are very large, but not uniform in size. Along each border of the branches runs a bundle of radical tubes, the number of which diminishes as the branch ascends, each terminating in a vibraculum.

2. *C. zelanica*, Busk.

Selbia zelanica, Gray.   Dieffenbach's New Zealand, Vol. ii. p. 292.

Crisia Boryi, Audouin.   (Savigny, Egypt, pl. 12, fig. 4.)

Biserial; opening of cell oval or elliptical, rounded at each end, crossed in front, and thus divided into two nearly equal parts by a transverse calcareous band, from the lower edge of which depends a pedunculate, falciform operculum.   Cells frequently produced upwards into a large arcuate ovicell.   Vibracula ovoid, setæ long, serrated.

Hab.—Off Cumberland Islands, 27 fathoms, fine grey mud.

Slender : sufficiently distinguished by the peculiar form of the operculum.   This part is so indistinctly represented in Savigny's figures, as to render it impossible to determine with certainty whether his species is the present one or not.   The posterior view is much more like, but that is insufficient of itself to afford a specific character.   The back of the branches exactly resembles an ear of barley. This species occurs in New Zealand, and also in South Africa.

b. Inoperculatæ; opening of cell without an operculum.

3. *C. lata*, n. sp?

C. dichotoma?, Lamouroux.

Branches 4—7 serial ; opening of cells in central rows, oval, sometimes square below; and the cell frequently produced into a shallow arcuate cavity.   A short blunt spine on each side of the mouth.   Marginal cells shallow, opening oval, margin much thickened, granulated : usually a short conical spine at the summit ; a very minute sessile avicularium behind the outer edge, superiorly. Vibracula very large : setæ serrated.

Hab.—Off Cumberland Islands, 27 fathoms fine grey mud.

Colour white or yellowish; forms close rounded tufts 2½ to 3 inches in height and width, composed of uniform dichotomously divided branches, about ⅛ of an inch wide, and which become wider towards their truncate extremities. The vibracula are very large, and though distinctly defined, are yet sufficiently transparent to allow a view of the lozenge shaped cells. The central rows of cells vary in number from two to five, and the cells composing them are arranged with extreme regularity. The marginal rows are placed in a plane posterior to the central, and as above noticed, the cells of which they are composed are widely different from the central.

The only other species with which the present can be confounded is *Caberea Hookeri* (*Cellularia Hookeri*, Fleming) a British form. The latter species appears to differ from *C. lata*, chiefly in its having a large tubular spine on each side of the mouth of the lateral cells, and in each of the central cells, or nearly so, being furnished with an anterior avicularium, below the opening and to one side. The lateral sessile avicularium on the marginal cells is also much larger.

Fam. 5. FLUSTRADÆ.

Polyzoarium expanded, continuous or encrusting. Cells disposed in straight series, which do not radiate from a centre.

17. FLUSTRA, Linn.

a. Cells on one side only.

1. *F. pyriformis ?*, Lamouroux.

Cells pyriform, or barrel-shaped, prominent, marked with transverse wrinkles. Ovicells lofty, keeled in front, with a strong central, and two lateral longitudinal ribs.

Hab.—Bass Strait, 45 fathoms.

Sometimes small and parasitic, upon Sertularians and Polyzoa—sometimes independent, then of large growth, forming dichotomously divided fronds, with strap-shaped truncate, unequal divisions.

b. Cells on both sides. (*Carbasea,* Gray.)

2. *F. denticulata,* n. sp.

Cells much elongated, narrow; sides parallel, ends square; an upturned spine on each side at the oval end; sides of cell denticulate, denticles very numerous, small, acute. Avicularia irregularly distributed on the surface of the frond.

Hab.—Bass Strait, 45 fathoms.

Frond divided into numerous strap-shaped, truncated segments, of various widths; it attains a height of several inches. In habit it is very like some forms of *F. truncata,* and there is a Mediterranean species (undescribed?) in which the cells are denticulate, much in the same way as in the present species, but otherwise quite distinct.

18. RETEPORA, *Lamarck.*

Char. (B.)—Polyzoarium foliaceous, calcareous, or horny, reticulate; cells only on one side.

1. *R. cornea,* n. sp.

R. ambigua? Lamarck.

Cells oval, not very regularly arranged, in a continuous, foliaceous, subcircular frond; reticulated with oval spaces, not as wide as the interspaces. Ovicells large, galeriform, immersed, smooth.

Hab.—Off Cumberland Islands, 27 fathoms, fine grey mud.

This remarkable species is so completely a Retepore in construction, that it seems impossible to separate it from that genus, merely from the circumstance that its composition is more horny than calcareous. The frond is more or less orbicular, or rather is composed of more or less orbicular or reniform folds, one over another, and attached as it were to a common centre. The substance is very thin and transparent, and the interspaces are much broader than the elliptical spaces.

2. *R. cellulosa.*

Hab.—Bass Strait, 45 fathoms.

Not distinguishable from a Mediterranean specimen.

3. *R. ctenostoma,* n. sp.

Frond umbilicate, irregularly infundibuliform, spaces elongated, narrow, margins subdenticulate; interspaces as wide as the spaces. Mouth of cells tubular, projecting; with six or seven unequal acute expanding teeth.

Hab.—Bass Strait, 45 fathoms.

A very distinct and beautiful species. The frond is about half an inch wide, and though really umbilicate and sub-infundibuliform, does not at first sight appear so, being much more expanded on one side of the centre than on the other.

19. Eschara, Ray.

1. *E. lichenoides,* M. Edwards. Mem. sur les Eschares. Ann. d. S. N. t. vi. p. 31. pl. 2. fig. 3.

Hab.—Australian Sea, probably Bass Strait. (It also occurs in Algoa Bay.)

20. Diachoris, n. gen. Tab. i. fig. 10—12.

Cells separate, each connected with six others by short tubes; disposed in a horizontal plane, and forming a continuous irregular frond; free, or partially adnate.

The mode of arrangement and interconnexion of the cells in this genus is remarkable, and highly interesting. It represents, in fact, a dissected Flustra or Membranipora. The cells are disposed in linear parallel series, and those of two contiguous series are alternate with respect to each

other.   Each cell is connected with one at either end in
the same linear series by a rather wide short tubular prolongation, and with two on each side in the contiguous
series by narrower tubes, so that each cell, except in the
marginal rows, is connected with six others.   It is this
mode of interconnexion of the cells that affords the diagnos-
tic generic character.   There is but one species in the
present collection, but in Mr. Darwin's there are two
others from the Straits of Magellan, as yet undescribed.

1. *D. Crotali*, n. sp.   Tab. i. fig. 10—12.

Cells erect, open in front, perforated on the sides and
bottom ; a lanceolate appendage articulated to each upper
angle.   Ovicell conical, placed on the upper edge.
Hab.—Bass Strait, 45 fathoms.
The frond, though not strictly speaking adnate, as it
seems to have no attachments, is usually spread loosely
over other polyzoa.   There is no appearance of a moveable
mandible in the lanceolate appendages, but which, never-
theless, most probably represent avicularia.   These organs
are of a lanceolate form, with an elevated ridge or keel
along the back, and slightly concave beneath.   They project in front, slightly depending ; and at the base of each
is a rounded eminence.

Fam. 6.   CELLEPORIDÆ.

Polyzoarium massive or crustaceous, composed of ovate
cells in juxta-position ; and arranged, more or less regularly, in linear series, radiating from a central point or
line.

21. CELLEPORA, Otho Fabricius.

1. *Cellepora bilabiata*, n. sp. ?
C. labiata ?, Lamouroux.
Cells deeply immersed ; mouths in some entire and un-
armed ; in others, with two acuminated conical lips ;

immediately beneath the apex of the posterior lip a small sessile avicularium. Ovicells subglobular, with a scutiform area on the upper surface, marked with several lines on each side, radiating from a central line.

Hab.—Bass Strait.

Parasitic on several zoophytes. This species to the naked eye exactly resembles *C. pumicosa,* but on closer examination several important differences will be observable. The cells in *C. bilabiata* are less rounded and less distinct than in *C. pumicosa.* As in that species, some of the cells are furnished with an avicularium, and others unprovided with that appendage ; and again, some cells support an ovicell, whilst others do not. The mouth of the unarmed cells in both species is more or less circular and plain, but in *C. bilabiata,* even in the unarmed cells, the mouth is occasionally distinctly bilabiate. In *C. pumicosa* the avicularium is placed subapically on a solitary posterior obtuse mucro, but in *C. bilabiata* there are two such processes longer and more pointed, one in front and the other behind the mouth; the avicularium, as in the former case, being placed immediately below the apex of the posterior mucro. The ovicells also differ very much. In *C. pumicosa* this organ presents several rather large circular spots or perforations?, whilst in *C. bilabiata* it exhibits a scutiform or horse shoe-shaped area, marked with several transverse lines on each side of a middle longitudinal line.

Fam. 7.   GEMELLARIADÆ.

Cells opposite, in pairs.

22. DIDYMIA, n. gen.   Tab. i. fig. 6.

Cells joined side by side; opening large, oval; mouth subapical, central. No avicularium. Ovicells contained within a cell, which is central at each bifurcation.

1. *Didymia simplex*, n. sp. Tab. i. fig. 6.

Cells oblong, narrowed below, broad and truncate, with an angle externally above. Back marked with transverse rugæ.

Hab.—Bass Strait, 45 fathoms.

A fine species, growing in loosely-branched phytoid fronds, to a height of several inches. In some (dried) specimens the branches are a little incurved, but not in all. The situation of the ovicell is peculiar. It is contained within the upper part of a cell placed between, or rather in front of the pair, from which the two branches at a bifurcation take their origin. The ovigerous cell differs widely in form from the others, being pyriform, and much attenuated below; and the orifice is below the middle. The upper compartment, in which the ovicell or sac itself is lodged, appears to be separated from the lower by a transverse diaphragm.

23. DIMETOPIA, n. gen. Tab. i. fig. 7—9.

Cells joined back to back; the mouths of each alternate pair looking in the same direction, and at right angles to the intermediate pair.

1. *D. spicata*, n. sp. Tab. i. fig. 9.

Cells infundibuliform. Margin of opening much thickened, with six equidistant, elongated pointed spines.

Hab.—Bass Strait, 45 fathoms.

White, transparent, forming thick tufts about 1½ to 2 inches in height. The same species also occurs in New Zealand.

2. *D. cornuta*, n. sp. Tab. i. fig. 7, 8.

Cells suddenly contracted about the middle. Opening oval, wide above; margins slightly thickened with a short thick conical horn on each side above, and a long projecting spine (rarely two) in front below.

Hab.—Bass Strait, 45 fathoms.

Branches narrower than in the preceding species. Colour

yellowish. Tufts loose; ovicell small in proportion to the size of the cells. It is placed immediately above and behind the upper margin of the opening of the cell to which it belongs.

Suborder III. CTENOSOMATA.

Fam. 1. VESICULARIADÆ. Cells tubular, horny.

24. AMATHIA, Lamouroux.

1. *A. biseriata*, Krauss. Corall. der Südsee, p. 23. Fig. 1. *a. b. c.*

Hab.—Swan Island, Banks Strait.

The biserial arrangement of the cells is not a sufficient character, because in *Amathia cornuta* (Lamouroux), the cells are also biserial as well as in another South African species, very like the Australian form probably intended by Krauss, but apparently different from it. In the South African form the cells are shorter, narrower, and more cylindrical, and the branches are terminated by two lanceolate tags, which are not present in the Australian species, in which latter the cells also are wider, longer, and prismatic, or subhexagonal, with very thin walls.

SERTULARIAN ZOOPHYTES.

The number of species of Sertularian Zoophytes comprised in this collection amounts to thirty-one, belonging to five genera, all of which appear to be common to both the Northern and Southern hemispheres; and four are European types. The fifth, *Pasythea*, is stated by Lamouroux, to be found on Fucus natans and in the West

Indics ; so that the present collection does not present any peculiar Australian generic form. It is far otherwise, however, with respect to the species. Of these three only are found in the European seas, viz. :

Sertularia operculata.
Campanularia dumosa.
　　　,,　　　　*volubilis ?*

Of which the first is a perfect cosmopolite, and the last is perhaps doubtful.

There are also, what is much more strange, not more than three species which I have been enabled to trace to any other locality, even in the Southern hemisphere. These are :—

Sertularia elongata.
　　　,,　　　*divaricata,* n. sp.
Plumularia Macgillivrai, n. sp.

The first occurring in New Zealand ; the second on the south coast of Patagonia and in the Straits of Magellan ; and the third (which, however, is not, strictly speaking, an Australian form, having been procured in the Louisiade Archipelago) in the Philippine Islands. With these six exceptions, the whole number of species would therefore, to a certain extent, appear to be characteristic of the Australian seas.

Of the thirty-one species, it appears strange that not less than twenty-five should here be described as new; and there can be no doubt many so described are included under the vague and uncertain descriptions of Lamarck and Lamouroux ; but, in the absence of authentic specimens, or trustworthy figures, I have found it impossible to identify satisfactorily the species described by them, and have therefore thought it better to assign new names rather than to apply former ones, which would in all probability prove incorrect. It is hoped, at all events, that the descriptions here given will be found sufficient to prevent any misconception of what is intended in the following catalogue.

The mode in which the species are arranged will be seen from the following synoptical arrangement :—

Synoptical Arrangement of the Genera and Species of Sertularian Zoophytes collected on the Voyage of the Rattlesnake.

Order. ANTHOZOA HYDROIDA.

Sub-order. SERTULARINA.

Fam. I. SERTULARIADÆ.

Gen. 1. Sertularia.

§ 1. Cells alternate (Sertularia.)

(*a*) Cells distichous.

1. *S. elongata.*
2. *S. divaricata,* n. sp.
3. *S. crisioides.*

(*b*) Cells secund.

4. *S. pristis.*

§ 2. Cells opposite (Dynamena)

(*a*) Cells distichous.

5. *S. subcarinata,* n. sp.
6. *S. patula,* n. sp.
7. *S. orthogonia,* n. sp.
8. *S. mutulata,* n. sp.
9. *S. operculata.*
10. *S. divergens,* n. sp.
11. *S. trigonostoma,* n. sp.
12. *S. digitalis.* n. sp.
13. *S. loculosa,* n. sp.
14. *S. unguiculata,* n. sp.
15. *S. tridentata,* n. sp.

2. Pasythea.

16. *P. hexodon,* n. sp.

2 c 2

3. Plumularia.

§ 1. Angiocarpeæ.

17. *P. Huxleyi*, n. sp.
18. *P. hians*, n. sp.
19. *P. delicatula*, n. sp.
20. *P. aurita*, n. sp.
21. *P. brevirostris*, n. sp.
22. *P. ramosa*, n. sp.
23. *P. divaricata*, n. sp.
24. *P. phœnicea*, n. sp.
25. *P. longicornis*, n. sp.
26. *P. Macgillivrayi*, n. sp.

§ 2. Gymnocarpeæ.

27. *P. effusa*, n. sp.
28. *P. campanula*, n. sp.

Fam. 2. CAMPANULARIADÆ.

4. Campanularia.

29. *C. volubilis* (?)
30. *C. dumosa.*

5. Laomedea.

31. *L. Torresii*, n. sp.

Order. ANTHOZOA HYDROIDA.

Suborder. SERTULARINA.

Fam. I. SERTULARIADÆ.

Gen. 1. Sertularia, *Linnæus.*

1. Cells alternate (Sertularia.)

a. Cells distichous.

1. *S. elongata*, Lamouroux.

Hab.—Swan Island, Banks Strait, thrown on the beach. Port Dalrymple, on stones at low water. (Also New Zealand.)

2. *S. divaricata*, n. sp.

Cells urceolate-subtubular, or very little contracted towards the mouth, often adnate to the rachis nearly their whole length; mouth looking upwards, with three large acute teeth, two lateral, and one rather longer than the others, and slightly recurved, above. Ovicells — ?

Hab.—Bass Strait, 45 fathoms, dead shells.

Colour dirty yellowish white; polypidom branched, from a common stem; branches irregular, (?) straggling, pinnate and bipinnate, pinnæ and pinnules divaricate at right angles, alternate; rachis flexuose, or with an angle at the origin of each pinna. The cells are placed at wide distances apart; small and adnate very nearly to the top. The mouth circular, with three large teeth, the one above frequently obscured by adventitious substances, very acute, ascending, and a little recurved.—*Sertul. Gayi*. (Lamouroux. Exp. p. 12. pl. 66. fig. 89 has four teeth.)

This species occurs also on the south coast of Patagonia, and the Straits of Magellan; in the latter locality, however, the habit is much more robust.

3. *S. crisioides*, Lamouroux. (Dynamena.)

Cells adnate, conical, slightly curved, truncate at bottom, narrow at top; mouth vertical, external.

Hab.—Off Cumberland Islands, 27 fathoms.

Very like a Thuiaria, but the cells are not immersed, though very closely adnate, and the outer angle of the square base of each cell is in contact with the upper and back part of the one below it, so that a small triangular space or opening is left below each cell. The branches are very regularly alternate; and the polypidom is of a light brownish colour.

b. Cells secund.

4. *S. pristis*, (*B.*)

Idia pristis, Lamouroux.

Cells tubular, all contiguous or adnate to each other, and to the rachis, upper half curved laterally, lower half closely adnate, almost immersed in the rachis; mouth looking upwards, rounded, expanded, almost infundibuliform, border slightly scalloped towards the rachis, and projecting externally. Ovicell cyathiform, long narrow with circular rugæ. Mouth as large as the diameter of the cup, margin very slightly everted.

Hab.—Prince of Wales Channel, Torres Strait, 9 fathoms. Off Cumberland Islands, in 27 fathoms, fine grey mud.

I see no reason why the present species should not come under Sertularia. It is peculiar from the position and extreme contiguity of the alternate cells. The ovicells arise from the back of the rachis towards the side. When viewed posteriorly, the cells are seen through the transparent rachis, and it might thus at first sight appear as if the rachis itself were cellular and not tubular, but such is not the case. The tube is wide and continuous from end to end.

2. Cells opposite—(sometimes alternate on the stem.) (*Dynamena.*)

a. Cells distichous.

5. *S. subcarinata*, n. sp.

Cells tubular, upper half divergent, ascending. Mouth looking upwards, circular, with an anterior and two lateral broad, expanding teeth. A narrow angular line or keel down the front of the cell. Ovicell— ?

Hab.—Bass Strait, 45 fathoms dead shells.

Colour white, transparent, growth small, straggling. Branches irregular, divaricate nearly at right angles, subalternate. The three expanding teeth and the anterior ridge or keel, besides its habit, distinguish it from a Tasmanian species with which alone can it be confounded. The cells are large.

6. *S. patula*, n. sp.

Cells tubular, upper third free, divergent ascending. Mouth perfectly round, looking upwards and outwards, margin entire everted. Ovicell— ?

Hab.—Bass Strait, 45 fathoms, dead shells.

Colour whitish. A small parasitic species, with opposite branches.

7. *S. orthogonia*, n. sp.

Cells tubular, nearly half free, divergent laterally at a right angle. Mouth looking directly outwards, border entire, slightly everted. Ovicell—?

Hab.—Prince of Wales Channel, Torres Strait, parasitic upon *S. pristis*.

Very like the preceding in habit and size, of which it may possibly prove to be a variety. The cells, however, throughout the whole of the polypidom are of precisely the same character, in each form, and exhibit no intermediate steps. In the present species the cells are much longer, rather narrower, and the upper half is turned out abruptly at a right angle, whilst in the former they ascend at an angle of 45°, and the free portion is much shorter. The branches in both are opposite; the ovicells are unfortunately absent in each.

8. *S. mutulata*, n. sp.

Cells compressed or flattened, from side to side; sometimes angular, lower half adnate, upper half divergent, projecting like a bracket. Mouth looking directly upwards, narrow oblong, quadrangular. Ovicells aculeate, with strong widely set spines, pyriform depressed.

Hab.—Prince of Wales Channel, Torres Strait, 9 fathoms.

Colour light olive grey. Polypidom about three inches high, irregularly? branched, branches not opposite. Thecells are distichous, and of a very peculiar form, but varying in some degree according to their situation. The younger (?) cells on the secondary branches are flat on the inferior or outer aspect, with two angles on each side, or are quadrangular; whilst the cells on the stems or older or fertile branches are usually rounded below, or on the outer side, and thus have only one angle on each side. The mouth varies in shape according to the cell; in the former case being a regular long rectangle, whilst in the latter it is rounded on the outer side. The ovicells are placed in a single series on one side of the rachis, as in *S. digitalis,* but are widely different in form.

9. *S. operculata,* Linn.

Hab.—Swan Island, Banks Strait.

This species occurs in all parts of the world. It is to be carefully distinguished from *S. bispinosa,* Gray,—also an Australian and New Zealand species, but which does not occur in the present collection.

b. Cells (on the branches) secund, contiguous.

10. *S. divergens,* Lamouroux.

Cells urceolate, much contracted towards the mouth; upper half free, divergent, projecting laterally almost horizontally; mouth small elliptical, with the long axis looking directly outwards; two lateral teeth. Ovicell smooth, rounded, ovoid; oral margin not elevated.

Hab.—Swan Island, Banks Strait.

Colour light yellowish: parasitic upon a fucus. Height from ¼ to ½ inch; simply pinnate, branches distant, regularly alternate. The stem is divided into internodes, from each of which arises a single branch. The cells on the stem are alternate.

b. Cells secund.

11. *S. trigonostoma,* n. sp.

Cells ovoid, gibbous, much contracted towards the mouth. Very small portion free, projecting forwards and outwards. Mouth looking outwards and forwards, triangular, with a short blunt tooth on the external angle. Ovicell—?

Hab.—Prince of Wales Channel, Torres Strait, 9 fathoms.

Colour very light yellowish. Polypidom simply pinnate, about two inches high: longest pinnæ about half an inch. Cells small adnate, projecting suddenly at top, and much contracted at the mouth. The mouth is of a triangular form, the longest side of the triangle being below. The cells are placed in pairs, but one is always a little higher than the other (subalternate), and one pair is placed on each internode on the pinnæ. The stem is also indistinctly divided into internodes, from each of which a single pinna is given off alternately on opposite sides, and besides the pinnæ there are three cells on each internode, two on the side from which the pinna springs, and on the opposite side alternate in position to the other two.

12. *S. digitalis*, n. sp.

Cells digitiform, slightly curved to the front, mouth circular, looking directly upwards. Margin entire, expanded. Ovicells long-ovoid, muricate, spines numerous crowded, mouth prolonged, tubular.

Hab.—Prince of Wales Channel, Torres Strait, 9 fathoms.

Colour dark grey, almost black. Stem two to three inches high, rising either from a strong main trunk (?) or from a mass of intertwined radical tubes. Stems or branches pinnate : pinnæ or branches alternate, straight, divaricate. The cells forming a pair, are, on the branches, adnate to each other throughout their whole length. But on the stem the cells are distichous and wide apart. The ovicells are peculiar in their long flask-like form, and tubular mouth. They are placed all on one side of the rachis, generally in single file, but sometimes in pairs.

13. *S. loculosa*, n. sp.

D. distans?, Lamouroux.

Cells completely adnate to each other, each apparently divided into two compartments by a transverse constriction. Upper half turned horizontally outwards. Mouth roundish, irregular, contracted : looking outwards, and a little downwards. Ovicell— ?

Hab.—Bass Strait, 45 fathoms.

Colour deep brown; polypidom simple unbranched (?) about half an inch high, parasitic upon a broad leaved fucus. The cells are so closely conjoined as to form but one triangular body, which appears as if divided into five loculaments by transverse constriction. The upper apparent constriction however seems merely to indicate the line of flexure of the upper part of the cell upon the lower. The form of the conjoined cells is not unlike Lamouroux's figure of *S.* (*D.*) *distans;* but the present is clearly not that species.

14. *S. unguiculata,* n. sp.

Cells urceolate, upper half free, projecting in front, and much contracted towards the mouth; elliptical, with the long axis horizontal, looking forwards and a little outwards; two long lateral teeth, the outer the longer and usually incurved. Ovicell ovoid; mouth wide, with a much elevated, thickened border.

Hab.—Swan Island, Banks Strait, thrown on the beach.

Colour bright brown; polypidom pinnate; the stems arising from creeping radical tubes, very thickly intertwined around a long slender body. The stems are from one to four inches long, the pinnæ about ¼—½ inch, alternate. The rachis of the stem is divided into distinct internodes, from each of which are given off two pinnæ, and upon which are also placed usually six cells, three on either side. The pinnæ are also divided, but less distinctly, into internodes of various lengths. The pairs of cells on the *pinnæ* are all secund, and in contact with each other at their bases, though widely divergent above.

14. *S. tridentata,* n. sp.

Cells urceolate, ventricose below, contracted towards the mouth. Mouth looking forwards and outwards, circular, with three acute teeth, two lateral, longer than the third, which is above.

Hab.—Bass Strait, 45 fathoms.

Colour yellowish white. Polypidom simply pinnate, about 2¼ inches high; pinnæ in the middle ⅜ of an inch. The cells are ventricose below, and almost flask-shaped.

The two lateral teeth are long, acute, and slightly everted; the upper third tooth is sharp, but not near as long as the others; the border of the mouth is as it were excavated below, so that the mouth is as nearly as possible vertical. Contrary to what is the case in *S. divergens*, but exactly as is represented in Savigny's figures of the so-called *S. disticha* (Egypt. pl. 14. fig. 2, 3.); and *S. distans* (Egypt. pl. 14. fig. 1, 3.) the lateral teeth are sloped or bevelled off from below upwards, and not from above downwards, as in *S. divergens* (Mihi.)

2. PASYTHEA, Lamoroux.

Cells in distinct sets, at some distance apart.

1. *P. hexodon*, n. sp.

Cells in sets of six,—three on each side; a single axillary cell in each dichotomous division of the polypidom. Ovicell pedunculate ovoid, adnate to the rachis, with a lateral opening.

Hab.—Off Cumberland Isles, 27 fathoms.

As this differs in the number of cells in each set, as well as in the form of the cells, and in the form and position of the ovicell, it appears irreconcileable with Lamouroux's *P. quadridentata*. According to the figure given of the latter the ovicell is not adnate, and is spirally grooved.

3. PLUMULARIA, Lamarck.

a. Angiocarpeæ—ovicells enclosed in siliquose, costate receptacles.

1. *P. Huxleyi*, n. sp.

Plumularia—Huxley, Philos. Trans. Part II., 1849, p. 427. pl. 39. figs. 43 and 45.

Cells cup-shaped, shallow; mouth nearly vertical, subquadrangular, margin subcrenate, plicate; with a small acute central denticle in front, and a wide shallow notch behind. Rostrum twice as long as the cell, arising from the rachis by a broad ventricose base, adnate the whole length of the cell, narrow upwards and slightly expanded again at the summit; lateral processes very short and wide, canalicular adnate. Costæ of ovarian receptacle numerous, each with a single branch near the bottom, and beset with small cup-like processes, and not connected by a membrane.

Hab.—Port Curtis. Off Cumberland Islands, in 27 fathoms fine grey mud.

Colour yellowish white. Polypidom about 6 inches high, rising with a single flexuose stem, which is naked at bottom, and afterwards gives off alternate branches, bifariously disposed at each angular fluxure. Branches simple, 2—3 inches long; pinnules about ½ inch. The construction of the ovarian receptacle in the present section of the genus Plumularia is well exemplified in this species, owing to the comparative simplicity of the elements of which it is composed.

2. *P. hians*, n. sp.

Cell cup-shaped, deep, cylindrical; mouth nearly vertical; margin with three teeth on each side, the middle one the longest, acute, much expanded, the other more rounded; a wide notch posteriorly. Rostrum, arising from the rachis, as long as the cell, slender, tubular, adnate; lateral processes very small, ovarian receptacles—?

Hab.—Prince of Wales Channel, Torres Strait, in 9 fathoms.

Colour bright brown, rachis shining, very dark brown; polypidom about six inches high, simply pinnulate, pinnules about half an inch; thickly and regularly disposed, alternate.

3. *P. delicatula*, n. sp.

Cell cup-shaped, rounded, mouth at an angle of 45₀; margin dentate, with two lateral teeth of equal size and a central one in front longer, all acute; entire posteriorly.

Rostrum a little longer than the cell, scarcely connected with the rachis, slender, and closely adpressed and adnate to the cell below, wide and projecting upwards; lateral processes large, rising above the margin of the cell, conical, tubular, or canalicular.

Hab.—Prince of Wales Channel, Torres Strait, in 9 fathoms.

Colour of rachis and pinnules, delicate yellowish white above; of rachis, light brown, inferiorly; polypidom about two inches high, rising in several straight simply pinnulated fronds from a common centre; pinnules ascending about ¼ inch.

4. *P. aurita*, n. sp.

Cells cup-shaped, tapering at bottom, constricted just below the top; mouth at an angle of 45°, circular; margin subcrenate, plicate, with three folds on each side, with a wide shallow notch in front and entire behind. Rostrum, slender, attenuated below, adnate up to the cell, summit contracted, tubular; lateral processes very long, expanding, rising far above the margin of the cell, conical, tubular.

Hab.—Off Cumberland Isles, 27 fathoms.

Colour bright brown; polypidom 2—3 inches high, consisting of straight pinnate fronds, pinnæ or branches not opposite, nor regularly alternate, divaricate at right-angles.

5. *P. brevirostris*, n. sp.

Cell sub-tubular, curved; mouth expanded with two equal acute teeth on each side, and a longer narrow and slightly incurved, central one in front. Rostrum small, conical, projecting, about half the length of the cell; lateral processes small, recurved at an angle, canalicular.

Hab.—Off Cumberland Isles, 27 fathoms.

Colour dirty white. In habit, and to the naked eye, very much like the last; its growth, however, appears to be longer and less regular. The difference in the cell is very great.

6. *P. ramosa*, n. sp.

Cells cup-shaped, deep, rounded at bottom; margin elevated on the sides, expanding, with four teeth on each side, the first and second in front much expanded, acute, incurved at the point; a long slender incurved central tooth in front; margin entire behind. Rostrum not continued to the rachis, adnate the whole length of the cell, wide and projecting, narrowed to the point, which is tubular, opening oblique, longer than the cell; lateral processes conical, short, tubular, closely adnate. Costæ of ovarian receptacle with short opposite tubular branches; *not* connected by a membrane.

Hab.——Swan Island, Banks Strait, thrown on the beach.

Colour greyish brown; polypidom 4——5 inches high, much branched, branches irregular, divaricate, rising in great numbers almost immediately from the mass of radical fibres. A beautiful species, and the ovarian receptacles very interesting.

7. *P. divaricata*, n. sp.

Cells cup-shaped, long, slightly contracted at bottom; mouth circular; margin sub-expanded, dentate, with three nearly equal upright teeth on each side, and a long, round pointed central tooth in front. Rostrum narrow at bottom, closely adnate, scarcely rising higher than the central tooth; lateral processes small, closely adnate.

Hab.——Bass Strait, 45 fathoms.

Colour dark brown, almost black when dry. In habit it is extremely like the preceding species, from which, however, it is quite distinct. The polypidom is five to six inches high, perhaps more; stem slender, branches long, divaricate at right angles, not opposite.

8. *P. phœnicea*, n. sp.

Cells cup-shaped, rounded, bent over in front, so that

the mouth is nearly vertical; margin with two folds, subcrenate, and with a broad, but pointed lateral lobe; entire posteriorly. Rostrum, arising solely from the cell, small, upper half free, projecting, tubular; lateral processes long, cylindrical, or tapering, free, projecting.

Hab.—Prince of Wales Channel, Torres Strait, in 9 fathoms.

Colour bright buff, many of the branches having a piebald aspect, or mottled with dark purple patches; when wetted these portions present a beautiful crimsom colour. Polypidom five to six inches high, rising with a strong, tapering, longitudinally grooved stem, which is sometimes sparingly branched, but more commonly simple. Stem and branches pinnate or bi-pinnate, the pinnæ and pinnules alternate. The latter are about ¼ inch in length.

9. *P. longicornis,* n. sp.

Cells urceolate, deep, upper half curved abruptly upon the lower, so that the mouth is vertical; margin subplicate, subcrenate, rising on each side into a broad angular lobe, entire behind, and quite free from the rachis. Rostrum, rising entirely from the cell, with a broad base, suddenly contracting into a long slender tube, which projects in front a long way from the cell; lateral processes very long, free, tubular, projecting suddenly forwards and a little upwards and outwards.

Hab.—Prince of Wales Channel, Torres Strait, 9 fathoms.

Colour pale buff. Polypidom five to six inches high, consisting of a strong straight, tapering stem, sometimes with a single ascending branch given off near the bottom; stem and branches pinnate; pinnæ 1¼ to 1¼ inches long; alternate, and arranged with the utmost regularity, of uniform length, till near the summit, when they shorten rapidly, so as to give the polypidom a rounded truncate end. The pinnules are excessively fine and delicate, not more than $\frac{1}{16}$ to $\frac{1}{12}$ inch long, and very closely set, so that the whole polypidom has the most exact resemblance to a beautiful silky quill feather.

10. *P. Macgillivrayi*, n. sp.

Cells campanulate, deep, rounded at bottom; margin subplicate, entire. Rostrum large, rising from the cell, adnate the whole length of, and as long as, the cell; the upper third constitutes a cup distinct from the lower portion; lateral processes adnate, wide, short, curved upwards, canalicular or tubular. Costæ of ovarian receptacle connected by a membranous expansion.

Hab.—Louisiade Archipelago, reefs at low water.

Colour bright brownish buff. Polypidom six to seven inches high, consisting of a strong central stem, giving off opposite branches, at regular intervals, and bifariously disposed. Pinnules about $\frac{1}{8}$ inch long, closely set.

b. Gymnocarpeæ—ovicels naked.

11. *P. effusa*, n. sp.

Cells urceolate; deeply emarginate posteriorly, entire in front, ventricose below; a small pedunculate infundibuliform process attached in front to the projecting portion of the rachis on a level with upper border of the cell. Ovicell—?

Hab.—Prince of Wales' Channel, Torres Strait.

Colour buff. Habit very peculiar. The polypidom rises to a height of seven or eight inches, with a long slender waving, but upright stem, which is naked inferiorly, and above gives off numerous straight or waving branches, again sub-dividing into other shorter straight ramules, about an inch long. The branches and branchlets are both pinnulated; the pinnules are not more than $\frac{1}{16}$ to $\frac{1}{12}$ inches long, extremely delicate and minute, so as in the dry state to be scarcely visible. The transition from the former section of the genus Plumularia to the present, is well shewn, through *P. Macgillivrayi* and the present species.

12. *P. campanula*, n. sp.

Cells campanulate, border entire; lateral and anterior appendages canalicular. Branches alternate. Ovicells—?

Hab.—Bass Strait, 45 fathoms dead shells.

There appear to be two varieties of this species, or that different portions of the same polypidom may assume very different characters. The larger and probably more common form, is at first sight extremely like *P. Catharina*, but it will soon be noticed that the branches are alternate instead of opposite. The shape of the cells and their average size is precisely the same as in that species. The lateral and anterior appendages differ in form very considerably. In *P. Catharina* these organs are longer, more slender, infundibuliform, whilst in *P. campanula* they are shorter and thicker and the terminal cup is open on one side or canalicular. The ovicells might perhaps afford a more striking characteristic, but they are unfortunately wanting in all the specimens of *P. campanula*. The second variety is much slenderer, unbranched, the cells and their appendages smaller but of the same form, and the cells usually contain a mass of opaque black matter. This species is parasitic, and appears to attain a height of several inches.

FAM. IV.—CAMPANULARIADÆ.

4. CAMPANULARIA, Lamarck.

1. *C. volubilis?* Ellis.

Hab.—Prince of Wales Channel, Torres Strait.

As one or two ovicells, parasitic upon *Sertularia pristis,* are the only evidences of this species that have come under observation, some doubt as to identity of the species with the British form may be entertained.

2. *C. dumosa*, Pallas.

Hab.—Bass Strait.

Parasitic upon *Sertulariæ.* Rather more slender than the usual British form, but otherwise identical.

5. LAOMEDEA, Lamouroux.

1. *Laomedea Torresii,* n. sp.

Cells campanulate, nearly sessile upon an incrassated collar projecting from the stem. Margin of mouth not thickened, with four shallow excavations.

Hab.—Prince of Wales Channel, Torres Strait.

Of a light brown colour, two or three inches high. At first sight it is very like *Laomedea antipathes,* Lamouroux, which occurs in New Zealand, but differs materially in its smaller size and in the four shallow emarginations of the mouth, which part in *L antipathes* is entire and with the margin a little thickened.

NOTE.—Circumstances having prevented the insertion here of descriptions of new species of Lunulites (Tab. I. fig. 13—16), and a few other Zoophytes of the " Voyage of the Rattlesnake"—examined by Mr. Busk subsequently to the preceding paper having been placed in the printer's hands—I may mention that the descriptions in question will shortly be published elsewhere.—J. M'G.

END OF VOL. I.

G. NORMAN, PRINTER, MAIDEN LANE, COVENT GARDEN.

THE UNIVERSITY LIBRARY
UNIVERSITY OF CALIFORNIA, SANTA CRUZ

This book is due on the last **DATE** stamped below.

REC'D BIOS

MAR 1 9 '04 -3 00 PM

1,'69(J5643ᴀ8)2373—3A,1

Check Out More Titles From HardPress Classics Series In this collection we are offering thousands of classic and hard to find books. This series spans a vast array of subjects – so you are bound to find something of interest to enjoy reading and learning about.

Subjects:
Architecture
Art
Biography & Autobiography
Body, Mind &Spirit
Children & Young Adult
Dramas
Education
Fiction
History
Language Arts & Disciplines
Law
Literary Collections
Music
Poetry
Psychology
Science
…and many more.

Visit us at www.hardpress.net

Im TheStory

personalised classic books

"Beautiful gift.. lovely finish.
My Niece loves it, so precious!"

Helen R Brumfieldon

★★★★★

UNIQUE
GIFT

FOR KIDS, PARTNERS
AND FRIENDS

Timeless books such as:

Alice in Wonderland · The Jungle Book · The Wonderful Wizard of Oz
Peter and Wendy · Robin Hood · The Prince and The Pauper
The Railway Children · Treasure Island · A Christmas Carol

Romeo and Juliet · Dracula

Highly
Customizable

Change
Books Title

Replace
Character Names
with yours

Upload
Photo into
inside page!

Add
Inscriptions

Visit
Im TheStory.com
and order yours today!